Immigrant Destinations

Jak Jechałem Z Ameryki
(When I Journeyed from America)

Jak jechałem z Ameryki,
Jak jechałem z Ameryki
I z tej żelaznej fabryki,
I z tej żelaznej fabryki.

Ręce moje dziękowały;

Do roboty zawsze stały.

Przyjechałem do Nef Jorka
Po szyfkartę do agenta.

Agenci się mnie pytali
Czy wiozę trzysta dolary.

"Nie pytajcie się mnie o to,
Bo ja wiozę srebro, złoto."

Wyjechałem w środek morza;
Nic nie widzę, Matko Boża.

Szyf kapitan się nie nudził,
Tylko chodził, cieszył ludzi.

Jakżem ujżał miasto Hamburg,
To myślałem że sam Pan Bóg.

A jakżem już wylądował,
Panu Bogu podziękował.

"Dziękuje Ci, wielki Boże,
Żem przepłynął wielkie morze."

A z Hamburga do Berlina,
"Szynkareczko, daj mi wina."

A z Berlina do Krakowa,
Bo tam była żona moja.

I dzieci mnie nie poznały,
Bo odemnie uciekały.

"Dzieci moje, ja wasz tata;
Nie był u was przez trzy lata."

When I journeyed from Amer'ca,
When I journeyed from Amer'ca
And the foundry where I labored,
And the foundry where I labored,

In pray'r my hands thanked our
  Father,
Hands that never shirked their labor.

Soon I came to New York City,
To the agent for my passage.

And the agents asked me if I
Had three hundred dollars with me.

"Ask me not such foolish questions,
For I carry gold and silver."

When I crossed the ocean midway,
No land could I see, sweet Virgin.

Our ship's captain was right busy,
Seeing, cheering all the people.

When I laid my eyes on Hamburg,
I thought I saw God Almighty.

When at last I landed safely,
"Lord," I prayed, "I thank Thee for
  this.

"O how grateful am I, dear God,
That I've crossed the ocean safely."

Berlin came next after Hamburg,
"Barmaid, I will have some good
  wine."

Then I left Berlin for Krakow;
There my wife was waiting for me.

And my children did not know me,
For they fled from me, a stranger.

"My dear children, I'm your papa;
Three long years I have not seen
  you."

—From *Merrily We Sing; 106 Polish Folksongs,* collected and edited by Harriet M. Pawlowska (Detroit: Wayne State University Press, 1961), pp. 154–55. (Sung in 1940 by Mrs. Sophia Dziob, who learned it from friends in Passaic, New Jersey.)

Immigrant Destinations

Caroline Golab

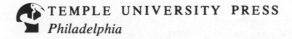

TEMPLE UNIVERSITY PRESS
Philadelphia

Temple University Press
© 1977 by Temple University. All rights reserved
Published 1977
Printed in the United States of America
International Standard Book Number: 0-87722-109-X
Library of Congress Catalog Number: 77-81334

For Busia Anna

Contents

Preface

This book has been in the making since I was six. On hot Chicago summer nights, while sitting on the front porch, I would listen to my grandparents and sundry other relatives and fellow villagers tell stories about the good life in the Old Country. The grass would be green now, the stream would be running with cool water, the orchards would be bursting with offerings and the stork would be returning to bless the family chimney. In contrast, the asphalt and cement of the Chicago streets and sidewalks, teeming with heat, would loom up at me, as would the smells of factories and foundries and the rumble of a not-too-distant locomotive. If everything is so beautiful in the Old Country, I would ask with unusual boldness, what are we doing here? I would be silenced by some adult who, bopping me firmly on the head, would tell me not to ask questions for which there were no answers.

With each passing year, however, I continued to ask such questions, in my heart and in silence. I discovered, through these early learning sessions on the front porch, that my grandfather had been quite the world traveler. He had worked in places whose names I couldn't pronounce, let alone locate on a map—Algeria, Tunisia, Silesia, Brandenberg. Only when I grew older did I appreciate the vastness of his sojourns. But why had he traveled so much, only to return home again and again to the family farm? And, then, why to America? And to Chicago, of all places, where there were no streams, no orchards, no stork?

I also learned of all those who had come to America only to return to the Old Country with their earnings from steel mills, tanneries, and slaughterhouses—three of my grandmother's brothers, two of my grandfather's, several from this village, some from that one. To my amazement, my grandparents, who had met and married here, had also planned to return with their American-born children. They had packed up all their belongings, bought ship tickets, and prepared for the journey, only to be prevented from sailing by last minute doubts. They remained, always dreaming of returning some day to the streams, orchards, and fields of wheat. Now they would be engulfed by the forces of an America they would never really understand. Had they sailed, how different the future would have been!

Many thanks to Charles Martin of the *Philadelphia Bulletin* for supplying back issues of the *Bulletin* and *Evening Ledger;* Thomas Slattery of the Philadelphia City Archives for his assistance in procuring Philadelphia maps and ward atlases of pre-World War I vintage; the Frankford Historical Society for sharing its storehouse of early twentieth-century Philadelphia history, especially its information on occupations and Philadelphia industries; Maxwell Whiteman, Librarian, Union League of Philadelphia, for his information concerning the Jewish peoples of Philadelphia; Richard Juliani, student of Philadelphia's Italian peoples, for sharing his research, information and expertise on this and other topics of immigration; the pastors and clergymen of Philadelphia's Polish parishes (Stanislaus A. Polityka, Anthony Ziemba, Sebastian P. Babiarz, Paul H. Lambarski, Joseph C. Klosinski, Francis S. Palecki, John J. Judycki, John A. Naja and Henry Krzywicki) who gladly and often enthusiastically let me use their parish records; Lawrence Schofer, Alfred Rieber and Alexander Riasanovsky, who generously read parts or all of the manuscript, offering wonderful suggestions; Edward P. Hutchinson and Seymour Mandelbaum, who first suggested the idea from which this book grew, and who continued to support it with time and ideas; and Edward F. Plocha, faithful soundingboard, who provided the support and encouragement for this endeavor. I am especially indebted to Melanie Piltch, the artist whose skill and patience during preparation of the maps was so valuable to me.

Finally, this book is dedicated to the one who taught me the true meaning of immigrant destinations.

CAROLINE GOLAB
Philadelphia, 1977

Introduction

The Wandering
of Nations

As yet it is impossible to assign any single factor or group of
factors as the primary force in the distribution of the foreign
stock in this country.

—Niles Carpenter[1]

After the Civil War Americans resumed their westward trek, initiating
a " 'wandering of the nation' that was none the less notable because
confined within the boundaries of a single country."[2] This westward
migration was paralleled by another movement, that of cityward migration. By 1880 the rural to urban flow had surpassed that to the frontier
and the farm. Rather than head West in search of fame, fortune or land,
the disillusioned farmer was more likely to set out for the nearest urban
center, whether hamlet, village, town or city. Farms from Maine to
Missouri were abandoned in increasing and alarming numbers; rural
townships everywhere recorded extensive depletions of population.
"It was the city rather than the unpeopled wilderness that was beginning to dazzle the imagination of the nation. The farmer, once the pride
of America, was descending from his lofty estate, too readily accepting
the city's scornful estimate of him as a 'rube' and a 'hayseed'."[3]

During the 1880s, a watershed decade for cityward migration, the
number of towns with 8,000 or more inhabitants rose from 286 to 448,
an increase of 162. During the previous decade, only 60 new centers
had appeared. Larger cities, especially those with populations exceed-
ing 100,000, grew even larger. By 1910 almost 48% of the nation's
residents were urban dwellers. American natives of rural origin accounted for one-third, or 14 million, of these 42 million urbanites; but it
was even more striking that almost 80%, or 11 million, of them had arrived after 1880. Finally, the urban population was not randomly dis-
tributed: it definitely favored the northeastern and northcentral states
and shied away from the West and South.[4]

During these crucial years, the nation's internal migration dis-
played several noteworthy characteristics. First, it consisted primarily
of short range rather than long distance movements, with individuals

3

seeking the nearest urban center regardless of size.[5] Second, individuals did not move "directly from the isolated farm to the huge
metropolis. More frequently, people moved from rural areas to a local
hamlet, then to a town or regional city, and then perhaps to Chicago,
New York, or another metropolis." In other words, the rural to urban
movement proceeded in steps—*Staffelweise,* Adna Weber called it.[6]

Finally, the ultimate distance traveled by the migrant varied in
direct proportion to the magnitude and size of the urban center. "The
larger the city, the greater its power of attraction (i.e., the larger its
proportion of outsiders, and the more distant the counties or districts
which contribute to it)."[7] Weber explains:

> Since, then, the current of migration is toward the cities and yet
> the bulk of migration is for short distances only, we can see the
> manner of the movement; it is a migration by stages having for
> its object the satisfaction of the demands for more labor in the
> cities. These demands are not met by the direct migration of
> superfluous labor from the fields to the cities, but by the flock-
> ing in of the inhabitants immediately surrounding the town; the
> gaps thus left in the rural populations are filled up by immigrants
> from more remote districts until the attractive force of a rapidly
> growing city makes its influence felt, step by step, to the most
> remote corner of the country.[8]

And, we might add, to the most remote corners of Europe and the
Near East. Indeed, despite the steady and significant movement of
rural Americans to urban centers, cities owed their rapid growth after
1880 in greater measure to an influx of European immigrants and
foreign migrant-laborers. Forty-one percent of 11,826,000 new city
dwellers in 1910 were foreign-born; only 29.8% were former rural
Americans.[9] By 1920 almost one-half of the nation's total urban population was composed of immigrants and their American-born children;
in the largest cities, those of 100,000 or more, immigrants and their
children constituted almost 60%.[10]

Like the urban population in general, the immigrant population
had distinctive and revealing locations. At least one-half of all the
foreign-born lived in the northeastern states and more than one-third in
the northcentral states; in comparison, the West and especially the
South were immigrant-poor. Moreover, the various immigrant groups
showed distinctive patterns of settlement; the Italians, Jews and Irish
favored the eastern cities, while the Germans, Poles and other Slavic
peoples favored the Midwest.

Table 1

PATTERNS OF IMMIGRANT SETTLEMENT

Area	% Foreign-Born			
	1850	1870	1890	1910
Northeast	59.0	46.9	42.6	49.7
Northcentral	29.1	42.4	44.6	35.1
South	10.7	7.2	5.6	5.4
West	1.0	4.5	7.3	9.8

SOURCE: U.S. Census.

NOTE: Figures do not total 100% due to rounding.

This rural to urban movement, whether from America's hinterlands or Europe's farms, was part of a larger fundamental reorientation and restructuring of the Atlantic Economy, that potentially integrated economic unit at first composed primarily of the United States, Canada and the countries of northern and western Europe, but which after 1870 gradually came to include the countries of southern and eastern Europe. The process of reorientation was a complicated one, now summarized neatly—perhaps too neatly—in the single term *industrialization*.[11] As David Ward, a leading authority on the subject, has shown, urban growth in the United States, its volume and location, responded directly to the spatial reorganization of the national economy; this reorganization established the northeastern and northcentral states as the industrial core or center of the economy. Moreover, "immigrants and their American-born children accounted for two thirds or more of the population of cities in the industrial center of the economy."[12] The immigrant's geographic distribution represented a positive adaptation to the reorientation of the American economy. There could be no adjustment to America (and hence no eventual creation of neighborhoods or communities) unless the immigrant found a proper "entrance status" via the economy.[13]

Although the peoples of the New Immigration followed the changing pathways of the national economy, they did not distribute themselves randomly or in equal numbers and equal proportions throughout the nation, its industrial core or its cities. Italians, Jews and Poles encountered similar situations and job offerings, but each responded differently. Jews, for example, were heavily concentrated in the garment industry, Poles in steel mills and coal mines and Italians in construction. The immigrants were not interchangeable. Their geographic distribution was a function of the precise nature of the industries which made up the national economy and the specific locations of these industries within the industrial core. It was the specific nature of the work to be performed which brought the immigrant to his geographic destination, whether that destination was the industrial core in general, a specific city within that core, or, finally, a specific area or neighborhood within the city.

To explain the distribution of immigrants within and among America's cities, therefore, it is first necessary to account for their distribution within industries. To do this, it is important to know the relationships prevailing among various groups (the work opportunities of one group often depended upon its ability to compete with other groups), as well as the cultural factors that prodded groups to emigrate and to seek out or to avoid certain occupations and forms of work. It is the latter considerations that offer the final clues to the ultimate distribution and initial economic adaptation of the immigrants and their children.

This study represents an attempt to account for the geographic distribution of America's immigrants in the period of their greatest influx, 1870 to 1920. It aims to answer the question: Why did certain immigrant peoples in certain numbers settle in certain places but not in others? This beginning analysis will not attempt a survey on a continental scale. I have selected for detailed study one particular geographic and temporal locus, the city of Philadelphia in the years 1870 to 1920, and tried to analyze the forces that determined the particular immigrant composition of this large northern center. If we can understand why certain peoples, in certain numbers, came or did not come to this city, perhaps we can also understand the forces which influenced immigrant distribution across the larger continent.

Philadelphia's experience with Europe's migrant peoples illustrates the interplay of factors at work in immigrant settlement after 1870. During this period Philadelphia was an industrial matrix of the nation, second only to New York City and neck and neck with Chicago, its upstart rival to the west. The city was also a chief port of entry for commodities and people, again second only to New York in most years and usually outdistancing competitors like Boston, Baltimore and New Orleans. Despite its lofty industrial status and prime port location, however, Philadelphia retained a relatively small immigrant population. The city achieved its peak foreign-born population in 1870, before the coming of the New Immigrants from southern and eastern Europe. Why did a city of such size, industrial magnitude and geographic accessibility remain, in Lincoln Steffens' words, "the most

American of our greater cities"? Philadelphia's uniqueness invites analysis.

Eastern European Jews and southern Italians were the chief groups of the New Immigration to settle in Philadelphia. Comparatively few Christian Poles stayed there permanently, although they used it as a port of entry. They actually appear to have avoided Philadelphia in favor of Chicago, Milwaukee, Detroit, Cleveland, Buffalo and the smaller cities and towns of western and northeastern Pennsylvania. In fact, Pennsylvania, exclusive of Philadelphia, received more Polish people than any other state. Eastern European Jews, in contrast, the largest immigrant group to settle in the city after 1880, disembarked at Philadelphia and stayed. Although relatively few Italians landed at Philadelphia before 1910, tens of thousands were present in the city by that date. Perhaps the very things that made Philadelphia attractive to Jews and Italians made it less attractive to Poles and other Slavs. Perhaps, too, differences in the historical and cultural backgrounds of the three groups were sufficient to explain their uneven response to the Philadelphia invitation.

In keeping with this thinking, a basic premise underlies the analysis in this book: immigrants did not exist in a vacuum. They brought much with them to America, even if they carried it within themselves: a rich cultural heritage, previous work experiences in an industrializing Europe, definite ideas about why they had come. They found much when they arrived here: other people as well as established social and economic structures. They could react and adapt to what they found only in terms of the experiences and values they had brought with them. Their coming to America; their settling in its cities; their settling in a particular city, region or neighborhood; their participation in certain occupations or industries and their lack of representation in others; these were not random or haphazard events. Demographic and cultural as well as economic forces propelled certain groups in predictable directions and into predictable occupations.

To solve the riddle of Philadelphia's uniqueness and to account for the particular composition of its foreign-born population, we begin by analyzing Philadelphia demographically and economically in order to recreate the structures into which any newcomers, native or foreign, would have had to fit themselves in order to survive. Next, by examining in greater detail foreign migrants, eastern European Jews, southern Italians and, especially one group, the Poles, we can see how intentions, desires, cultural belongings and pre-emigration experiences helped or hindered their attempts to adapt to established economic and demographic structures. The Poles are singled out for greater study because, as the least responsive of the New Immigrants to the Philadelphia situation, they exemplify the phenomenon that made the city unique: the Poles may have avoided Philadelphia, but so did others. After 1870, the city never supported a foreign-born population commensurate with its size, seaport location and industrial magnitude. The Poles' generally negative response can help us to understand what made the Jews and Italians respond more favorably. In this sense, the Jews and Italians are the foils for the Polish experience.

Finally, any meaningful interpretation of the distribution of immigrants must eventually come to grips with the formation of the immigrant neighborhood. The ethnically defined neighborhood long remained, and in many instances remains today, the defining characteristic of the twentieth-century American city. Once again, it was primarily work that brought together the immigrant and a particular piece of the city. If the conditions of work remained favorable long enough to keep the newcomers rooted to their piece of city-space, the ethnic neighborhood and community could be formed, complete with its unique industrial and occupational structures. The ethnic neighborhood is the final product of the process of geographic distribution. It represents the positive and successful adaptation of foreign-born peoples to the vagaries and inconsistencies that were America in what, for the purposes of further argument, will be called the Age of the Early Industrial Economy.

PART I
The Context

1   Philadelphia— Corrupt, Contented but Definitely American

> New York is excused for many of its ills because it is the metropolis, Chicago because of its forced development; Philadelphia is our "third" largest city and its growth has been gradual and natural. Immigration has been blamed for our municipal conditions; Philadelphia with 47 percent of the population native born of native parents, is the most American of our greater cities.
>
> —Lincoln Steffens[1]

In his 1902 edition of *Philadelphia and Notable Philadelphians,* Moses King, the city's foremost social critic, remarked with relief and pride that "the tide of newcomers flowed to New York and Philadelphia became the one northern city in which the native-born American was in an overwhelming majority."[2]

King's observation was accurate: from 1870 to 1920 Philadelphia supported a smaller proportion of foreign-born residents than any other large northern city. During these years the city's foreign-born population never exceeded 27%, a peak which was reached as early as 1870. Boston and New York were also old seaports, but, unlike the City of Brotherly Love, they continued to support substantial foreign-born populations—34% and 40% respectively—throughout the entire fifty-year period.

The proportions were even larger in the newer inland cities of America. In 1870 almost one-half of all Chicago and Milwaukee residents were foreign-born, as were 45% in Detroit and 42% in Cleveland. If we include the immigrants' American-born children, three-fourths or more of the inhabitants of Buffalo, Chicago, Cleveland, Detroit, Milwaukee and New York City were of "foreign stock," whereas almost one-half of Philadelphia's population remained "native born of native parents." To determine why Philadelphia's situation was unique, it is necessary to examine the city's immigrant population in detail and to compare its composition and proportions with those of other cities.

Philadelphia's Immigrants

According to the 1920 census (see Appendix A for full listing), Philadelphia's foreign-born population numbered 400,744 and was composed of

Russians	95,744
Irish	64,500
Italians	63,723
Germans	39,766
Poles	31,112
English	30,886
Austrians	13,387
Hungarians	11,513
Rumanians	5,645
Lithuanians	4,392

Forced from their homelands by poverty, persecution and famine, and able in America to find employment in iron and textile manufacture and railroad and building construction, the Irish had been coming to Philadelphia in considerable numbers since the early nineteenth century.[3] By 1870 they constituted more than half the city's foreign-born population, making Philadelphia a large, viable and self-sustaining Irish center. Only New York City hosted a larger Irish population. Boston, despite its reputation, was a distant third. The Irish influx diminished after 1890, but the Hibernian presence persisted. In 1900 more than one-third of Philadelphia's immigrants were Irish; in 1910, more than one-fifth; and in 1920 the Irish still comprised the second largest foreign-born group in the city. Between 1870 and 1910, one of every four Philadelphians was born outside of the United States, but it was because of the foothold secured by the Irish at an earlier date. The dwindling of the Irish flow was a major factor in reducing the city's proportion of foreign-born residents.

New immigrant peoples—southern Italians, eastern European Jews and Slavs—moved into the city after 1870, but their numbers were not enough to compensate for the decline of the Irish. Although not recorded as such, almost all of the Russians listed for Philadelphia were Jews, as were most of the Austrians, Hungarians, Rumanians, Lithuanians and Poles. The estimated number of eastern European Jews in Philadelphia by 1920 amounted to 120,000, perhaps even

135,000. The number of foreign-born Christian Poles (31,112 less the Jewish segment) amounted only to 15,000 to 18,000 by 1920.[4] Proportionally, for every Pole in Philadelphia there were eight eastern European Jews, four Irishmen and four Italians.

The number of Christian Poles in Philadelphia was also small in comparison with the Polish populations of other American cities. In 1903 Wacław X. Kruszka, an early chronicler of the Poles in America, estimated that there were 250,000 Poles and Polish-Americans in Chicago, 70,000 in Buffalo, 65,000 in Milwaukee, 50,000 in Detroit and Pittsburgh and 30,000 in Cleveland. He did not even mention Philadelphia. In 1908 the Polish *Press* estimated that the Chicago group numbered 350,000 and the New York City group 250,000. There were then 80,000 Poles in Buffalo and 75,000 in Detroit and Milwaukee. Again, Philadelphia was not mentioned, not even as a minor Polish center. By 1920 Chicago's Polonia numbered 400,000; the Pittsburgh and New York groups totalled 200,000 or better; and Detroit, Buffalo and Milwaukee each harbored 100,000 Polish immigrants and their children. Philadelphia's Polish community, finally mentioned, was listed at 50,000.[5] This figure, however, reflects Polish migration to the city between 1915 and 1920, a period during which industrial activity was spurred by war orders pouring into city factories. The demand for labor, especially unskilled labor, was keen. The Poles who settled in Philadelphia after 1915 in response to this demand drifted in from the coal and steel regions of Pennsylvania or from other parts of the country; they did not come directly from Poland.

Table 2

POLES IN U.S. CITIES*

City	1903	1908	1922
Chicago	250,000	350,000	400,000
Detroit	50,000	75,000	100,000
Milwaukee	65,000	75,000	100,000
Buffalo	70,000	80,000	100,000
Toledo	14,000		30,000
Cleveland	30,000		50,000
Pittsburgh	50,000		200,000
New York		250,000	200,000
Philadelphia			50,000
Baltimore			35,000
Boston			25,000

*The figures include both foreign-born and native-born of foreign parentage.

Philadelphia and Its Peers

A deeper examination of major American cities and their foreign-born populations during the period 1870 to 1920 provides the first clues to why Philadelphia, a key industrial city and chief port, supported a relatively small foreign population and why its ethnic configuration consisted so largely of eastern European Jews and southern Italians and so meagerly of Poles. Taking fifteen major cities, this probe analyzes total growth rates, immigrant growth rates, composition of the foreign-born population and the timing of its arrival (see Appendixes B and C). The findings enable us to place the cities into three categories: (1) five older cities of the eastern seaboard—Boston, New York, Newark, Philadelphia and Providence; (2) seven newer cities, all inland and most in the Midwest—Buffalo, Chicago, Cleveland, Detroit, Milwaukee, Minneapolis and Pittsburgh; and (3) three older semi-southern cities that had been leading urban centers since the early days of the Republic—Baltimore, Cincinnati and St. Louis.

In total growth, the newer cities tended to grow more rapidly than the older ones. Nevertheless, the older cities of the East were very dependent on immigrants for even their relatively low rates of total growth. Of all cities, those of the semi-South were the least indebted to the foreigner for their total population increase. In fact, with each passing decade, these cities were expanding more and more slowly.

A city's ability to attract and keep a foreign-born population is best measured by its immigrant growth rate, the extent to which the foreign-born population continues to expand. The decade of the 1880s is important because it established three distinguishable patterns of immigrant growth: the fast pace of the newer cities, the slower pace of the older cities, and the declining pace or stagnation of the semi-southern cities. This decade also provides the first indications of which groups were going to which cities, patterns that were to become increasingly prominent in succeeding decades.

The newer cities were inundated with foreigners. Chicago's immigrant population, totalling 204,859 in 1880, more than doubled (to 450,666) by 1890. Germans, Czechs, Swedes, Norwegians and Poles were the major contributors. Minneapolis scored even higher, quadrupling its immigrant population in ten years. Swedes and Norwegians represented more than one half of this increase, British Canadians and Germans together made up another 25%. The immigrant populations of Buffalo, Detroit and Milwaukee, while not growing as rapidly as those of Chicago and Minneapolis, increased by more than 75%; the Cleveland and Pittsburgh groups increased by more than two-thirds.

Originally, the newer cities were strongholds of German settlement and remained so until 1890. In that year Germans comprised 68% of the foreign-born community in Milwaukee, 47% in Buffalo, 43% in Detroit, 41% in Cleveland, 35% in Chicago and 34% in Pittsburgh. After 1890 these cities began to absorb increasing numbers of Slavic immigrants: Poles, Czechs, Slovaks, Ukrainians and Lithuanians. The chief losers in the newer cities during the 1880s were the Irish, Scottish and English. Having peaked ten to twenty years earlier, these groups were to join the Germans in becoming smaller and smaller fractions in each succeeding census. The Italian and Russian groups, in contrast, were beginning to increase in numbers but in 1890 were not yet formidable contributors to the newer cities.

The immigrant populations of the older cities of Philadelphia, Boston, New York, Newark and Providence continued to increase during the 1880s but more slowly than those of the newer cities. An immigrant growth rate of 33% was the average for the older cities, with Providence at 44% recording the highest rate. The immigrant composition of these Eastern cities also differed from that of the newer cities. The persistent Irish were almost one-half of Boston's foreign-born in 1890, Canadians were 25% and Germans only 7%. Italians and Russian Jews were 3% each. In Philadelphia the pattern was similar: Irish 40%, Germans 25% and the Italians and Russians nearing 3% each. In New York the Irish and Germans together comprised two-thirds of the foreign community; the Russians had reached 8% and the Italians with 6% were gaining. Providence owed its relatively high immigrant growth rate to continuous Canadian and British immigration in addition to the arrival of large numbers of Swedes and Italians. The Irish, nonetheless, remained one-half of Providence's foreign population in 1890; the English were one-fifth, and the Germans were only 4%. The Italians, less than 1% of the foreign-born in Providence in 1880, were almost 4% by 1890.

The semi-southern cities illustrate a third pattern of immigrant growth during the 1880s: low or decreasing rates of increase of the immigrant population. Baltimore's foreign-born population increased by only 23% between 1880 and 1890. St. Louis barely increased its immigrant colony by 10% during this decade, and the rate of immigrant growth was negative in the following decade, 1890 to 1900. Cincinnati's foreign-born population, like that of St. Louis, was more than one-third of the city's total in 1870; however, Cincinnati experienced a continuing decline in the absolute numbers of its foreign-born population, and it was the only city to do so. Its immigrant growth rate was negative for the entire fifty-year period.

Table 3

TOTAL CITY GROWTH RATES AND IMMIGRANT GROWTH RATES, 1870–1920*

City	1870–1880 TCGR (1)	IGR (2)	1880–1890 TCGR (3)	IGR (4)	% Δ (5)	1890–1900 TCGR (6)	IGR (7)	1900–1910 TCGR (8)	IGR (9)	% Δ (10)	1910–1920 TCGR (11)	IGR (12)	% Δ (13)
Baltimore	24.3	-0.6	30.7	22.9	12.6	17.2	-0.6	9.73	13.2	18.3	31.4	9.2	4.1
Boston	44.8	30.5	23.6	37.8	50.7	25.1	24.6	19.6	23.5	42.2	11.6	-0.3	
Buffalo	31.8	10.9	64.8	74.5	38.0	37.8	16.5	20.2	13.9	20.2	19.6	2.6	3.8
Chicago	68.3	41.7	118.6	120.0	41.2	54.4	30.3	28.7	33.4	40.3	23.6	3.2	4.9
Cincinnati	18.0	-10.0	16.4	0.0	0.0	9.8	-18.8	11.6	-1.9	-2.9	10.4	-24.5	
Cleveland	72.5	5.3	63.2	63.4	37.2	46.1	28.4	46.9	57.4	40.0	42.1	22.4	18.6
Detroit	46.2	29.0	77.0	79.0	40.3	38.8	18.1	63.0	63.2	33.9	113.3	84.7	25.3
Milwaukee	61.8	36.4	76.9	72.7	37.7	39.3	11.8	31.0	25.3	25.5	22.3	-1.2	
Minneapolis			251.4	303.4	38.6	23.1	0.8	48.7	41.1	25.4	26.3	2.5	2.7
New York	28.0	13.8	25.6	33.7	52.2			38.7	53.1	50.7	17.9	4.3	9.8
Newark	29.9	12.4	33.2	37.8	33.6	35.3	28.4	41.2	55.6	39.1	19.3	-5.9	9.8
Philadelphia	25.7	11.3	23.6	31.9	32.6	23.6	9.6	19.7	30.3	35.0	17.7	4.2	5.8
Pittsburgh	81.7	60.3	52.6	64.3	34.9	34.8	15.8	18.2	22.7	31.7	10.2	-14.3	
Providence	52.2	63.4	26.0	43.8	45.1	32.9	38.4	27.8	36.6	42.0	5.9	-8.4	
St. Louis	12.8	-6.4	28.9	9.4	9.7	27.3	-3.1	19.4	13.4	13.3	12.5	-17.9	

KEY: TCGR = total city growth rate; IGR = immigrant growth rate; % Δ = % total increase due to immigration.

*See Appendix B.

By 1900 the semi-southern cities had the smallest proportion of immigrants of all cities under review. Thirty years earlier they had been strongholds of Old Immigrant peoples, especially Germans and Irish. In 1870 almost two-thirds of Cincinnati's and Baltimore's foreign-born populations were German and one-fourth was Irish. In St. Louis one-half of the foreign population was German and one-third was Irish. When these groups stopped receiving overseas reinforcements and older members died or moved, the foreign-born populations of these cities could increase only if replenished by members of new groups. Because the immigration of newer groups was not enough to make up for the decline in older groups, southern cities continued to house comparatively small foreign-born populations throughout the period 1880 to 1920. As we have seen, the same was true of Philadelphia.

The immigrantization of America's cities continued during the depression decade of the 1890s but more slowly. The semi-southern cities showed negative immigrant growth rates. Cincinnati's loss, for example, was 19%. Philadelphia's immigrant growth was very low, 9.6%. Only Minneapolis, with less than a 1% increase, recorded a lower rate, as Scandinavian immigration halted because of the depression.

The first decade of the twentieth century saw a renewal of immigrant expansion. With their foreign populations increasing by more than 50%, Cleveland, Detroit, Newark and New York were in the forefront of the revival. Minneapolis, with the Scandinavians on the move again, increased its immigrant population by more than 40%; Chicago and Providence increased by one-third. Philadelphia's growth rate was 30%. St. Louis and Baltimore continued to gain slowly (13%) while Cincinnati's foreign community continued to decline (−2%). The migration patterns established in the 1880s persisted more vigorously after 1900: the Italian and Jewish populations of the eastern cities grew rapidly while the Poles and other Slavic peoples continued their trek to Chicago, Detroit, Cleveland, Milwaukee and Pittsburgh.

Immigrants and the South

Because of their declining or stagnating rates of immigrant growth, and because they were once strongholds of older immigrant groups, the semi-southern group of cities merits additional consideration. What set Baltimore, Cincinnati, St. Louis, and all large cities of the South apart from their northern counterparts was the presence of large black populations, either in the city proper or in adjoining hinterlands. The black population of Baltimore averaged 15% of the total for the 1870 to 1920 period while Cincinnati and St. Louis were approximately 6% black by 1910.

There was an inverse relationship between the foreign-born and black populations of America's cities. Baltimore, with the largest percentage of blacks, had the smallest percentage of immigrants. St. Louis and Cincinnati had relatively large black populations and smaller immigrant populations. New York, Chicago, Cleveland and Detroit had very high proportions of immigrants but very small proportions of blacks. If Philadelphia's foreign-born representation was low compared with other cities, its black representation was high—almost 6% by 1910 (84,459). In that year only three southern cities—Baltimore (84,749), Washington, D.C. (94,446) and New Orleans (89,262) had larger absolute black populations. To repeat the common cliche of the period, Philadelphia had much in common with her southern sisters.[6] (See Appendix C.)

The inverse relationship prevailing between blacks and the foreign-born holds for the United States in general. It becomes very evident when the foreign-born/black distribution is viewed by states or regions, as in Table 5. This inverse relationship is easily explained. The two groups were competitors in the nation's unskilled or secondary labor market.[7] The presence of a substantial black population worked to depress the foreign-born representation of a city or region, since cities with large pools of black labor had little need for unskilled immigrant labor.[8] The reverse was also true: blacks had difficulty in securing entrance to areas where immigrants were more accessible and had thus become entrenched. As the foreigner was at a competitive disadvantage in the South, so was the black in the North.

Southern blacks were very much involved in the redistribution of population that occupied the nation after 1870. Spurred by the same conditions as native white and foreign migrants—"the difficulty of making a living at home and the prospect of an improved economic status in other regions"—they were moving in greater numbers. They were no exceptions to the rule that migrations consisted primarily of short-distance movements while longer distances were covered in several stages over a greater period of time. Before the First World War the ultimate destination of black migrants was usually the nearest southern city, the site of potential economic opportunities, for blacks were a chief source of unskilled labor.[9] If blacks did move to a northern city, it was to one that happened to be only a short distance away. One-half of all southern-born blacks living in the North in 1910 came from two states, Kentucky and Virginia, and only 18% came from the eight

Table 4
BLACK POPULATION OF SELECTED CITIES, 1890–1920

City	1890 No.	1890 %	1900 No.	1900 %	1910 No.	1910 %	1920 No.	1920 %
Baltimore	67,104	15.44	79,258	15.57	84,749	15.52	108,322	14.80
Boston	8,125	1.81	11,591	2.06	13,564	2.00	16,350	2.20
Buffalo	1,118	.43	1,698	.48	1,773	.40	4,511	.90
Chicago	14,271	1.29	30,150	1.77	44,103	2.02	109,458	4.10
Cincinnati	11,655	3.92	14,482	4.44	19,639	5.40	30,079	7.50
Cleveland	2,989	1.14	5,988	1.56	8,448	1.50	34,451	4.30
Detroit	3,431	1.66	4,111	1.43	5,741	1.20	40,838	4.10
Milwaukee	449	.21	862	.30	980	.30	2,229	.50
Minneapolis	1,320	.80	1,548	.76	2,592	.90	3,927	1.00
New York	23,601	1.55	60,666	1.76	91,709	1.90	152,467	2.70
Newark	4,141	2.27	6,694	2.72	9,475	2.70	16,977	4.10
Philadelphia	39,371	3.76	62,613	4.83	84,459	5.50	134,229	7.40
Pittsburgh	7,850	3.28	17,040	5.30	25,623	4.80	37,725	6.40
Providence	3,963	2.99	4,817	2.74	5,316	2.40	5,655	2.40
St. Louis	26,865	5.94	35,516	6.17	43,960	6.40	69,854	9.00

SOURCE: U.S. Census.

Table 5

FOREIGN-BORN/BLACK DISTRIBUTION BY GEOGRAPHIC DIVISION, 1920

Geographic Division	% Black	% Foreign White Stock
United States	9.9	34.4
New England	1.1	61.0
Middle Atlantic	2.7	54.0
East North Central	2.4	42.6
West North Central	2.2	37.9
South Atlantic	30.9	6.2
East South Atlantic	28.4	3.1
West South Atlantic	20.1	11.3
Mountain	0.9	36.3
Pacific	0.9	44.3

SOURCE: Niles Carpenter, "Immigrants and Their Children," *U.S. Bureau of the Census Monograph,* No. 7 (Washington, D.C., 1927), p. 34.

states of the Deep South—Georgia, Florida, South Carolina, Alabama, Mississippi, Arkansas, Louisiana and Texas. Kentucky's blacks tended to move across the river to cities and towns in Ohio (Cincinnati, for example), while Virginia's blacks moved to the urban centers of adjacent Pennsylvania, New Jersey and Delaware. The overwhelming majority of Southern-born blacks living in Pennsylvania in 1910 had moved there from the neighboring state of Virginia. These are the figures: 48,995 were Virginia-born, 9,735 were from North Carolina, 2,113 from South Carolina, 1,578 from Georgia, 393 from Florida, and 545 from Alabama.[10]

The development of railroad transportation reinforced this early pattern of black migration. Until well into the twentieth century, railroad links between southern points and northern points were primitive or nonexistent. Unless they were willing to walk to Chicago, Detroit, Cleveland or Milwaukee, it was very difficult for large numbers of poor southerners, black and white, to reach such places. For this reason northern cities found it easier to import migrant workers from Europe than to bring blacks up from the South. After 1870, major ports within the European portion of the Atlantic Economy (Bremen, Hamburg, Antwerp, Rotterdam, Naples, Palermo) became accessible via railway and highway, and transatlantic steamship service was increasingly available. Once landed in the United States, foreigners found that the railroad network would propel them with relative ease to most points in the North (but not the South).[11]

In addition to the southern black, there was another group whose presence helps to explain the unattractiveness of the South for European immigrants. The southern rural white, like his black counterpart, was increasingly mobile and available after 1880. During this period, for example, Cincinnati owed its growth primarily to the influx of rural whites from adjoining hinterlands. The South differed from the North chiefly in its surplus of rural farmers, both black and white, who could serve as potential urban workers. The North had largely exhausted its supply of available native workers. There, the number of nonagricultural job openings expanded faster than the number of available native workers. The South, in contrast, did not produce enough nonagricultural jobs to absorb its surplus rural populations, much less to attract foreign labor. The South's predicament was further complicated by the inadequate integration of its transportation and communication facilities with the North. Because of the North-South transportation problem, surplus southern farmers of either race could not easily take advantage of or even learn about job opportunities in the North.

Urban centers with surplus populations in their hinterlands employed these excess people before recruiting any others. Philadelphia was in a position similar to that of Cincinnati, St. Louis and Baltimore. Even before the Civil War, the Quaker City's prime location in a free state bordering the slave South made it an easily reached gathering place for blacks, freed and fugitive, and a key terminus of the Underground Railroad. Geography was important in determining the city's unique mixture of foreign and black populations: Philadelphia faced two hinterlands, one supplying black labor and one bringing foreign labor via a major port and an integrated northern railroad network.

Blacks and Philadelphia

From the time of the Civil War and before, blacks were employed in all aspects of Philadelphia's economy—manufacturing and mechanical operations, transportation, trade and domestic and personal service. Unlike other large northern cities, Philadelphia's blacks were not confined to domestic and personal service, the traditional "entrance status" of blacks heading north before the First World War. In New York and Chicago, 50% of all black males were in domestic and personal service; in Philadelphia only 29% were so employed. In New York less than 14% and in Chicago less than 17% were in manufacturing and mechanical pursuits; in Philadelphia, 25% found employment in manufacturing. Philadelphia also had substantial portions of blacks

Table 6

DISTRIBUTION BY CHIEF OCCUPATION OF BLACK MALE WORKERS,
1910

City	% Black Male Workers in			
	Mfg/Mech.	Transportation	Trade	Domestic/Personal
New York	13.6	15.7	9.3	49.0
Philadelphia	25.1	19.2	11.5	28.8
Chicago	16.7	10.0	8.2	51.1
Detroit	17.4	7.7	4.6	33.4
Pittsburgh	28.8	12.4	8.2	30.4
Cleveland	21.6	11.8	8.3	32.9
Cincinnati	24.7	20.7	7.1	23.6

SOURCE: L. V. Kennedy, *The Negro Peasant Turns Cityward: Effects of Recent Migrations to Northern Centers* (New York, 1930), p. 75.

employed in trade and transportation. The occupational distribution of the city's blacks resembled that of southern or semi-southern cities like Cincinnati, where blacks had also been employed in manufacturing, transportation and trade as well as domestic and personal service since at least 1870.

Blacks' ability to compete with foreign laborers in the secondary labor market is also evidenced by their distribution within Philadelphia's industries. Blacks were significantly employed in those unskilled occupations and industries that, elsewhere in the nation, relied very heavily on foreign-born workers and their children. In the building trades in 1915, blacks constituted one-fifth of all brick, cement, stone, paving and road construction laborers, 13% of those in building construction and 10% of those in railway construction. They accounted for one-third or more of all workers employed in the manufacture of grease, tallow and paving materials; one-fifth of those working with oils and manufacturing bricks, 16% of those making iron and steel forgings, 13% of those working with flour, grist mill products and ice cream and 12% of those in fertilizer production. The steam railroads also employed substantial numbers. Outside of industry, blacks were street and sewer cleaners, trash collectors, livery men, hostlers, laundresses and domestics.[12] (See Appendix E.)

The reciprocal relationship between foreign and black labor was further illustrated when the First World War temporarily halted large-scale immigration from Europe. Northern industries found themselves in great need of unskilled laborers. With foreign workers lacking, agents representing railroads, employment agencies and large corporations began to recruit blacks in the South and to send them to Pennsylvania, New Jersey, New York and, to a lesser extent, to Illinois and Michigan. The same institutions and organizations perfected to recruit and route foreign labor were turned to southern labor. By now the railway network had been much improved. Industries and occupations usually the preserve of unskilled foreign workers were employing increasing numbers of blacks. There were, for example, only seventeen black laborers in Detroit auto factories in 1910; in 1920 there were 3,870. Pittsburgh blast furnaces and rolling mills employed 507 blacks in 1910 and 4,350 in 1920. The Chicago stockyards experienced a similar upsurge. At least 40,000 southern blacks moved to Philadelphia between 1916 and 1918 and, for the first time, more black males were employed in manufacturing than in domestic and personal service. Most found work in steel manufacture, chemical and oil refining, railroad maintenance and in other war-related factories. So great was the influx and so urgent the demand that blacks employed in Pennsylvania industry increased by 151% while the number employed in domestic and personal service actually decreased by 23%.[13]

It is estimated that more than 250,000 blacks moved North in the two-year period between spring 1916 and spring 1918, making these years important ones in the history of black migration. Twenty percent of the nation's blacks were living outside the states in which they had

Table 7

BLACK MALE WORKERS TEN YEARS OF AGE AND OVER, PHILADELPHIA, 1920 and 1910

Occupation	1920		1910	
	No.	%	No.	%
Agriculture	310		259	
Extraction of minerals	27		80	
Mfgr. and mechanical	27,702	45	7,407	25
Transportation	10,103	20	5,676	19
Trade	4,342	8.5	3,393	11.5
Public service	1,686		674	
Professional	870		538	
Domestic and personal	9,378	18.5	8,509	29
Clerical	1,391		929	
Total male workers	50,809		29,561	

SOURCE: L. V. Kennedy, p. 74.

Table 8

BLACKS LIVING IN PENNSYLVANIA, BY BIRTHPLACE, 1920

Birthplace	1910	1920	% increase
Virginia	48,995	60,843	25
North Carolina	9,735	16,664	78
South Carolina	2,113	11,624	475
Georgia	1,578	16,196	910
Florida	393	5,370	1,350
Alabama	545	9,994	1,818

SOURCE: L. V. Kennedy, p. 29.

been born. For the first time, Philadelphia and New York City housed the largest black populations of the nation, pulling ahead of all southern cities; this was evidence of the improved transportation and communication networks that had penetrated the South. In 1910 only 18% of northern blacks had been born in the Deep South, but in 1920, 40.5% listed one of these eight states as their birthplace.[14]

Immigrant Relationships

The racial composition of a city or region was not the only demographic factor influencing the settlement patterns of foreign workers. There were some specific relationships between immigrant groups. An older group helped to determine, for example, not only which group or groups came to an area but how many eventually stayed. A large pool of labor remaining from an earlier period of immigration often kept unskilled laborers of subsequent migrations away from that location in the same way that large pools of black or native white laborers deterred foreign workers. Workers of previous immigrations tended to be called upon first to fill jobs that required unskilled muscle; only if their supply fell short or if their wage demands were too high were other unskilled laborers brought into the city. Thus, the large numbers of Irish and Irish-American workers in Philadelphia meant fewer opportunities for newer migrants like the Poles to find unskilled employment in the city. The Irish presence, added to that of the black, further reduced the city's need for additional unskilled labor.

Labor market competition was not the only way in which the Old Immigration influenced the pattern of the New. It was no accident that cities with large German populations—Milwaukee, Chicago, Cleveland, Detroit—tended to receive the greatest number of Poles and other Slavic migrants. America's first Poles came from areas that had been absorbed by Prussia in the late eighteenth century. Often fluent or conversant in German, these Poles followed the paths blazed earlier by their German conquerors, who had been making the journey to America since the early nineteenth century. The Prussian Poles, in turn, passed information along to their compatriots in the Austrian and Russian sections of Poland. Nor should the influence of Bremen and Hamburg upon ultimate destinations be overlooked; virtually all Poles sailed for America from these two ports and, in addition, used the efficient German railroad network to reach them. In emigrating, not only did Poles from Poznań, Silesia and Prussia usually seek out German cities but, once there, they inevitably settled in German sections.[15]

Relationships between groups that migrated during the same period also influenced settlement patterns (see Appendixes B and C). In earlier decades Germans virtually monopolized Chicago, Milwaukee, Cincinnati, Detroit and St. Louis, while the Irish populations of these cities were comparatively small. In Boston, Providence and Philadelphia, on the other hand, the Irish were dominant and the Germans, in comparison, were few. The Irish secured an early foothold in these cities and stayed there, saturating the market for laborers. No Germans needed to apply. Finding the Eastern cities crowded and also more physically mobile and better off financially than the Irish, the Germans headed West, where they made a strong showing in the burgeoning cities of the midcontinent. In short, there was an inverse relationship in the settlement patterns of the Germans and Irish.

Among the newer migrant groups, Italians and Poles often competed for the same unskilled jobs. If one group secured a foothold in the unskilled labor market of a city, the other would be forced to try elsewhere. In part, this accounts for the large numbers of Italians and relatively few Poles in Philadelphia and for the Polish predominance and relative paucity of Italians in Chicago, Milwaukee and Detroit. The Poles, lacking the Italians' labor institution, the *padrone*, had a decided disadvantage in securing jobs in public works projects and were frozen out of this very large sector of Philadelphia's unskilled labor market. In Chicago, Milwaukee, Cleveland and Detroit, on the other hand, the largest sectors employing unskilled laborers were not public works projects, but heavy industries like steel, oil, chemicals and leather that did not rely on *padrone*-type systems to secure workers. Employers in those industries strongly tended to favor Slavic workers, and Italians on their part did not find such work attractive.

Immigrant Destinations: The General Pattern

The presentation thus far has indicated the discernible patterns of foreign settlement in America's cities from 1870 to 1920, and has showed how relationships between various immigrant peoples encouraged movement to certain areas and discouraged it in other places. Foreigners were largely responsible for the growth of the nation's cities during these years, but they were especially responsible for maintaining the growth of the older cities of the East. Foreigners preferred the cities of the North and avoided those with large or significant black and southern white populations. Moreover, they tended to prefer cities that did not have surplus pools of unskilled labor remaining from earlier eras of foreign migration. Finally, each group had its own pattern. Eastern European Jews concentrated in the large eastern cities where they had disembarked—New York, Philadelphia and Baltimore. Economically more mobile than other immigrant peoples, the Jews were not as geographically mobile. Southern Italians also showed a clear preference for the older cities of the eastern seaboard; comparatively few Jews and Italians found their way to the Midwest. Poles, however, definitely favored the newer cities of an industrializing America (see Appendix C).

The same forces that gave rise to these national trends were at work within each city. Whether Jewish, Italian or Polish, the migrant who came to Philadelphia before the First World War had to contend with an old eastern city already housing large numbers of Irish, Irish-Americans and blacks, the city's usual unskilled laborers. The presence of these older foreign and indigenous groups discouraged the settlement of newer peoples. All groups had to compete with each other for space and for jobs.

The Poles' behavior in Philadelphia, therefore, was partially determined by how well they competed with the established Irish and blacks and with their contemporary arrivals, the eastern European Jews and southern Italians. How well they competed depended on two things: (1) the type and number of jobs available in the city and (2) their qualifications for these jobs—their skills or lack of skills, previous work experiences and occupational preferences. A city's job openings might require a definite type of labor. If so, only certain types of immigrants could fill the need and only these would come and stay.

Philadelphia's age, racial composition, previous ethnic make-up and seaboard location may have influenced the composition of its foreign peoples, but these factors alone did not determine the city's final ethnic configuration. Philadelphia's economic structure and the foreigners themselves were also important in determining who came, how many, and why.

2   Philadelphia in the
         Land of the Titan

Fifteen cigars are made in Philadelphia every second of the
working day. In every second of time there are also made
twelve loaves of bread, ten pairs of stockings, one steel saw,
one man's hat, fifty newspapers, one and a half yards of
carpet. Every hour a new dwelling house is completed and a
new trolley is ready for the tracks.
                                    —*Philadelphia Yearbook*[1]

Almost one half of our population is of alien origin. It is
found upon investigation that except for the usefulness of
this one half in our industries, the other half pays little attention to it.
                —Pennsylvania Department of Labor and Industry[2]

Philadelphia was once the largest city of the colonies, the second
largest city of the British empire and the first capital of the new republic, but during the course of two more centuries it developed
certain physical, social and economic rigidities that greatly restricted
its ability to maintain its role of economic leadership. Many of the advantages enjoyed in earlier decades were lost as the nation moved from
a technology based on steam, water and iron to one based on electricity, steel and petroleum. What had once been economies of
concentration eventually became diseconomies of congestion.

Philadelphia's major industries had established their grip on the
city's economy before the coming of large scale mechanization and factory-type production. New technologies, techniques and systems had
to make their way amid economic conditions and industrial institutions
already fully formed and functioning. Land, especially in the central
parts of the city, was scarce and expensive; as a result, rents were
high. There was a tendency to squeeze all the people and buildings
possible into the available space. This brought about extensive industrial and residential overcrowding and inadequate air, light and
ventilation at home and work. It is not surprising to find that Philadelphia began to decentralize its industries and residences much

28

earlier than other cities; it began the process as early as 1870. The replacement of steam power by electricity and the accompanying improvements in transportation made such rearrangement increasingly feasible. Many industries and firms moved from the oldest parts of the city to its periphery; later, they sought vacant areas just beyond the city limits.[3]

Old firms found it difficult to expand and new firms found it difficult to locate in the central areas of the city because of the age and obsolescence of the buildings there, and because land to build on was scarce or extremely high priced. Industrialists also had to contend with high taxes, high insurance rates, high utility costs, a higher cost of living and bothersome nuisance legislation regulating smoke and noise. All these conditions especially affected those new industries essential to full scale economic growth, the ones that stressed bigness and freedom of experimentation. These tended to prefer areas unencumbered by archaic buildings and obsolete technologies, ones relatively free of taxes and restrictive financial and welfare legislation. Industries or firms usually chose to locate where production costs were lowest and where there were the greatest advantages in physical plant, transportation, markets, labor supplies and accessibility to ancillary industries and services. For iron and steel manufacturers, among others, accessibility of raw materials was important.[4]

By the late nineteenth century, Philadelphia's economy, old and firmly structured, had lost much of its adaptability. It could not compete with centers like Chicago, Cleveland, Detroit, Milwaukee, or Pittsburgh, all of which enjoyed advantages that Philadelphia no longer possessed. Because of their still fluid structures, the newer cities were better able to accommodate the beginnings of massive, full-scale industrialization.

> With the growth of the nation as a whole, new industrial regions were developing in competition with the older East. An inevitable result was a decline in the proportion of the nation's industrial production accruing to the older sections. It is significant that within Pennsylvania the decline was due largely to the passing of the great industrial preponderance of Philadelphia. Between 1869 and 1899 Philadelphia lost about three percent in percentage value added to manufacture, while Pittsburgh increased in value nearly two percent. Almost exactly the same ratio prevailed in terms of percentage of wage earners. . . . Of course, Pittsburgh's rise was related to the steel industry and its

expansion, while Philadelphia's decline was associated with a shift in the textile industry.[5]

What was true of Philadelphia was also true of Boston and New England, which "suffered a still more serious loss of relative position during the same period, as compared with Philadelphia and eastern Pennsylvania." This phenomenon, however, characterized all older cities:

> In general, the newer industrial regions and cities showed relative growth during this period, while the older areas, including some of the older midwestern industrial cities such as Cincinnati and St. Louis, experienced a relative decline in importance.[6]

If Cincinnati and St. Louis, like Philadelphia, did not receive new immigrants to the same extent as did other major cities, it was because these cities, with their more mature economic structures, did not have new openings for masses of unskilled male laborers and, when unskilled openings did appear, they were readily taken up by either the surplus black and white populations or the children and grandchildren of earlier immigrants. In short, the economic needs of these cities were not met by unskilled male immigrants, especially the Slavs, who were streaming to America in search of work after 1880.

Philadelphia's Industries

Philadelphia's economy was distinguished by the diversity and quality of its product, the smallness and plentitude of its business establishments and the bias it showed for female and skilled male labor. Textiles, including clothing manufacture, metal products manufacture, printing and publishing and leather manufacture were the city's major industries. Except for printing and publishing, all these industries had some place for immigrants, as did a host of smaller industries such as oil and sugar refining, chemical manufacture, meatpacking and furniture making. In 1915, 25% of Philadelphia's 250,000 industrial workers were foreign-born, but their patterns of distribution and the nature of their work tended to vary from industry to industry. Moreover, Philadelphia's preference for female labor was quite strong: women comprised 27% of the city's total workforce, in contrast, for example, to the 8% in Allegheny County (Pittsburgh). Philadelphia, perhaps, was more appealing to immigrant groups, like the Jews and Irish, that included large numbers of women and was less appealing to groups like the Italians and Poles that consisted primarily of men, unless, of course, the city was deliberately attracting those male immigrants, regardless of origin, who were accompanied by women or who had made the decision to marry and remain in America.

Textile and clothing manufacture, Philadelphia's largest industry, normally employed one-fourth to one-third of the city's work force. In textile manufacture the foreign-born predominated only as wool pullers and makers of yarns, cordage, twine and jute products. They were not extensively employed in the industry's largest branches, namely, the production of woolen cloth, cotton piecegoods, carpets and rugs. The textile industry remained largely in the hands of native Americans and the children and grandchildren, mostly women, of earlier immigrants. Only clothing manufacture was different. Here, in the "needle trades," foreign-born workers, the vast majority of them "Hebrew" women, comprised one-half or more of all those making men's, women's and children's clothing and hosiery and knit goods. Outside of clothing manufacture the city's major industry offered limited opportunities to the peoples of the New Immigration (see Appendix E).

Metal products manufacture, employing more than 54,000 men, was the second major bulwark of Philadelphia's economy before the First World War. The workers tended to be skilled and semi-skilled men employed as machinists and tool and die makers. Their industries turned out foundry and machine shop products, including machinery; locomotives; rolling mill products; electrical machinery and supplies; steel ships; saws; stoves; cutlery; hardware and tools; files; safes and vaults; agricultural implements; bolts, rivets and washers. Philadelphia had only two major steel rolling mills during this period—Midvale Steel Company and Disston Saw Works. These plants were excellent examples of vertical integration, producing acid and open hearth ingots not for general sale but for use in the manufacture of their own products.[7] Both plants employed thousands of unskilled laborers, primarily Slavs and blacks, in the making of steel. For this reason, and because they were basic steel producers, these plants were the exceptions which proved the rule: Philadelphia never housed a basic steel industry able to match those of Pittsburgh, Chicago or Cleveland. Most metal manufacture was of the highly specialized, machine-shop variety. The skilled immigrants usually found in such industries tended to be German and British.

Printing and publishing required large numbers of skilled persons to serve as printers, pressmen, proofreaders, editors and writers. Because these individuals had to read, write and speak English fluently, this industry remained the preserve of native Americans or of native-born English-, Irish-, Scottish- and German-Americans. Of 11,935 workers employed in the printing and publishing industry in 1915, only · 397 were foreign-born. One of Philadelphia's most important industries offered virtually no opportunities to the peoples of the New Immigration.

The last of Philadelphia's major industries, leather and its products, employed more than 15,000 men in tanning and finishing and in the manufacture of boots, shoes, trunks, bags, belts and purses. Tanning was nasty, often disgusting work, and was a chief occupation of unskilled laborers. In Pennsylvania, first the Irish and later the blacks and newer immigrants like the Slavs monopolized it. The manufacture of leather goods was usually a skilled or semi-skilled activity, however, and it relied on native American or skilled immigrant labor.

Thus, Philadelphia's major industries were long established institutions that required skilled, semi-skilled or female labor. Only in the initial stages of leather manufacture and the primary stages of the metal industry were substantial numbers of unskilled male workers employed. Within manufacturing, unskilled jobs requiring male labor were most often found in industries of less city-wide significance than the Big Four—the manufacture of fertilizers, glue, gelatin, grease, tallow, sulphuric and nitric acids, bricks, lime and curled hair; slaughtering and meatpacking; rubber manufacture; sugar and oil refining.

There were other areas of employment open to unskilled male laborers but not directly within manufacturing. Construction was the area of prime importance. Three great continental trunk lines—the Pennsylvania Railroad, the Philadelphia and Reading and the Baltimore and Ohio—employed thousands of laborers in Philadelphia in repairing and laying ties and tracks and in building depots, stations and crossings. Construction of streets, sewers, public buildings and subways was also constantly in progress throughout the period. The East-West subway, for example, built between 1903 and 1905, required thousands of unskilled laborers to dig ditches, pour concrete, raise beams and rivet girders. Private building construction and contracting kept pace with public construction and in many years employed more laborers than public projects. In 1915, 15,000 men found employment in railroad and building construction, both public and private, within the city.[8]

Philadelphia's standing as a major port meant additional opportunities for unskilled male workers, primarily in construction and maintenance but also as stevedores and longshoremen. Before the First World War more than 6,000 vessels engaged in foreign and coastwise shipping docked in Philadelphia harbor annually. Thousands of men unloaded these ships and loaded the railroad cars and drays that conveyed their cargoes to final destinations. Some used direct muscle power and others operated cranes, pulleys and machines. Many more facilitated the movement of 4 million tons of anthracite and bituminous coal through the port annually, often as employees of railway companies which operated innumerable marine terminals.

Port business required that docks, piers, wharves, dikes and bridges be kept in repair and that new ones be built. City officials were continually letting contracts for the construction of municipal piers and bulkheads and for the cleaning and dredging of the river and harbor system; in the four-year period 1908–1912, the Department of Wharves, Docks and Ferries removed "1,676,367 cubic yards of material from the Delaware and Schuylkill Rivers, channels, city docks and private docks where municipal sewers empty." Because of its importance for ship building and commerce, state officials and congressmen as well as city fathers were interested in the welfare of the Delaware River port. The river sheltered two major shipbuilders—Cramp's Ship and Engine Company, one of the world's largest private shipyards, and the Philadelphia Navy Yard. It was said that the Delaware carried more commerce and did a greater business for the government than any other river in the United States. To enhance the port and the river, Smith's Island and Windmill Island were removed from Philadelphia harbor in 1898. The Delaware River channel was deepened to 30 feet and widened to 600 feet over a period of 12 years (1899–1912). No sooner was it done than the city decided to extend the channel as far as Trenton, New Jersey, and to widen it an additional 5 feet. A U.S. River and Harbor Act of 1909 provided for the extension of dikes on the Delaware to control tides and a 1915 act authorized monies to construct these dikes and to dredge the 35-foot channel then under construction.[9]

All these public and semi-public projects—harbor and river improvements, subway, street and sewer construction—required that large amounts of unskilled male labor be assembled at a certain point in space and time. The employment offered was usually limited in duration, and the employer was usually the federal, state or city government. In Philadelphia, as elsewhere throughout the industrial core, most forms of public work tended to be the preserve of Italian immigrants and their children. Poles and other Slavs, in contrast, tended to predominate as stevedores, longshoremen and loaders and unloaders of warehouses, terminals and freight cars.

Pennsylvania's Industries

Pennsylvania attracted the peoples of the New Immigration to an extent that Philadelphia never matched. More Poles, Slovaks, Croatians, Slovenes and Ukrainians found their way to Pennsylvania than to any other state; Pennsylvania drew twice as many Slavs as did New York and Illinois. Pennsylvania's Italian and Jewish groups were also very large; only the state of New York had greater numbers.[10]

The distribution of Pennsylvania's immigrant peoples was interesting, perhaps unique. A hefty majority—71%—of the state's Italians and Poles preferred smaller towns and villages to the two largest cities, Philadelphia and Pittsburgh. In New York and Illinois, on the other hand, two-thirds of the Italians and Poles settled in the principal metropolises of New York City and Chicago. The Jewish pattern, however, did not vary from state to state. Seventy percent of Pennsylvania's Jews lived in Philadelphia and the rest in Pittsburgh and smaller cities, just as the overwhelming majority of Jews in New York and Illinois lived in New York City and Chicago.[11]

The arrival of large contingents of Poles, Lithuanians and Slovaks in the 1870s inaugurated the great eastern and southern European migration to Pennsylvania. Although Magyars, Croatians, Slovenians and some Italians followed in the 1880s, the Poles remained the leading group until 1901, when southern Italians and Sicilians pushed them into second place. The most intense years of immigration were 1899 to 1914 when 2,328,788 foreigners entered the state. Southern Italians made up 510,000 of these newcomers; Poles, 337,000; Slovaks, 240,000; Croatians, 182,000; and "Hebrews," 150,000. English, Scottish, Welsh, Dutch, Scandinavian, German and Flemish immigrants were conspicuously scarce, marking a dramatic change in the nature of immigration after 1870. Only 10% of the immigrants who arrived in Pennsylvania in 1914 were from northern and western Europe; 85% were from southern and eastern Europe. Fifty years earlier the proportions had been reversed: more than half of Pennsylvania's immigrants then had come from those countries which in 1914 accounted for only 10%.[12]

Pennsylvania became the home of these vast numbers of southern

Table 9

NUMBER OF IMMIGRANTS ADMITTED TO PENNSYLVANIA, BY
NATIONALITY, 1899–1914

Nationality	No.	Nationality	No.
Italian (South)	509,914	Welsh	9,023
Polish	336,961	Finnish	5,656
Slovak	210,295	Dalmatian	5,580
Croatian	181,882	Dutch	3,038
Hebrew	150,385	Armenian	1,851
German	139,892	Turkish	1,783
Magyar	133,815	African	1,138
Ruthenian	113,204	Spanish	915
Italian (North)	79,043	Cuban	815
Irish	773,359	Chinese	664
Lithuanians	70,019	West Indian	607
English	63,057	Spanish American	563
Russian	40,939	Portuguese	192
Rumanian	31,152	Mexican	186
Bulgarian	29,562	Japanese	185
Greek	22,797	East Indian	71
Scottish	22,735	Korean	2
Scandinavian	22,536	Pacific Islander	2
Bohemian	11,244	Other	1,803
Syrian	11,140	Not specified	2
French	10,781	Total	2,328,788

SOURCE: Pennsylvania Department of Labor and Industry, "Report of Division of Immigration and Unemployment," *First Annual Report* (Harrisburg, 1913), p. 233.

and eastern Europeans because of its undisputed status as the "titan of industry."[13] Coal, iron and steel, railroads, cement and glass were the state's major industries and employed immigrants and their children in overwhelming numbers. Mining, for example, employed more persons than any other Pennsylvania enterprise and was heavily, perhaps totally, dependent on foreign labor. According to the 1915 *Annual Report* of the Pennsylvania Commissioner of Labor and Industry, 64% of 159,170 anthracite workers, 68% of 153,753 bituminous workers, and 50% of 13,345 coke company employees were foreign-born; inclusion of American-born children pushed the percentage up to 90% or better. (See Appendix F.)

The original anthracite miners were Welsh, Scottish, English, Irish and German, groups that were in the majority until 1875 when Poles and Lithuanians began to outnumber them. Slovaks, Ukrainians, Syrians and Italians (in that order) began to arrive after 1880. At the

Table 10

FOREIGN-BORN EMPLOYEES, PENNSYLVANIA ANTHRACITE FIELDS,
1880–1900

Nationality	1880	1890	1900
Ireland	45,330	42,374	31,349
England		24,575	21,225
Wales	33,214	24,140	20,220
Germany*	20,686	28,534	24,086
Scotland	3,191	4,013	3,389
Total English-speaking	102,421	123,636	100,269
Poland†	1,925	15,142	37,677
Austria‡		9,226	17,876
Russia§		4,474	10,283
Hungary		9,931	13,534
Italy		4,234	9,958
Total non-English speaking	1,925	43,007	89,328
Total foreign-born	108,827	170,582	193,692

NOTE: The Pennsylvania Anthracite Region was composed of three "fields"—
Luzerne County, the largest; Lackawanna County; and the "Schuylkill Field," which included Carbon, Dauphin, Northumberland and Schuylkill Counties.

*Germany included a small portion of Poles from those provinces of Poland directly
annexed by Germany.

†Primarily Polish persons from the Congress Kingdom of Poland.

‡Austria included Ukrainians, Ruthenians, Slovaks, Czechs, Slovenes, Slovenians,
Servians, etc., and Poles from Galicia.

§Russia included Russians, Ukrainians, Lithuanians and Poles from provinces
directly annexed by Russia.

SOURCE: F. J. Warne, The Slav Invasion and the Mine Workers: A Study in Immigration (Philadelphia: Lippincott, 1904), pp. 51, 58.

height of the influx to the anthracite fields, the U.S. Immigration Commission reported a definite ethnic hierarchy:

> Managers and superintendents, Welsh; foremen and bosses,
> Irish; contract miners, Poles and Lithuanians; inside laborers,
> Slovaks and more recent Poles and Lithuanians; and outside la-
> borers, Slovaks, Ruthenians and Italians.[14]

Employment opportunities in anthracite mining were the single most
important factor initiating the Polish influx to Pennsylvania. The
state's first Polish settlements were all in the heart of the anthracite
belt: Shamokin (1870), Shenandoah (1873), Excelsior (1875), and
Mount Carmel (1877) in Northumberland County; Nanticoke (1875) in
Luzerne County; and Blossburg (1875) in Tioga County. By 1900 the

Poles were the largest single group employed in the anthracite fields. The Philadelphia and Reading Coal and Iron Company, the largest anthracite firm in Pennsylvania, employed 7,000 Polish-born workers out of a total of 26,000; if American-born sons are included, "Polish stock" accounted for more than half of all the company's employees.

The pattern in the bituminous fields was similar to that in anthracite. Soft coal miners of the 1870s were largely native Americans or members of older immigrant groups—English, Dutch, German, Welsh, Scottish and Irish—most of whom had been miners before coming to the United States. Because of the demands of the steel industry, bituminous mining continued to grow very rapidly. In many years, demand for laborers far outstripped supply. In response, the first eastern Europeans were solicited as early as 1870, and by 1880 Slovaks and Magyars were displacing English-speaking workers. Poles, more Slovaks, Croatians and Slovenians arrived in the 1890s. The first Italians appeared about 1895, but were not employed in large numbers until many years later. The greatest influx of immigration came after 1900 and did not peak until the war years. More Slovaks and Poles came, as did large numbers of Russians, Bulgarians, Rumanians, Ruthenians, Syrians, Armenians, Macedonians, Croatians and Servians. By 1910 75% of all bituminous employees were foreign-born with Slovaks and Poles the leading groups.[15]

Table 11

NATIONALITIES WORKING FOR 116 ANTHRACITE COMPANIES IN PENNSYLVANIA, 1905

Nationality	No.	%
Slavic and Hungarian	36,049	39.0
Italian	3,975	4.3
American, mostly of Slavic and other foreign parentage	25,905	28.0
Irish	6,351	6.8
Welsh	2,397	2.6
English	2,497	2.7
Scottish	289	0.3
German	4,003	4.4
Other	10,989	11.9
Total	92,455	100.0

Source: Pennsylvania Department of Internal Affairs, *Annual Report, 1905* (Harrisburg, 1906), pp. 448–49.

The story in the manufacture of metal and metal products was the same. Native Americans and the Welsh were the chief ironworkers of the 1850s; English, Scottish, and Germans joined them in the 1860s. With the rise of steel and its new technologies demanding less skilled labor, workers of western European origin turned their attention to other fields. To remedy the shortage of unskilled labor that gradually occurred, many steel firms began in the 1870s to recruit workers in Europe. Their agents no longer had success with western and northern Europeans on their home grounds; workers there were too skilled and preferred to seek opportunities at home or, when they came to America, to go into industries where their abilities would be used. The recruiting agents looked to southern and eastern Europe.

About 1880 the first Poles and Magyars arrived in the mills, followed by Slovaks, Croatians and Italians. By 1915 the Pennsylvania Department of Labor and Industry could declare that the "normal working force" in the iron and steel industry was "now made up of Magyars, Poles, Italians, Slovaks and Russians."[16] Of the more than 367,000 persons employed in iron and steel in Pennsylvania in 1915, 36% were foreign-born. Immigrants constituted one-half to two-thirds of those employed in smelting and refining and in the manufacture of billets, blooms, slabs, ferro alloys, pig iron, pipes and tubing, the percentage varying according to the amount of skill required. Fitch saw the trend in 1910:

> Fifteen or twenty years ago, the labor force was largely Irish.
> Now it is made up almost entirely of Hungarians and Slavs, an
> interesting example of the shifting of races that is going on to a
> greater or less degree in all departments of the iron and steel in-
> dustry. Irishmen still hold the better positions such as those of
> blower and foreman. In other departments of the industry the
> shifting has not gone so far; yet it seems to be only a question of
> time when in all but the most highly skilled positions the Anglo-
> Saxon, Teuton and Celt will be displaced by the Slav; nor have
> we any reason to think it will stop short there.[17]

Pennsylvania's railroads, essential to the nation's economic welfare and indispensable to the mines and steel mills, were an endless source of employment: laying and repairing tracks; stoking coal furnaces, maintaining locomotives, tenders, flats, frogs and switches; loading and unloading railroad cars, barges and lorries; building bridges, cross-ings and tunnels. According to the 1910 census, 29,000 foreign-born whites found work constructing and maintaining Pennsylvania's rail-

Table 12

DISTRIBUTION OF MALE EMPLOYEES OF THE BITUMINOUS COAL
INDUSTRY OF PENNSYLVANIA, BY RACE AND NATIONALITY, 1910

Origin	%
Native-born of native father:	
White	13.1
Black	1.9
Native-born of foreign father, by country of birth of father:	
Austria-Hungary	1.2
England	2.0
Germany	2.5
Ireland	1.6
Scotland	0.9
Wales	0.4
Other	0.7
Foreign-born, by nationality:	
Bohemian/Moravian	0.9
Bulgarian	0.1
Croatian	4.0
English	2.7
French	0.7
German	3.1
Irish	1.3
Italian, north	6.9
Italian, south	4.6
Lithuanian	1.3
Magyar	7.2
Polish	12.3
Russian	2.6
Scottish	1.0
Slovak	20.3
Swedish	0.4
Welsh	0.4
Other	5.9
Total	100.0
Totals:	
Native-born of foreign father	9.3
Native-born	24.3
Foreign-born	75.7

SOURCE: Immigration Commission, 1907–1910, *Abstracts of Reports* (Washington, D.C., 1911), p. 506.

roads, while another 1,300 performed the same services for urban
street railways. By 1915, the railroads that reported construction
activities to the Pennsylvania Department of Labor and Industry listed
almost 38% of their employees as foreign-born. Most of these were
southern Italians and Sicilians.[18]

Pennsylvania's Lehigh Valley was the source of Portland cement,
which revolutionized construction because it was fireproof, sturdy and
partial to unskilled labor. Demand for unskilled workers accelerated
with its increased use. Pennsylvania was also the center of the
American glass industry; Pittsburgh alone had twenty-seven glass
manufacturing plants and twenty-four glass cutting, staining and orna-
menting firms. Almost two-fifths of those employed in cement, glass
and related industries were foreign-born. Those working with stone,
granite and marble were mostly Italians; those in glass, lime and cruci-
bles were most often Poles, Slovaks, Ukrainians, Lithuanians, Hungarians and Croatians.[19]

Although coal, iron and steel, railroads, cement and glass were the
Pennsylvania industries that employed foreign labor in the largest numbers, smaller concerns also depended upon immigrant workers. In the
manufacture of chemicals and allied products, for example, 28% of the
32,000 workers were immigrants, but in the more unpleasant aspects,
working with hazardous chemicals, fertilizers, wood alcohol and
acetate of lime, 50% to 75% of those employed were immigrants. The
more distasteful or dangerous the work, the more likely were Slavic
immigrants and blacks to be the chief performers.

Twenty-eight percent of the 50,000 workers employed in Pennsylvania's building and contracting industry in 1915 were foreign-born. In
certain activities, such as paving and road construction, miscellaneous
contracting and private housing construction, foreigners were one-half
or more of those employed; in railway construction they were more
than one-third. Most foreign-born road, public works and railroad
construction workers were Italians; in private housing construction the
Irish and their American-born children continued to be dominant.

Twenty-six percent of Pennsylvania's leather and rubber goods
workers were foreign-born, but in the primary stages of leather production immigrants and their children accounted for almost all workers. In
tanning and curing, Slavic groups generally predominated. In lumber
and its remanufacture, the foreign-born represented more than 16% of
all workers; in branches of the industry that relied on unskilled male
workers, they accounted for one- to two-thirds of all those employed.

Finally, certain food processing industries were strongly dependent on immigrant labor. Sugar refining employed Poles and Lithuan-

ians in overwhelming numbers, as did slaughtering and meatpacking. In fact, wherever there was a slaughterhouse in Pennsylvania, Poles and other Slavs were invariably among its chief workers. Italians predominated in preserving and canning fruits, truck farm vegetables and fish, and also provided the bulk of the migrant workers who harvested fruits and vegetables.

Summary

The massive influx of Slavs and Italians coincided with Pennsylvania's industrialization. The consolidation and technological advances in coal mining, the beginnings of iron and steel production and its innumerable manufactures, the incessant demand for railroads and more railroads to facilitate the inflow and outflow of coal and iron, the perpetual need to repair and to maintain the railways and to load and unload freight cars, the manufacture of glass, cement and chemicals—all demanded huge armies of laborers whose primary qualifications were strength and availability rather than knowledge and skill.[20] Slavs and Italians were particularly active in these fields because they were unskilled, plentiful, available, mobile and most often single or unaccompanied by wives and children; 71% of them lived outside of Philadelphia and Pittsburgh precisely because of the direct relationship of industry and immigration in Pennsylvania.

Moreover, the state's enterprises were enormous in size and extent. Companies like Carnegie Steel, Pittsburgh Plate Glass, the Pennsylvania Railroad, H. C. Fick Coke Company or Westinghouse Air Brake were often vertically or horizontally integrated and composed of many plants. Because of economies of scale, they were able to employ thousands of workers at a place or time. They could afford to employ their own recruiting agents as well as exercise great leverage with New York employment agencies. For groups like the Italians who arrived in large numbers and often relied on a *padrone* to channel them, or the Poles and Lithuanians who often relied on company agents and employment agencies, it was much easier to be put in contact with bigger firms (exactly the ones needing large numbers of unskilled workers) than with smaller ones that had no agents of their own or no access to New York employment agencies. Smaller firms in need of laborers relied on newspaper advertising, word of mouth communications and traffic off the streets.

Pennsylvania's economy stressed bigness, required large numbers of unskilled workers and was devoted to the more primary forms of industrial activity. Philadelphia's economy relied on old, well-established industries that stressed diversity, precision, smallness and quality and relied on female, skilled and semi-skilled labor. In number and type of expanding work opportunities, Philadelphia could not compete with newer cities such as Chicago, Cleveland, Milwaukee or Pittsburgh, or with the myriad of smaller towns and cities that dotted Pennsylvania's coal regions.

Table 13

INDUSTRIAL COMPARISON, 1915

Category of comparison	Allegheny County		Philadelphia County	
	No.	%	No.	%
Total population	1,018,463		1,549,000	
Total workforce	212,694	100	321,181	100
Male	196,248	92	233,630	73
Female	16,446	8	87,551	27
% of total population in workforce		21		21
Firms with 10,000+ employees	4		0	
Firms with 5,000+ employees	5		2	
Firms with 1,000+ employees	27		23	
Firms with 500+ employees	66*		68	

*The Carnegie Steel Company is listed as one entity; if its individual plants employing 500+ employees were counted separately, the total number of plants in Allegheny County employing more than 500 workers would be more than 80.

Of the 27 industrial firms in *Allegheny County* that employed more than 1,000 persons, 17 were iron and steel manufacturers, 3 were railroad companies and 2 were coke companies. The rest included manufacturers of cork, electric supplies, glass and refractory brick and a food processor. Only 2 of these 27 firms—the food processor and cork manufacturer—employed women to any considerable extent.

Of the 66 firms that employed more than 500 persons, 37 were primary metal manufacturers, 5 were railroads, 5 were coke manufacturers and 4 were food processors; there were no textile or garment firms.

Of the 23 industrial firms in *Philadelphia County* that employed more than 1,000 persons, 9 were textile and garment makers, 6 were manufacturers of metal products, 2 were tobacco processors and 2 were railroad companies. The remainder included a publishing house, sugar refinery, leather processor and manufacturer of electric batteries. The textile, garment and tobacco firms were large employers of women.

Of the 68 firms that employed more than 500 workers, 26 were textile manufacturers, 12 were metal products manufacturers, 5 were cigar and tobacco makers, 4 were printers and publishers, 4 were food processors, 4 were chemical makers and 3 were construction firms.

SOURCE: *Second Industrial Directory of Pennsylvania, 1916.*

3   The Atlantic Economy and Its Migrant Workers

We get, if only through the Stock Exchange, some idea of
the industrial resources and economic exploitation of
Mexico and Persia; but we read very little about the
enormous and astonishing material development between
the Oder and the Dwina, within a couple of days travel from
London. We realize the rapid growth of Chicago and Win-
nipeg and Oklahoma, but forget that of Lodz, where a city
which began to grow only half a century ago now counts
800,000 inhabitants. How many Englishmen realize that
Lodz has become more populous than either Liverpool or
Manchester? How many Scotchmen are prepared to find it
as a manufacturing center vying with Glasgow? But the
mineral resources of Poland are greater even than its manufactures. The oil and salt and coal and iron with which Poland now supplies Europe constitute no small percentage of
the total world resources. . . .

—Stanislaw Posner[1]

The Philadelphia that greeted newcomers after 1880 had an established
economic and industrial structure as well as a settled ethnic and racial
composition. These two structures, invisible but pervasive, were crucial in determining who, and how many, came to Philadelphia to stay.
Whether they realized it or not, the immigrants were constantly
interacting with others—with the Irish and their descendants, with the
blacks who were there before them, and with the Jews, Italians and
Slavs who arrived at the same time. Moreover, without knowing it,
they were reacting to the city's particular economy which relied on
older industries biased toward skilled or female labor and which, unlike
Pittsburgh or Chicago, was not adding many new industries requiring
large quantities of unskilled male labor.

Exposed to the same economic and demographic structures, each
immigrant group responded differently. The variations depended on
such things as the nature of the group's migration (whether it was

forced or voluntary), the idiosyncracies of its culture and its work and migration experiences within the Old World of the Atlantic Economy. All these affected the competition among newcomers and their ability to fit themselves into the economic needs of the city. Occupational differences may have been the key, but the final variable in the riddle of immigrant destinations was the immigrants themselves. The Jew, the Italian and the Pole tended to choose certain occupations more than others—why? To answer this, we must establish what was unique to each group. The contrasts between them will act as a spotlight, isolating the qualities we seek.

Immigrants and Migrant-Workers

Throughout the nineteenth century, Europe and America had a special economic interdependency of labor, capital and resources. This relationship is best viewed in the context of what Brinley Thomas has called the "Atlantic Economy"—a large, potentially integrated economic unit encompassing the United States, Canada, Great Britain and northern Europe.[2] By 1880, if not before, the countries of central and southeastern Europe—Russia, Poland, Austria-Hungary and Italy—were ready to join the Atlantic Economy. In the throes of early industrialization, they were experiencing some of the highest rates of urban growth ever recorded, investing foreign and domestic capital in expanding industries, and, most important for our purposes, injecting surplus populations into the marketplace of the Atlantic Economy. Considered purely economically, the surplus southern and eastern European was a factor of production seeking the highest and best use, a result of differentials within a large Atlantic labor market.

In keeping with the rules of industrialization, Europeans, like Americans, were migrating. Their moves were usually short ones, with long distance migration occurring in stages over greater periods of time. Regardless of distance, these movements were centripetal: the thrust was to cities and smaller urban centers rather than to "open spaces." The European city, like its American counterpart, was feeling the effects of an expanding economy that was establishing new centers in areas rich in natural resources and industrial potential.[3]

One major difference distinguished the European from the American experience. Where Europe struggled to cope with surplus rural populations that could not be absorbed by the continent's expanding industrial and urban activities, America had to contend with the opposite problem—extensive shortages of native rural labor available for industry. In Europe, populations continued to grow more rapidly than industries and cities. Long distance or overseas migration, the "spill-over," occurred when native industry and local opportunities could no longer absorb the surplus. Frank Thistlethwaite has observed that "in country after country, beginning with Ireland and ending with Italy and Greece, there is a direct correlation between rates of emigration and rates of natural increase twenty years previously, which represents the migration of the surplus proportion of a larger age group at the point when it was ready to enter the labour market."[4] When an area could absorb its surplus population in local industry, emigration ceased or never occurred. Overseas migration of Poles, Slavs, Italians and Jews was part of, or peripheral to, the larger demographic and economic changes overpowering southern and eastern European society. The forces keeping people at home or urging them to move and to concentrate were equal to, if not greater than, the forces propelling them abroad: "In short, a consideration of the phasing of overseas migration both places it within a limited time-scale and reduces its significance in relation to intra-European migration. . . . We are, again, a long way from the America fever."[5]

By the late nineteenth century all of the conditions necessary for emigration from southern and eastern Europe were present. There was a surplus population unable to make ends meet in a changing society. There was freedom to migrate; serfdom had been abolished and governmental restrictions on emigration had been eased or removed for most groups. There were opportunities to earn money by working away from the farm in industrial and urban activities, many of which required temporary laborers with no skills. These opportunities were scattered throughout the Atlantic Economy, as close as the nearest town or provincial capital or as far as the industrial center of another country or another continent. Finally, for the first time, the means to learn about and reach these opportunities were readily available: steamships, trains, roads, banks, post offices and newspapers.[6] These were both the products and the symbols of a changing society, but they in turn became further instigators of change (see, for example, the accompanying map and Table 14 of railroad mileage in Poland).

Because of the fundamental changes occurring within Europe, it is misleading to speak of "immigrants" or "emigrants." From the perspective of the Atlantic Economy, there were only migrant-laborers who, in essence, constituted a "peasant proletariat, roaming the countryside, indeed the world, in search of employment in agriculture

Table 14

RAILROAD MILEAGE IN THE KINGDOM OF POLAND, 1845–1911

Year	Mileage
1845	72.70
1850	204.44
1855	204.44
1860	214.38
1865	408.88
1870	560.50
1875	580.39
1880	925.26
1885	1,112.31
1890	1,153.94
1895	1,384.48
1900	1,575.87
1905	1,873.52
1910	1,963.62
1911	2,103.44

SOURCE: *Polish Encyclopedia* 3 (Geneva, Switzerland: Atar Ltd., 1922–1924): 448–49.

and industry."[7] It is the entity of the migrant-laborer and not time (before or after 1880), origin (northwestern v. southeastern Europe), or destination (farm v. city) that distinguishes the New Immigration from the Old.

The new migrant-laborers were not totally unprepared for the type of work or style of living they would find in America. They had already been exposed to cities, factories, machines and life away from the farm. In leaving their own rural areas they realized only too well that they most likely were going to perform nonagricultural employment and that they would find it in urban centers. Because of their experiences in an industrializing Europe, they would seek and perform the same type of work as they had done in Europe. If they were skilled, they would seek jobs that matched their skills; if unskilled, they would seek the basic forms of industrial or nonagricultural labor. If, for personal or cultural reasons, they avoided certain types of work in Europe, they would do the same in America.

From the point of view of the Atlantic Economy, all those Jews, Italians, Poles or Armenians who traveled to America were essentially migrant-laborers searching for work, people displaced by a changing, industrializing society. From the American point of view, they were "immigrants," persons who would make new lives in the New World.

WATERWAYS AND RAILWAYS IN THE KINGDOM OF POLAND, 1911

The Atlantic Economy saw migrant-laborers as factors of production; America saw "huddled masses" and the "wretched refuse" of Europe. The distinctions in perspective are important because the differences between immigrants and migrant-laborers were real and often accounted for divergencies in action and behavior.

In the truest sense of the term, immigrants were people who had left their homelands with no intention of returning, either because they did not wish to return or because there was nothing to return to. True immigrants saw their futures as being elsewhere and planned accordingly. They usually came as families or sent for the rest of the family soon after arrival, so that women and children were always well represented. Finally, they carried their most precious possessions with them as well as whatever funds they had managed to raise before their departure. The Irish of the Old Immigration and eastern European Jews of the New are classic examples of immigrants. Forced from their homelands by famine, poverty, persecution and pogrom, they had no intention of returning to Ireland or Russia, and very few of them did— less than 11% of the Irish and less than 5% of the Jews. Many Germans and Scandinavians, especially those who came before the Civil War, were also immigrants: they came intending to make new lives for themselves in America because opportunities for improvement at home were few.

In contrast, migrant-laborers did not come to stay. Their stay was to be temporary: "As is perfectly well known, many (a very large proportion) of these unskilled men, especially the Slavs, have no 'stake' in the country and do not expect to remain in the United States."[8] Their aim was to earn money to send home to parents or to use upon their return to reestablish themselves in the traditional system of farm and village. Accordingly, the overwhelming majority (80%) of migrant-laborers—Poles, Greeks, Italians, Slovaks, Chinese—were young unmarried men, eighteen to forty years of age. If they happened to be married, they traveled alone, leaving wives and children in Europe or Asia. At the height of the movement, they were joined by young single women in need of money for dowries (or in search of husbands without dowries). Unlike immigrant-refugees, migrant-laborers usually paid for their own passage. They were not the most impoverished people of their societies; that element did not emigrate because it lacked the economic means and ambition to do so. Depending on the group, 50 to 85% of migrant-laborers returned to their native lands. More were intending to do so had not the First World War and, ultimately, better economic prospects in America intervened. Migrant-laborers became immigrants only when conscious choice or force of circumstance caused them to see their futures as being in America rather than in their native lands. Many of those who converted to immigrant status nevertheless remained migrant-laborers in attitude and psychology.

The differing psychologies and attitudes of the two groups, immigrants and migrant-laborers, often affected destinations and distributions in America. Their view of themselves as temporary or permanent influenced their goals and behavior. The migrant-laborer, in considering many alternatives, ultimately opted for destinations where work would be plentiful and well-paying. If America was within his range of possibilities, he invariably headed for the large urban centers of the North because of their enormous potential for job offerings. The migrant-laborer did not go into farming like many of the Old Immigration, nor would he have done so had land been given to him without charge.[9] The land he coveted was in Europe or Asia. Moreover, it was not possible to transport his whole social system to the isolated, detached farms of America. Individuals may move easily, but institutions, structures and social networks do not. The migrant-laborer was very much a part of a strong social network; this network propelled him to search for work and, enriched, to return home rather than to leave his country permanently.

Second, because the migrant-laborer was usually young, male and single or traveling alone, he was free and willing to go anywhere within his range of "equal accessibility." Unlike immigrants with spouses, children and belongings, he was geographically mobile and not confined to his port of entry. He also had sufficient money to take him to his destination or, because of his youth, lack of encumbrances and minimal needs, he could easily work his way along. The true immigrant, in contrast, had expenses and other persons to consider. From the very moment of disembarkation spouses, children and/or aging parents needed food, shelter and clothing.

Third, the migrant-laborer would accept any type of work, no matter how disgusting, because he was not intending to stay; the work was temporary, only a means to the money that was his goal. "The Slav was willing to work for longer hours than the English-speaking laborer, to perform heavier work, to ply his pick in more dangerous places, and stolidly to put up with inconveniences that his English-speaking competitor would not brook."[10] Thus, migrant-laborers, especially Italians and Slavs, performed work that to native-Americans and older immigrant groups had become untouchable, "work no white man could stand."[11] This work was found in slaughterhouses, tanneries, abattoirs, grease mills, foundries, rolling mills, blast furnaces, coal, mercury and asbestos mines. In the South this work was reserved for black labor.

Fourth, the migrant-laborer's expenses were minimal: "he had a lower standard of living; he could produce his labor at a less cost and sell it at a lower rate. He was a cheap man, and it was to the interest of . . . the capitalists . . . to secure and give employment to cheap men."[12] He was willing to live in conditions considered abhorrent by middle-class Americans because his stay was to be temporary and his aim was to save money. Once the migrant-laborer stopped thinking of himself as a "temporary worker" he no longer would accept the lowest grade of job or the poorest housing. Changing his status from temporary to permanent meant that he was planning a future in America; he began to aim to improve himself here. He sought better work, and, perhaps, a wife; or he might send for his family in the Old Country.

The Jews of Eastern Europe: True Immigrants

Unlike the Polish and southern Italian peasants who were their contemporaries, eastern European Jews were fugitives and refugees. If they came to the United States it was to remain forever, for they were seeking life in addition to livelihood. Usually arriving penniless and with families in hand or soon to follow, they had to succeed in the New World because there was no other place for them to go. While the German Jews had come primarily from large urban centers, their poor cousins of eastern Europe were products of the small towns and rural villages of the Russian Pale, Austrian Galicia and Rumania. As a whole, they possessed skills and trades and were more literate than other migrant groups.[13] Throughout the Pale and cities of Eastern Europe they had been merchants, artisans and craftsmen, leaving their gentile neighbors to work the land.[14]

Two characteristics of their migration were especially important in directing the distribution and development of eastern European Jews in America. First, their status as refugees made them less spatially mobile than others and contributed to their overwhelming concentration in the port cities of the East—New York, Philadelphia and Baltimore. Second, they possessed crafts, trades and mercantile skills. Rather than an urban people (those of the Pale and Galicia were often as rural as their peasant compatriots), the Jews are best seen as the traditional performers of nonagricultural tasks that were essential to both

Table 15
OCCUPATIONS OF JEWS AND NON-JEWS IN RUSSIA, 1897

Occupation	No.		%	
	Jews	Non-Jews	Jews	Non-Jews
Manufacturing and artisans	542,563	4,627,356	37.9	15.2
Commerce	452,193	804,137	31.6	2.7
Service	277,466	4,872,546	19.4	16.2
Professions	71,950	916,863	5.0	3.0
Transportation	45,944	688,801	3.2	2.2
Agriculture	40,611	18,204,676	2.9	60.5
Total	1,430,727	30,114,379	100.0	100.0

SOURCE: Compiled from the *Premier Recensement General de la Population de l'Empire de Russie, 1897;* reported in Isaac M. Rubinow, *Economic Condition of the Jews in Russia,* U.S. Bureau of Labor bulletin no. 15 (Washington, D.C.: GPO, 1907; rpt. New York: Arno Press, 1975), p. 500.

rural and urban, industrial and preindustrial societies: making clothes and shoes, working with wood and metals, building houses and wagons, selling and marketing produce and wares, butchering and baking, hostelry and livery.

Arrivals and Departures

True to the mythic image, the Statue of Liberty welcomed most newcomers who came to America from all points of the world. In some years hundreds of thousands of people were processed through Ellis Island. In 1907, for example, more than one million people were deposited in Battery Park at the tip of Manhatten Island. If New York

Table 16
PERCENTAGE OF JEWISH WORKERS IN VARIOUS OCCUPATIONS, 1900

Occupation	West Galicia	East Galicia
Agriculture	0.8	1.8
Industry	21.0	38.7
Commerce	59.2	74.0
Services Auxiliary to Industry and commerce	22.9	40.4
Public services	13.4	27.4
% of Total population	7.7	12.9

SOURCE: *Polish Encyclopedia,* 2:536.

endured as the perennial city of immigrants, it was because it was the major gateway to the New World (see Appendix G).

Not all newcomers, however, arrived at New York harbor. Many disembarked at Philadelphia, Boston or Baltimore—not the vast numbers that beset New York City but enough to merit recognition. Like New York, Philadelphia was altered by the hoards of people who landed there and went no farther. The average annual influx through the Port of Philadelphia after 1880 was 20,000 to 25,000 persons; during the five years before the First World War, it was more than 46,000. One of the more prominent groups to use the Port of Philadelphia, especially after the turn of the century, was the Jews of eastern Europe.

Very few eastern European Jews found their way to Philadelphia before 1880. Those who did were adventurous individuals who had left Europe because of a cholera epidemic, Polish famine or occasional pogrom like the one in Odessa in 1871. Omnipresent poverty was also a constant incentive to move. During these early years "only the poorest Jews carrying on a retail trade emigrate . . . to the United States, being chiefly compelled to do so by the compulsory military service and particularly by the difficulty of earning their livelihood, though they represent a sort of people of so limited wants that they surpass even the Chinese in their extreme frugality, feeding merely on bread and onions." These early Jewish immigrants were rarely married, and if they were, "they are then mostly childless."[15]

After 1880 the situation in eastern Europe worsened. Proclamation of the Russian May Laws in 1882 contributed to substantial Jewish emigration; 2,052 Jews disembarked at Philadelphia in that year. Between 1890 and 1894 thousands of Jews were expelled from Moscow, St. Petersburg and Kiev, again resulting in heavy emigration. Renewed troubles and persecutions came when the czar nationalized the liquor trade in 1897, depriving Jewish innkeepers and dependents of their livelihoods. More pogroms and the Kishinev massacre occurred in 1903. A revolution erupted in Russia in 1905. Conditions continued to deteriorate until the war in 1914. Jewish immigration to America grew accordingly, and increasing numbers disembarked at Philadelphia.

When utilizing major passenger steamship lines servicing Philadelphia before the First World War, Jews, Poles, Ukrainians, Slovaks and other Slavs preferred German companies (*North German Lloyd* and *Hamburg-American*) which sailed from Bremen and

Table 17

JEWISH IMMIGRATION TO THE UNITED STATES, 1880–1920

Year	No.	Year	No.
1881	5,692	1905	129,910
1882	13,202	1906	153,748
1883	8,731	1907	149,182
1885	16,892	1908	103,387
1890	28,639	1909	57,551
1890	28,639	1910	84,260
1891	51,398	1911	91,223
1899	37,415	1912	80,595
1900	60,764	1913	101,330
1901	58,098	1914	138,051
1902	57,688	1915	26,497
1903	76,203	1916	15,108
1904	106,236	1920	65,000

SOURCE: Mark Wischnitzer, *Visas to Freedom,* prepared by the Hebrew Immigration Assistance Society (Cleveland: World Publishing Co., 1956), p. 32.

Hamburg. On occasion, Jews sailed from Antwerp and Rotterdam (*Red Star* and *Holland-American* Lines) or from Southampton (England) and Christiana (Sweden).[16] Not everyone, however, made use of scheduled steamship services. Many made the crossing in the numerous cargo ships bound for the United States. These vessels, *towarowi* as the Poles called them, often provided accommodations that were less crowded and cheaper than regular passenger runs, although the journey might take slightly longer. The cargo ships usually took passengers on a first come–first serve basis. Emigrants who found room on a cargo vessel at the last minute simply went where the cargo went.[17]

Philadelphia was one of the nation's chief importing and exporting centers, second only to New York City; in certain commodities she outdistanced her archrival. Persons leaving Europe by way of Bremen and Hamburg had the greatest opportunities to board cargo ships bound for Philadelphia. German ships carried calfskins and "skins for morocco"; silk, wool and cotton knit goods; flax, hemp and jute products; glass and glassware; cutlery; chemicals such as potash and nitrate of soda; coal tar colors and dyes such as logwood, indigo and licorice root; and, most often, sugar beets and cement. All these products reflect Philadelphia's industries: glazed kid, chemicals, textiles, hosicry, carpets, rope and twine.

From Antwerp and Rotterdam, Philadelphia received unmanufactured leaf tobacco, coffee and some tin—and more immigrants, especially eastern European Jews. From England came "tin in bars, blocks
or pigs, grain or granulated"; tin plate, terne plate and taggers tin; large
quantities of goatskins; unmanufactured wools and cotton; cloth of all
kinds—wool, cotton and silk; leather; malt liquors; machinery; pig
iron—and more immigrants, primarily English, Irish and Welsh, but
with substantial numbers of Jews who often made England an interim
stop in their journey to America. Swedes, Norwegians and Russian and
Polish Jews made good use of ships leaving Christiana and Copenhagen
laden with bar iron and more goatskins for Pennsylvania's factories.[18]

Passage on cargo boats bound for Philadelphia by large numbers of
eastern European Jews in the early 1880s and 1890s is the principal
reason that the city became a major center of Jewish settlement. Had
the Jews boarded boats bound for other ports, their future and the
city's would have been very different. Needing to leave Europe as
soon as possible, they were unconcerned about their destinations in
America. They took whatever boats and ships were available, whether
passenger or cargo carriers. Wherever they disembarked—Philadelphia, New York, Boston or Baltimore—there they tended to stay.
Usually arriving with families and little money, they simply began to
seek work and shelter wherever they found themselves.

The Jews at Work

The Jews who came to America had long worked in the urban
centers of an industrializing Europe. As conditions had worsened in
the late nineteenth century, they had moved from village to village
thoughout the Pale, from village to town, from town to city and finally
to the major industrial centers of eastern Europe—Warszawa, Łódź,
Bialystok, Grodno, Kreslawki and Czestochowa. Many gradually
worked their way further west to Berlin, Vienna, Antwerp, Rotterdam,
London and the smaller cities in between. They were tailors and
seamstresses and workers in cigar and toy factories, leather tanneries
and textile mills. Many were peddlers and hucksters, some of whom
became small businessmen or merchant capitalists. Rapid urbanization
and city-building demanded skilled artisans and service personnel such
as carpenters, joiners, roofers, masons, coppersmiths, blacksmiths,
shoemakers, bakers and butchers. More often than not, it was the Jews
who performed these functions because "throughout the Pale virtually

all artisans were Jews . . . the Russian peasant aspir[ing] neither to commerce nor to the handicrafts."[19]

The Jews of eastern Europe performed the same tasks in America as they had throughout the Pale and cities of Europe. Philadelphia's Jews were often peddlers, hucksters, merchants and shopkeepers. Charles Bernheimer, a contemporary student of the city's Jewish community, reported that as early as 1905 there were almost 1,000 Jewish "peddlers and keepers of stands, the number varying according to the season of the year." In industry Jewish men were operatives in tobacco and cigar factories ("in various branches of the cigar trade there are about 1,000 employed"); women, too, were hucksters, peddlers and, on occasion, workers in cigar factories.[20]

In the 1880s and 1890s almost 40% of Philadelphia's Jewish immigrants were employed in some aspect of the garment industry, or "needle trades," neatly defined in one account as "the manufacture of cloaks, waists, wrappers, shirts, skirts, overalls and underwear." After examining factory inspectors' reports and making personal inquiries, Bernheimer concluded that for 1905 an estimate of 10,000 Jews in these trades "would not be an exaggeration." A Metropolitan Life Insurance Company survey ten years later found that the men's and women's clothing industry alone employed 15,000 persons, most of whom were "Hebrew" and most of whom were women.[21] The relationship between the Jews and the garment industry was very close; not only did eastern European Jews constitute the vast majority of workers in this industry but this one industry employed more of Philadelphia's Jews than any other industry or occupation.

In the United States, as in Europe, Jews avoided unskilled jobs in heavy industry and construction, turning to them only as last resorts or temporary expedients. Although 10% of all foreign-born persons were classified as general laborers by the 1900 census, only 2% of the Jews were so recorded. According to the Dillingham Commission, a survey of the occupations of immigrants entering the United States between 1899 and 1910 showed that 67% of all Jews were skilled workers before their arrival, whereas fully 75% of the Poles and southern Italians were either laborers or farmers. The Jews, therefore, competed neither with Italians in building and railway construction nor with the Poles in the heavier manual industries of coal, steel, cement and glass.[22]

Because of their pre-industrial origins, the older cities of the East had more to offer the Jews than did the newer cities of the West. The older cities remained centers of commerce and continued to support what had once been the nation's handicraft and household industries—

Table 18

OCCUPATIONS OF IMMIGRANTS ENTERING THE UNITED STATES, 1899–1910

Previous Occupation*	Jews	Northern Italians	Southern Italians	Irish	Poles	Germans	Scandinavians	English	All Immigrants
Professional	1%	1%	0%	1%	0%	4%	1%	9%	1%
Skilled worker	67%	20%	15%	13%	6%	30%	20%	49%	20%
Merchant or dealer	5%	1%	1%	1%	0%	5%	0%	5%	2%
Laborer	12%	48%	42%	31%	45%	20%	36%	18%	36%
Farmer	2%	21%	35%	7%	31%	21%	11%	4%	25%
Servant	11%	8%	6%	46%	17%	19%	30%	5%	14%
Other	2%	1%	1%	1%	1%	1%	2%	10%	2%
No.	590,267	296,622	1,471,659	376,268	748,430	458,293	475,094	249,998	7,048,953

*Excludes those without occupations, including most women and children.
SOURCE: Compiled from Reports of the Immigration Commission 1 (1911), 100.

the making of clothes, shoes, silverware, wooden toys, and the like. As long-established urban centers, their need for skilled artisans and craftsmen was very great. Commerce and handicraft industries, traditionally the preserves of the Jews throughout eastern Europe, continued to be their mainstays in the United States.

Thus, the disembarkation of large numbers of Jewish refugees in the port cities of the East, cities with economic structures established in preindustrial times, accounts in large measure for the settlement and overwhelming concentration of eastern European Jews in New York City, Philadelphia, Baltimore and Boston. Although the nature of their migration rendered them less geographically mobile than Poles or Italians, who were the truly professional migrant-laborers of the Atlantic Economy, the very timelessness of their skills and attitudes facilitated Jewish adjustment to an industrializing, urbanizing America.

The Peoples of Southern Italy and Sicily: Professional Migrant-Workers

The southern Italians and Sicilians who crowded Philadelphia's streets after the turn of the century were not refugees deposited at Delaware River docks. Few Italians entered the United States by way of Philadelphia. No regularly scheduled steamship service was established until the *Italia Line* initiated operations between Genoa and Philadelphia in 1909; nor were many cargo boats available, as trade between southern Italy and Philadelphia was not substantial. Nevertheless, by 1910 the city's southern Italian community, including American-born children, approached 100,000.[23]

Unlike the Jewish refugees, the peasant-farmer of southern Italy and Sicily was the consummate migrant-laborer of the Atlantic Economy. He sold his labor cheaply and abundantly (employers and contractors simply bought a product, cheaper by the dozen, and discarded it after use); and he was incredibly mobile, willing and able to go anywhere for work with decent pay.

Fundamental changes in social and economic structures were responsible for his existence. Traditional Italian village society was undermined by rapidly increasing population, shrinking land holdings, deteriorating agricultural conditions, the introduction of factory-style industry (at least in the north) and the occasional political upheavals attending national unification. Migration in search of work was the only possible way under these conditions to attempt to maintain a traditional lifestyle. "Generally, their aspiration was not to rise in status in this country [the United States] but to secure sufficient funds with which to increase their land holdings and therefore their economic status in the homeland." Many men journeyed to the United States two, three or more times during a single decade; in 1904, for example, 10% of Italians entering the United States had been here before; by the 1920s the percentage was even higher. More than half of all Italians who made the crossing to America returned to Italy. For southern Italians and Sicilians, who comprised the vast majority of the migration, the percentages were higher: 63% of those who came between 1902 and 1924 eventually repatriated.[24]

Abundance and willingness to migrate had made Italian laborers a well-established European institution by the end of the nineteenth century. Their specialty was construction. They built roads and tunnels through the Swiss Alps and returned later to lay that country's railroad tracks. They performed these same services in France and were specially helpful to Baron Hausmann in laying the sewers and constructing the streets of Louis Napoleon's new Paris. By 1886 there were 250,000 Italians in France; by 1911, 500,000. French entrepreneurs like Ferdinand de Lesseps employed Italians by the thousands to build the Suez Canal in the 1860s and the Panama Canal after 1900.[25] Given such preeminence in Europe, it was only a matter of time before Italians in quantity found their way into the American labor market. In 1876, 82% of all Italian migrants went to countries in Europe and North Africa; in 1913, 36% reported the same destinations. Between 1876 and 1926, 7.5 million Italians traveled to places in Europe and the Mediterranean and 8.9 million journeyed to America.[26]

In the United States Italians undertook the type of work that had earned them a reputation in Europe: "Work that is simple and monotonous . . . that can be performed by men disposed in a gang, under the more or less military supervision of a foreman, so that the worker becomes himself like a part of a machine, set in motion only when other parts are active, such work the Italians, helot-like, have performed satisfactorily."[27] Italians were considered to be ideally suited for construction of roads, tunnels, canals, bridges and railroads.

The Italian reputation in construction was enhanced by the institution of the *padrone,* by which their labor was initially channeled. As an institution, the *padrone* can be traced in early form to ancient Mesopotamia where gangs of workers constructed roads and earthworks. Most Mediterranean peoples appear to have employed the *padrone,* but the Italians perfected the system.

The *padrone* was a professional labor broker who brought a supply of unskilled labor together to meet specific demand. Usually he operated on his own, as an entrepreneur promoting his "product," seeking big construction contracts or making deals with government officials. Occasionally he worked directly with company agents or employment agencies, serving as the chief channel to the general pool of Italian labor. The *padrone* came in all sizes, ranging from the big operator with international or nationwide connections to the small-time contractor who often doubled as a laborer himself, donning the *padrone* role when the opportunity appeared.

Italian peasants saw the *padrone* as an important and powerful person, someone who could secure what they most dearly wanted—work. To the railway agent, building contractor or government official, the *padrone* was indispensable: a person who could provide cheap labor in bulk when and where it was needed. Moreover, he handled all arrangements, including food, housing and transportation, and spared both the employer and employee the headaches of such responsibilities. Unfortunately the *padrone* was not always altruistic; exploitation of both his fellow countrymen and their employers was common.

Regardless of the merits and drawbacks of the institution, the *padrone* is essential for understanding early Italian work distribution and settlement patterns in the United States. Italian laborers knew that they could rely on a *padrone* to find them work, and that the work would be the most elementary form of human labor, ageless and endlessly adaptable, in which "whatever their tasks, skill, judgment, and responsibility are but an insignificant element, and they fulfill their functions when a number together contentedly and unintermittently ply shovel and pick."[28]

Thus underemployed agricultural workers and insufficient employment opportunities in industry at home established the conditions for Italian emigration. Accessible work opportunities abroad provided the spark for the Italian's career as migrant-laborer. Two factors were principally responsible for Italian distribution throughout the United States: (1) the availability and location of work requiring the hiring of laborers in quantity to perform tasks of short or limited duration; and (2) the use of established institutions, especially the *padrone,* to secure Italian labor and to channel it to potential employers.

Italians at Work in the United States

After 1880 Philadelphia's Italians came exclusively from the south of Italy, primarily from the provinces of Abruzzi and Campania, and Sicily.[29] The pioneers were adventurers and free spirits who found work as musicians, peddlers, organ grinders, "dealers in plaster statuettes" and general laborers. The railroad, however, with its voracious appetite for unskilled labor, was the single entity most responsible for the Italian influx to Philadelphia. The Pennsylvania and Philadelphia and Reading Railroads had miles of tracks, acres of rail-yards and numerous terminals throughout the city, all of which had to be maintained, repaired or constructed. These roads also used Philadelphia as a staging and rerouting center for labor destined for other parts of the state and nation. In the mid-1880s railroad management began the practice of hiring gangs of Italian laborers on contract, usually in New York City, and dispatching them to Philadelphia. Many who came to the city in this manner did not remain with the railroad but found better opportunities in public works construction or as craftsmen and petty merchants. When defections were heavy, more Italians would be recruited and transported to Philadelphia.

Italians became identified with railroad work after supplanting the Irish as the major source of unskilled labor in the 1890s. So essential were they to the industry that the Industrial Commission concluded that "it would be a difficult thing at the present time [1905] to build a railroad of any considerable length without Italian labor." Between May 1, 1904, and July 3, 1906, 76% of those who secured employment in railroad construction through New York employment agencies were Italians. The Pennsylvania Railroad alone employed an average of 10,000 Italians yearly after 1900; in its peak year it employed 13,500. Italians generally were used to construct and repair tracks and to maintain roadbeds. They avoided work with timber but specialized in "quarrying and blasting" as well as surfacing, ditching, grading and tunneling.[30]

Italian labor was also vital to the nation's public works projects. Italians built municipal halls, public utility plants, harbor works, bridges, dams, canals, subways, roads and highways. They built Washington's Union Station, New York's Grand Central Station, and Philadelphia's City Hall, Reading Terminal, and the Broad Street and Market Street subways. They cleaned up Galveston after the devastating hurricane of 1900 and were the first to be recruited to clean up and rebuild San Franciso after the earthquake of 1906. Almost all of the 12,500 men hired to enlarge the Erie Canal were Italians. Excavation, especially street surfacing and grading, laying gas and water pipes and digging sewers, was their exclusive preserve; as early as 1890, 90% of New York's public works employees and 99% of Chicago's street workers were Italians.[31]

Although American employers, like their European colleagues, considered Italians to be ideal for public works and railway construction, they did not consider them suitable to work in mines and steel mills. Italians were thought to be "less robust than the Slav, less hardy than the Irish," and were "rare in the rolling mills, whether because of their physical lightness, or as has sometimes been said, [because] of a lack of nervous strength." Slavs, thought to be stronger and more enduring, were preferred in these industries. The claim that "steel companies have definitely sought this class of labor" is supported by advertisements like one in a Pittsburgh newspaper in 1909 which solicited "Tinners, Catchers and Helpers. To work in open shops. Syrians, Poles and Romanians Preferred."[32]

Poles and Slovaks were preferred in the mines because Italians consistently avoided underground work. In the anthracite fields, Italians were mule drivers, culm men, car loaders, haulers, repairmen and slate pickers, all above-ground tasks. In the bituminous fields, they were more numerous because stripping operations took place in the open air. According to the Industrial Commission, Italians would not work underground because they were timid and unwilling to face danger. For a group reputed to be expert in blasting and explosives and the only one, according to employers, unintimidated by nitroglycerin, this explanation leaves much to be desired. More likely, Italians avoided steel mills and underground mines because culturally they were a highly peer-oriented people who preferred to work in the company of others where talk and social exchange were constantly possible rather than in the isolation typical of underground mines and steel mills.[33]

Whether or not Italians were especially suited for railroad and construction work or the Poles for mines and metal work, by the late nineteenth century employers thought so and hired accordingly. When applying to employment agencies for bulk labor, they would indicate the race or nationality of laborers preferred for the job. In 1906, for example, major railroad companies filed applications specifically requesting thousands of Italian laborers. One New York agency received applications for 8,668 Italians from 165 employers in New York, New Jersey, Connecticut, Pennsylvania and Virginia. Another agency received requests for 37,058 Italian workers. Demand for Italians was so high in some years that agencies were unable to fill even one-third of requests.[34]

Italians at Work in Philadelphia

Brought to Philadelphia by railroad and public works construction, by 1915 Italians dominated the city's unskilled labor market in street grading and surfacing, sewer and subway construction, building construction, street cleaning, street railway and steam railroad construction and maintenance, snow shovelling and scavenging. They secured this work because at some point a *padrone* had made a deal with local political bosses, promising Italian support in exchange for city contracts. As early as 1897 the Italians, "through one of these arrangements, acquired an exclusive claim on the work of keeping the streets of Philadelphia clean." Another agreement secured them a virtual monopoly of street grading and construction and maintenance of the city's railway lines. Because the *padroni* were able to make these political accommodations, often in the form of monopolies, it was almost impossible for unorganized groups, especially those lacking the institution of a professional labor broker, to gain access to city contract work. Moreover, the *padroni* maintained control by assuring that no Italian would be employed in city work unless a member of the *Societa Operaja di Mutuo Soccorso,* a *padroni*-dominated organization.[35]

Philadelphia's *padroni* were enterprising, but their abuses never became as great as those of *padroni* who operated in central Pennsylvania or New York City. In Pennsylvania's mining regions and railroad camps Italian laborers depended on *padroni* for food, lodgings, banking and postal services as well as for jobs. Because Philadelphia was not a major port of disembarkation for Italians, there was no mass of naive recruits in need of "organizing." The availability of cheap housing also took away much of the power of the *padroni*; Italians did not have to depend on them for room and board.

Finally, Philadelphia's occupational and industrial diversity meant that substantial portions of Italians were independently employed as merchants and craftsmen or worked in skilled industries not under *padroni* control. Philadelphia's *padroni,* therefore, confined themselves to their traditional roles as brokers of unskilled bulk labor. Eventually they established Philadelphia as a staging area for Italian labor destined for inland towns and cities or for the truck and vegetable farms and canneries of New Jersey, Delaware and Maryland.[36]

Whatever brought Italians to Philadelphia, the diversity of the city's industry was instrumental in persuading them to stay. Once in Philadelphia many Italians abandoned their status as common laborers and used their skills as artisans and craftsmen or became independent businessmen and small merchants. Like the Jews of eastern Europe, Italians possessed skills and performed roles equally adaptable to rural and urban, pre-industrial and industrial societies. Thus, if they were not laborers and if they did not return to Italy (two categories which accounted for the majority), Philadelphia's Italians were peddlers, hucksters, fruit and vegetable vendors (the famous Ninth Street Market was their creation), shoemakers, waiters, confectioners, musicians, masons, stone cutters, plasterers, tailors and barbers.[37]

By the First World War, the garment industry was an important user of Italian labor. Italian men, unlike their Polish counterparts, were not adverse to working with a needle and were second only to Jews in the number so employed. Many Jews relied on the garment industry for their sole income, but Italians often used it as an adjunct, turning to sewing and tailoring during lulls in construction or during inclement seasons. It was because of its reliance on female labor that the garment industry became important to the Italians. While husbands and fathers were paving streets, digging sewers or unloading freight cars, wives could supplement family income by taking needle work into the home.

By 1915 one-half of all women employed in the men's clothing industry were Italians. After basting and machine work were completed, usually by Jewish workers, Italian women did the delicate handwork of attaching linings, tacking seams and hemming. This work was done at home, often with the help of young children who played hookey from school. The practice gave rise to the notorious "sweated homes of Philadelphia . . . an unwelcome corner of industry upon which the law has turned its back." On occasion, an Italian woman could be seen nursing a baby and sewing trousers at the same time. A popular magazine of the day pictured three smiling Italian children sitting in front of a South Philadelphia row house and carried this caption: "Behind the door the mother finishes trousers at eight cents per pair. By fourteen hours work she makes forty-eight cents a day." Despite such exploitation, Italian women favored needle work precisely because it enabled them to remain home with children and relatives. They deliberately avoided domestic service and work in factories where they would not be adequately chaperoned. If not engaged in sewing at home, Italian women were hucksters and peddlers or operatives in cigar, silk, artificial flower and candy factories, industries that tended to rely almost exclusively on female labor.[38]

Philadelphia's occupational and industrial diversity, which broadended the range of work opportunities open to Italian men and provided supplemental forms of work for Italian women, helped to anchor the migrants to the city and to moderate the conduct of local *padroni*. Philadelphia's unique housing situation worked toward the same end. Unlike New York City or Chicago, Philadelphia had few tenements and apartment buildings. One- and two-family brick row houses on narrow grid-patterned streets were the dominant pattern. These homes were relatively inexpensive and roomy; they provided privacy while allowing high density and concentration of population. The immigrant family could enjoy its own private space and at the same time have the ambience and conviviality of a busy neighborhood. Because prices were low and financing via two mortgages was a common practice peculiar to Philadelphia and Baltimore, Italians often owned their homes or at least aspired to that end.

Summary

The migration experiences of the Jews and Italians differed from those of the Poles in several important ways. The Jews were true immigrants, permanent residents who came with skills, crafts and merchandising experience. Because they avoided unskilled manual labor, they offered no competition to the Poles.

The Italians were potential competitors of the Poles but they had at least three advantages: the *padrone* for channelling workers to public works and other construction projects; a long history and reputation of migratory labor throughout the Mediterranean Basin; and, like the Jews, a tradition of performing nonagricultural roles such as artisan and merchant. It can be argued that each unskilled Italian construction worker was a potential mason, shoemaker, tailor, merchant or musician, having done such work on occasion in his native village. Choice of occupation in America often depended upon whether the worker saw himself as a permanent immigrant or as a migrant-laborer who would return to Italy with American funds to set himself up as an independent shopkeeper, artisan or farmer. Finally, perhaps for personal or cultural reasons, the peer-oriented southern Italians normally avoided work in which they would be alone or isolated from their companions for long periods of time (as in underground mining, steel smelting and furnace tending). The Poles had no such aversions.

PART II

The Polish Experience

4   The European Background of Polish Migration

> A man without land is like a man without legs; he crawls
> about but never gets anywhere.
>
> —Władisław Reymont[1]

The Polish presence in the United States was directly related to the important changes taking place in Polish society during the three or four generations preceding emigration. These changes gave rise to a new creation, the rural proletarians, institutionalized their migration in search of work, and, acting with the legacies of a feudal past and peasant heritage, prepared them for the type of work they were eventually to perform in the industrial centers of the American economy.[2] The Polish experience has much to tell us about how the impetus of a group's migration, the idiosyncracies of its culture and the nature of its experiences in the Old World of the Atlantic Economy all worked to determine immigrant destinations, either by influencing the group's ability to compete with others or by providing incentives and inclinations for certain forms of work and not for others.

Feudal Past and Peasant Heritage

Of overriding importance is the Polish peasants' beginning as serfs. Whether "freed" in 1808, 1848 or most likely, after 1861, their lives remained enmeshed with complex relationships, diverse roles and innumerable duties and obligations, all stemming from this dominant experience of their history. Although, as serfs, they could be bought and sold, peasants were considered an immovable fixture of the land unless freed or evicted by legal decree. Under the system of *folwark-panszczyzna,* a nobleman (or abbot, bishop or rich burgher) owned land in the form of a large manor-farm, or *folwark,* which included an allotment of serfs. The master allowed the serfs to till part of the manor lands for their own use and granted them certain "servitudes" or rights

67

to take fish, game, water, wood, kindling, litter and fruit from common grounds. In exchange for these servitudes and the use of land, the serfs were required to work the fields of the master (*panszczyzna* or compulsory labor), to pay taxes and to submit to conscription for military service and public works construction. In many provinces the state operated coal, salt or iron mines and lumber camps and owned the serfs who worked in these enterprises. Because the peasants' function was to work the land, there was no need for them to read or write. Indeed, literacy was considered a hindrance and was discouraged. Unfortunately, the peasants themselves often held this belief.

Despite their rural or agricultural occupations, the serf-peasants lived in highly clustered agglomerates or villages. More than a geographic pattern of settlement, the village or commune was a close-knit network of roles, expectations and familiarities. It included gentry, peasantry, clergy, laity, Jews, and, depending upon the locality, Ukrainians, Russians, Bylo-Russians, Germans and Moslems. Thus, in its physical closeness and social network, the village represented an ancient "urban" tradition, very different from the tradition of isolated farms common in Anglo-Saxon America and parts of northern and western Europe.

Polish society was strongly polarized between nobility and peasantry, which was to prove a source of economic and political turmoil. The nobility, ranging from high princes to countless lower gentry or *szlachta,* comprised perhaps 10% of the Christian population and constituted the *naród* or "nation." The functions of the *naród* were to rule the peasantry, to defend the state and to engage in war and interna-

Table 19

POLAND: COMPOSITION OF POPULATION, 1791

Group	No.	%
Clergy	50,000	.57
Nobility	725,000	8.25
Middle class (Christian)	500,000	5.69
Peasants	6,365,000*	72.40
Jews	900,000	10.24
Tartars, etc.		2.85

*Of 6,365,000 peasants, 1,000,000 were "free" peasants; 1,030,000 were serfs of royal domains and households; 921,300 were serfs of ecclesiastical domains; and 3,400,000 were serfs of hereditary (i.e., noble) estates.

SOURCE: *Polish Encyclopedia* 2: 115, 119–20.

tional diplomacy. The peasantry in turn constituted the *lud* or
"people," the masses who by definition were excluded from the *naród*
and its functions. Their role was to work the land and to be subject to
the nobility. Because the relationship between the two groups was so
rigidly fixed, the status of the peasant and that of the nobleman were
secure and the identity of each was clear. The existence of the one both
assured and necessitated the existence of the other.

Unfortunately, the rigidity of the relationships between peasantry
and nobility, manor and village, prevented other roles from being
filled. Neither the peasant nor the nobleman were readily inclined to
perform the middle or intermediary tasks of artisan, craftsman and
merchant which were crucial to economic growth and stability.
Peasants were serfs who must work the land of their masters, while the
nobility could maintain power and status only by controlling the serfs
who were bound to them through their relationship to the land. If
peasants were allowed to be artisans or merchants, this relationship
would be jeopardized. The nobility, however, considered the middle
roles to be demeaning and also a threat to their superior status. So
strong was the feeling on this subject that at one point in its history the
Polish Diet actually issued an edict forbidding the nobility to practice
any trade or craft. The peasants, like the nobility, had also internalized
the rigid social values of the society: for them, working the land
remained the highest calling. Their desire, if not their dream, was to
have enough land to make them independent. All their plans and ambi-
tions were aimed in this direction.[3]

Nevertheless, spurred by the demand for their services and encouraged by necessity, a small population of indigenous Christian burghers managed to survive in Poland's few towns and small cities. There
were never enough of them, however, to meet the demands of the society or the economy because the nobility continually tried to suppress
them. Throughout their centuries of conflict, the nobility resorted to innumerable measures to restrain the influence of towns and cities.
Heavy taxes were imposed on the goods of towns; burghers were forbidden to own land; all burghers and nonnobles were forbidden to
engage in the rich grain commerce of the Vistula; special "suburbs"
and shops within cities were established and given extraterritoriality so
that they would be exempt from municipal or burgher jurisdiction;
various attempts were made to lower the social standing of burghers,
the most ingenious being sumptuary laws.

For centuries, however, the nation's rulers had recognized the
need for a middle class to perform the roles of merchant and craftsman;

as noted, demand for such services was great. The usual solution was
to encourage outsiders to fill the void so as not to disturb existing social
relationships and prevailing attitudes. Wandering gypsies performed
these necessary functions on occasion, as did Germans and a few
German Jews who were coaxed or bribed into the Polish domain by
desperate princes. The Tartar invasions of 1240 devastated Polish
cities and provincial towns, wiping out whatever small middle class
had previously existed. The situation, always acute, was rendered in-
tolerable and was alleviated only by the arrival, beginning in the latter
half of the thirteenth century, of large numbers of Jews. Repeatedly
persecuted and finally expelled from German provinces and other parts
of western Europe in the wake of the Crusades, the Jews were
welcomed into Poland by a special decree of Boleslaus the Pious in
1264. The privileges of the decree were expanded by Casimir the Great
in 1354, reportedly because of the influence of Esther, his Jewish
mistress.

Following their expulsion from Spain, France and England, more
Jews arrived in the fifteenth and sixteenth centuries. Totalling approximately 50,000 persons in 1500, their numbers grew to one-half
million by 1650. During the next several centuries Jews would continue
to settle in those areas which, by the late nineteenth century, constituted the Russian Pale or Ukraine, Lithuania and Austrian Galicia, all
of which had once been part of ancient Poland.[4] Totally and eternally
extraneous to the Polish social structure, Jews could take on the
necessary middle roles of artisans and merchants without threatening
the status of the nobility and without jeopardizing the age-old relationship between lord and peasant. In fact, their presence reinforced the rigidity and permanence of the two-class system and enabled the nobility
to consolidate its position vis-a-vis the peasantry.

For its existence the peasantry depended upon land—land to farm
and, in the best of all possible worlds, land to own. Land was much
more than an economic necessity; it was the crux of the peasant's complex social system. Although many changes took place in Polish social
relationships as the peasant moved from serf to freeman, the role of
land remained constant or even increased in importance.

To freed peasants, land was important because it was the social
unit that determined the status and position of their families within the
community. If at all possible, land was not divided but was passed on
in its entirety to one son (not necessarily the eldest), who was obliged
to settle in cash or kind with his brothers and sisters. Thomas and

Znaniecki correctly observed that "sale, division, or mortgaging of the farm means a lowering of the social standing of the family," and had, therefore, to be avoided.[5] It is no exaggeration to say that the peasant of late nineteenth century Poland had little or no identity and security apart from the family. Because peasants defined themselves, first and foremost, as members of a family, their life was crowded with immense obligations, loyalties and responsibilities. Children, for example, were expected to contribute to the family's upkeep before and after marriage. If a son or daughter worked before marriage, it was only to gain money or other wages to support the entire family. Earnings were automatically turned over to the father for management and disposition. After marriage, the child continued to contribute to the support of the family (both blood and law relatives) according to his or her ability. When parents were old, sick, or retired, aiding them financially was accepted without question: "it is now a consciously moral duty powerfully reinforced by the opinions of the familial group."[6] Marriage was essential to the solidarity and the status of the family. Married persons possessed higher status than unmarried ones; an individual could not manage money and property unless married, because money, property and land were controlled only by families. It followed that an individual could not have influence or be important unless married and controlling property as part of a family. The peasant's goal, therefore, was always to improve the position of the family. This could be done only by augmenting or acquiring land holdings and other property, usually through a beneficial marriage or, if necessary, by purchase.

Two censuses taken in the Duchy of Warsaw, a Napoleonic creation that, with the later addition of the province of Kraków, comprised most of Central Poland, illustrate that, as early as the beginning of the nineteenth century, the Polish peasant's relationship to the land was undergoing auspicious changes. The censuses of 1808 and 1810 identified three groups of peasants in relation to land tenure: those who, in theory, possessed sufficient land for subsistence; those who did not have sufficient land for subsistence and so were forced to seek additional sources of work; and those who possessed no land.

The fully self-sustaining peasant, known in ancient times as *kmieć* but increasingly referred to as *gospodarze,* fulfilled his obligations to the master by paying rent, providing his compulsory labor or offering some combination of rent and labor. According to tradition, the *kmieć* worked a whole *łan* or *włoka* (41.5 acres) with his own yoke of oxen or pair of horses. He also employed hired help, most often his sons or sons-in-law. Although the size of his landholdings eventually diminished, the distinguishing characteristics of the *gospodarze* remained ownership of oxen or horses and employment of others.

The intermediate group of peasants, those with too little land to be self-sustaining, were called *małorolni* or "little land possessors." There was the *ogrodnik,* who possessed only a little garden around his house; the *zagrodnik,* who had a house and some farm buildings but no garden; *chałupnik,* who possessed only a *chałupa* or cabin but no other farm buildings; the *komornik,* who didn't even have a *chałupa,* but lived in a *komora,* the "smaller room of a peasant house belonging to someone else"; and finally, the *kątnik* who lived with his family in a *kąt,* a corner of someone else's room. In time these names lost their literal meanings, but, as Stefan Kieniewicz observes, "the common features of the whole group" were that "they used exiguous lots of land (not always the same every year); they did not have their own horses and oxen; they performed compulsory labor only as 'workers on foot'—and above that, they were expected to perform some obligatory work for hire, because, otherwise, they could not support their families."[7]

The landless peasants, or *bezrolni,* consisted of permanently employed farmhands and occasional workers. The former were employed by manor farms or by independent peasants, sometimes on yearly contract. The latter were assigned the lowest social standing in the village and were usually employed only at harvest time. The landless peasantry, or rural proletariat, formed a large group. In the early nineteenth century the majority were single persons who were earning a living as farmhands before marriage and whose landless condition tended to be temporary. After marriage the landlord would give the young couple a portion of their parents' lands and establish new obligations and duties.

Kieniewicz, who studied the 1810 census in some detail, delineates three types of peasant social structure: "proletarization," as in the province of Płock where 62% of all heads of household, or 39% of the total peasant population, were landless; the predominance of small landholders, as in Kraków, where 55% of the population struggled to support itself on small holdings, 27% were in households headed by a full or self-sufficient peasant and 18% were without land; and the traditional pattern represented by Lublin, where 10% of the peasant population was landless, 15% worked small farms and a hefty 75% were apparently self-sufficient.[8]

The 1810 census thus indicates that large segments of the Polish population were landless or possessed insufficient landholdings to support themselves and a family. The situation deteriorated as the century progressed. The rural proletariat ceased to be temporary and became a permanent institution. Proletarization and parcelling (the division of manor estates into small plots) became the norm and the traditional pattern of Lublin became the rarity. The shrinking landholdings were a problem that had no solution until the last quarter of the nineteenth century. Until then, there would be no work opportunities in local industry nor any means of learning about or getting to jobs that might exist elsewhere. In any event, in most areas the peasant was not yet free to move but was literally bound to the land and burdened with obligations of compulsory labor or military service. Finally, in many provinces the population remained stable and even declined because of high death rates, low birth rates, famines and epidemics; only after 1850 would this pattern begin to change. To the Pole, landlessness remained the omen of future ills.

The legacies of a very recent serfdom combined with certain values of peasant culture greatly influenced the Pole's subsequent career as migrant laborer. As the product of a rigidly stratified and highly class conscious society, he saw his ideal role as that of an independent and self-sufficient land owner. Since land was primarily a social unit embodying the status of the family, any threat to the land, its loss or diminution, seriously jeopardized the peasant's way of life. By the mid-nineteenth century it was becoming increasingly difficult to hold onto land, to support a wife and children by means of it or to buy more of it. Consequently, the peasant-farmer was very willing to exchange his unskilled labor for wages. The money would enable him to contribute to the support of his parents, an inherent and inescapable obligation in his social system; to support his wife and children; to rescue family property from debt; or to buy land in order to re-establish himself within the solidarity of the familial community.

To give labor in exchange for something was the accepted and proper way of doing things. As a serf, the peasant had given his labor in exchange for servitudes and the privilege of farming patches of the master's land. The transition from the feudal to the capitalistic concept of exchange was perfunctory; by the 19th century the peasant would increasingly exchange his labor for money or goods rather than for rights and privileges. Moreover, centuries of serfdom had taught him that work, especially physical work requiring strength and endurance, was good and honorable. It did not matter if the work were unpleasant, disagreeable or menial; what counted was that one performed it to its conclusion and received some rightful compensation.

In search of work, the peasant farmer exhausted all possibilities in the villages and neighboring farms before proceeding to nearby towns, cities or provinces. The next stage of his journey would be to the large agricultural estates of Prussia, Russia and Denmark, or to the growing industrial centers of Silesia, Moravia and the Ukraine. These migrations exposed him to new ideas and experiences. For the first time, perhaps, he lived in towns and cities and encountered machines and factories. He carried these experiences home to his family and village. The Pole, accustomed to agglomerated settlements in which everyone knew everyone else, was so much a network person that isolated settlement, at home or abroad, was not possible for him. He needed others of his group in order to maintain identity and status. In a village-oriented oral culture, exchange of information and sharing of experiences was the lifeblood of community.

In his life as a serf and a villager, the peasant was exposed to various forms of nonagricultural work—commerce, industry and construction—some of which were suitable to his role as serf and some of which were not. As the only source of unskilled labor, the peasant was familiar with extractive industries, such as coal, iron, salt and lumber, as well as with road and earthworks construction. The other type of industry that included commerce and the making of clothes, shoes, utensils and weapons was not compatible with the terms of his serfdom. It was simply not his role to perform them, nor were they socially or culturally preferable to physical labor. There were also many occupations, such as weaving, sewing, cooking, cleaning and laundering, that Slavic culture defined as women's work; no Polish male would consider these except under duress or after exposure to different cultural norms.

Eventually, the peasant's search for work brought him to the United States, Canada, Brazil, Argentina, Germany or France. America was an alternative, perhaps a final and more profitable one, available to those absolutely in need of work to preserve a fading way of life. Before sailing for America, however, the Pole became accustomed to migrating throughout an industrializing Europe. It was rare to find a Polish immigrant who had not migrated to some other part of Europe or within his own country before coming to America. During his European sojourns he performed countless fundamental tasks, either in industry or agribusiness, requiring little skill but much muscle and effort—mining; street, road, railroad and bridge construction; steel and iron manufacture; oil and sugar refining; tanning; slaughtering and meat packing; painting, chopping, digging, dredging, hauling, loading and unloading. A topsy-turvy world forced new experiences on the Polish man of the soil long before he had heard of the New World. Always, however, his desire was to augment or redeem his landholdings so as to reinstate himself in the traditional life style and family structure of the village. The peasant left only so he could return a better man.[9]

Polish Society in Transition

In the fifteenth century Poland was the largest state in Europe. Subsequent centuries saw its power diminish and its territories reduced until finally the once proud country was dismembered by Austria, Russia and Prussia in the Third Partition of 1795. Additional adjustments, made in 1815 at the Congress of Vienna, reapportioned territories among the three powers and created an ersatz "Kingdom of Poland" under the full control of Russia. The Pole who immigrated to America before 1914 was leaving a country that had been incorporated into the political, social, economic and administrative policies of Germany, Austria-Hungary and the Russian Empire. The differences in development caused by this arrangement influenced not only the timing and origin of emigration but also the subsequent distribution and work preferences of the Poles in the United States. In general, Polish emigration progressed from west to east, from the provinces of German Poland to Galicia or Austrian Poland, and on to the Congress Kingdom and other Polish provinces of Russia.

German Poland

The German sections of Poland—Poznań, Silesia, West Prussia and East Prussia*—were the first to send Polish migrant workers and permanent settlers to the New World.[10] The earliest pioneers, leaving Europe in the 1850s, 60s and 70s, tended to emigrate as families and often came in response to the promise of land; a goodly number

*These are the Polish territories as defined by the Prussian Government. In traditional Polish nomenclature they were the provinces of Poznań (Posen). Bydgoszcz (Bromberg), Gdańsk (Danzig), Kwidzyń (Marienwerder), Olsztyn (Allenstein), (Gąbin (Gumbinnen), Królewiec (Königsberg), Opawa (Troppau), Opole (Oppeln) and Wrocław (Breslau).

ADMINISTRATIVE DIVISIONS
OF POLAND, 1912

ADMINISTRATIVE DIVISIONS
POLAND 1912

Frontiers of States — Limits of Gov'ts
and Regencies
Limits of Countries ◎ Chief town-Province
and Provinces and Regency
o Chief town of Government
and Regency

SCALE
15 0   30   60

possessed skills and craft knowledge in addition to farming expertise and they were conversant in German. Many were not migrant laborers but intended to settle in America. For these reasons they resembled their German neighbors and emigrants of earlier decades more than they did their compatriots in Austria and Russia. Speaking of these early Polish emigrants, the American consul in Wrocław (Breslau) reported that

> their social condition is as good as can be expected, and if they were not thrifty, they would lack the means to emigrate. It is notoriously one of the reasons why the Prussian Government looks with disfavor upon emigration, that only the industrious and economical among the population are able to turn their backs upon their native land, while the idle, the shiftless, and brawlers remain.[11]

Caught in the crossfire of Bismarck's *Kulturkampf* or unable to compete with larger landowners, the greatest numbers came to the United States during the 1880s. Although Prussian Poles constituted three-quarters of all Poles in the United States at that time, within a few years they would be so outnumbered by migrations from Austrian and Russian Poland that they would never again constitute more than 8 to 10% of the total Polish population in the United States. Nevertheless, their migration was vital to the whole; as the initial phalanx they founded the first churches, parishes and organizations, developed channels for disseminating work information and established patterns of distribution, thereby easing the way for Russian and Austrian Poles to come.

Of Germany's Polish provinces, Poznań, West Prussia and East Prussia (the latter two were sometimes referred to, incorrectly, as Pomerania) were the chief suppliers of emigrants. They were agricultural regions traditionally controlled by *Junkers,* local aristocrats who had large landholdings. Taking advantage of Prussian land and serf reforms beginning with the Regulation Reform of 1807, the *Junkers* consolidated and enlarged their estates by buying up the smaller farms of indebted peasants. By century's end they controlled more than half of the best land in Poznań and Pomerania. Only peasant farmers owning fifty or more acres were able to survive. Positive state support in the form of credit and banking facilities, low taxes, and especially, subsidies to protect German wheat from foreign (that is, American) competiton, encouraged the *Junkers* and many of the larger peasant-farmers to employ scientific farming techniques and to invest in machinery. Wheat and grain production was fully mechanized and steam plows were in common use by the 1880s. Improved seeds, mineral fertilizers and crop rotation increased productivity significantly. Advantageous market conditions encouraged diversification, cattle breeding became popular and sugar beets and clover were planted with prospects of good profit.

By 1880 the situation in the agricultural provinces was characterized by "polarization" *(rozwarstwienie):* on one side there were very large landholdings controlled by *Junkers* and smaller, but nevertheless viable, holdings of well-to-do peasants; on the other there was a mass of landless or nearly landless peasants. Four-fifths of the agricultural populations of Poznań and Pomerania were wage earners

Table 20

POPULATION GROWTH IN PRUSSIAN POLAND, 1816–1912 (in thousands)

Year	Prussian Poland (total of nos. 2-5) (1)	Poznania (2)	West Prussia (3)	East Prussia (4)	Upper Silesia (Regency of Opole) (5)	Regency of Olsztyn (6)
1816	2,802	820	571	886	525	
1831	3,812	1,056	782	1,244	730	
1840	4,450	1,234	916	1,394	906	
1849	4,809	1,353	1,028	1,462	966	
1858	5,239	1,417	1,136	1,609	1,077	405 (1861)
1871	6,025	1,582	1,312	1,821	1,310	461
1880	6,474	1,700	1,406	1,927	1,441	492
1890	6,728	1,753	1,434	1,963	1,578	517
1900	7,317	1,886	1,561	2,002	1,868	520
1905	7,691	1,987	1,642	2,026	2,036	533
1910	8,076	2,100	1,704	2,064	2,208	544
1912	8,205	2,136	1,727	2,078	2,264	548
Increases:						
1816–1858						
No.	2,437	597	565	723	552	
%	87.0	72.8	98.9	81.6	105.1	
1858–1912						
No.	2,966	719	591	469	1,187	143
%	56.6	50.7	52.0	29.1	110.2	35.3
1816–1912						
No.	5,403	1,316	1,156	1,192	1,739	
%	192.8	160.5	202.5	134.5	331.2	

SOURCE: *Polish Encyclopedia* 2: 133.

or "farmhands." These included peasants without any land who were steadily employed on large estates or peasant farms; peasants who owned very tiny plots and earned the bulk of their wages by working on larger farms; and *komornicy,* peasants who were given a plot of ground in exchange for working a specified number of paid days during the busy season. In addition, there was a growing representation of seasonal workers who came to harvest wheat or to dig and weed sugar beets, a tedious task not given to mechanization. Farmhands, especially those who worked on *Junker* estates, were routinely exploited. Housing and wages were seriously inadequate and the Journeyman's Law of 1854 made workers' contracts inviolable, forbad strikes, outlawed unions, denied legal redress for wage grievances and sanctioned physical punishment by employers.[12]

Given these conditions, it is not surprising that the landless and nearly landless populations supplied the sources of emigration; lacking machinery and access to credit and capital resources, they were unable to compete with large landowners who were subsidized by the state. The first heavy outmigrations of Germans and landless Poles (as well as Jews) came in the 1870s. By 1914, 4.5 million people, including 1.2 million Poles from Pomerania and Poznania, had left the Prussian provinces east of the Oder-Neisse line. Although the bulk of this emigrating population relocated in other German areas, the Polish portion followed a somewhat different pattern. At its height, 1881–1890, 232,300 persons, virtually all Poles, emigrated from Poznań and 197,600 from West Prussia, but unlike their German counterparts, the majority of these Poles headed for the United States.[13]

The loss of rural population in these years contributed to severe shortages of agricultural labor. To fill the void, increasing numbers of foreign (Polish and, later, Ruthenian) workers were imported. In 1905 the Central Farmhand's Board was established as the sole agent for recruiting foreign workers. On the eve of the First World War, German agriculture was employing a half-million foreigners as seasonal farmhands; four-fifths came from Congress Poland and one-fifth from Galicia. Less than half worked in Pomerania or Poznań; the majority went west to the estates of Brandenburg and Saxony. German agriculture could not have functioned without these *Sachsengänger,* or cheap Polish laborers.[14]

After 1890 distressed Polish farmers in Poznań and Pomerania no longer went abroad. German industrialization had so progressed that it was able to absorb surplus German and Polish farmers in local industry, mining and construction. The mining and steel industries of the

Table 21

EMIGRATION FROM POZNANIA AND WEST PRUSSIA, 1841–1910*

Years	Actual nos.		Per 10,000 inhabitants per annum	
	Poznania	West Prussia	Poznania	West Prussia
1841–1850	− 9,200	+ 11,800	− 7	+ 12
1851–1860	− 12,000	+ 13,700	− 9	+ 12
1861–1870	− 90,300	− 32,000	− 59	− 26
1871–1880	− 135,300	− 104,900	− 83	− 78
1881–1890	− 232,300	− 197,600	− 135	− 140
1891–1900	− 217,000	− 137,800	− 118	− 92
1901–1910	− 180,300	− 156,800	− 90	− 96
Total	− 876,400	− 628,100		

*Excess of emigration over immigration.
SOURCE: *Polish Encyclopedia* 2: 138.

Ruhr Valley, the center of German industrialization, employed hundreds of thousands of Poles. Silesia, particularly Upper Silesia, was also integral to German industrialization. Accordingly, this province experienced little or no Polish emigration; to the contrary, it witnessed a modest Polish influx from East and West Prussia, Poznań and, increasingly after 1906, a seasonal flow from Congress Poland and Galicia. Upper Silesian coal mining employed more than 100,000 men, mostly Poles, and metal foundries and manufacturers employed approximately 75,000, again primarily Poles. By the eve of the 1914 war it was to safe to say that German industries, especially coal and iron mining and steel manufacture, depended heavily upon Polish labor.[15]

Thus, because of large farm-factories, heavy industries and myriad city-building activities, German Poland was able to absorb its surplus of landless and nearly landless Polish peasants; after 1890 very few of them emigrated abroad. Indeed, so great was the demand for industrial and agricultural labor that not only did emigration cease but inmigration accelerated. Hundreds of thousands of Poles from Austria and Russia made their way to Poznań, West and East Prussia, Silesia and the industrializing centers and agricultural estates of central and western Germany.

Galicia

By agreement reached in Vienna in 1815, Austria retained control of Galicia (geographically, southern Poland), which consisted of two provinces, Kraków and Lwów.[16] The history of Galicia in the years between the Congress of Vienna and the peasant uprisings of 1846–1848 is a litany of recurrent woe. Galicia was the most backward of all Polish regions and one of the most poverty-stricken pockets in Europe. In some areas agriculture bordered on the primitive; the three-field system predominated in a "natural" economy and the peasants burned manure for fuel. Peasant landholdings were too small for subsistence, although in theory, since the Austrian government forbad evictions, no one was landless. There was little agricultural production for market or for export even among the gentry; customs barriers prevented produce from using the Vistula, its only outlet.

The worst elements of serfdom prevailed. Relationships between peasantry and gentry were riddled with deep and ingrained hatreds. Ethnic rivalries compounded class hostilities; the Poles shared the region with Jews, Russians, Moslems and Ukrainians, the latter group comprising 40% of the population. Tensions were especially severe in eastern Galicia where the majority of serfs were Ukrainians serving Polish landlords. Illiteracy was universal. Ignorance and suspicion exacerbated the class and ethnic anxieties and encouraged parochialism. Drunkenness and alcoholism were chronic. Because of *propinacja,* the aristocratic monopoly of the production and distribution of liquor (the latter function was leased to Jews who operated village taverns, another source of ethnic conflict), it was often cheaper for the peasant to drink vodka than to eat bread.

Finally, a series of natural disasters descended upon the province like the plagues of ancient Egypt—floods, famines, bad harvests and epidemics. Tuber rot destroyed the potato crops of 1847–1849, causing the widespread famine traditionally referred to as the "Great Hunger." During those three years, 400,000 people, out of a population of less than five million, died of typhus triggered by the famine. In parts of the mountain areas the Great Hunger persisted until 1855, resulting in a decade of mass starvation. The consequences of the famine and its ensuing typhus were prolonged by a cholera epidemic that carried off hundreds of thousands between 1852 and 1855. In some years the number who died exceeded the number who were born so that the population actually declined. In 1847, for example, the death toll was a quarter-million higher than in any of the previous fifteen years. Western Galicia, the Polish portion of the province, suffered most: between 1846 and 1847 its population decreased by 181,449 or 11%.[17]

Faced with the same potato famine and similar ensuing conditions, the Irish fled their country. They made their way to the larger towns and cities of an industrializing England where they hoped to find work or at least the assistance of the English Poor Laws, or they sought

Table 22

POPULATION INCREASE AND DECREASE IN GALICIA, 1810–1910

Year	Population	Increase or Decrease	
		Actual nos.	% per annum
1810	3,086,000		
1817	3,717,000	631,000	2.92
1827	4,382,000	665,000	1.79
1837	4,241,000	− 141,000	− .32
1846	4,774,000	533,000	1.40
1857	4,597,470	− 176,530	− .34
1869	5,444,689	847,219	1.54
1880	5,958,907	514,218	.86
1890	6,607,816	648,909	1.09
1900	7,315,939	708,123	1.07
1910	8,029,387	713,448	.98

NOTE: During the nineteenth century in Galicia there were eight years in which the death rate exceeded the birth rate: in 1831 the difference was 163,271; in 1847, 188,403; 1848, 140,696; 1853, 12,215; 1854, 68,855; 1855, 141,901; 1866, 1,892; and 1873, 63,982. SOURCE: *Polish Encyclopedia* 2: 142, 141.

ports with ships to take them to Canada and the United States. The English parliament provided passage for many. The Church and sympathetic citizens of western Europe and North America organized relief missions.[18] In Galicia, however, there were no ports, no industrializing cities or regions, no state assistance, no charity. There simply was no place to go and no way to get there. No one in western Europe or North America organized relief missions or sent aid, for very few had even heard of Galicia. For Galicia, unlike Ireland, massive emigration was no solution. The opportunity, the means and even the freedom to migrate did not exist. For the peoples of Galicia, God remained the only consolation. Fortunately for the Poles, but not for others, Austria was officially Roman Catholic, so they were at least spared the added burden of religious persecution.

The complex of adverse conditions, both natural and man-made, led to peasant uprisings that resulted in the major reforms of 1848. The serfs were freed, but more often *de jure* than *de facto*. An effort was made to grant each peasant a plot of land, usually less that fourteen acres, too little for subsistence. The nobility retained 43% of usable land and 90% of the forests. Under these circumstances, it was virtually impossible for the peasants to support themselves. Not only were landholdings too small, but they were denied their ancient servitudes, the rights to pastures and forests. Disputes over *"lisy i pasowyska"*—woods and pastures—were to assume major proportions in later years, often climaxing in bloodshed.

The nobility remained steadfast in refusing to relinquish any of its lands to the peasantry. Hope of self-sufficiency shattered, the peasants were forced to work for the former landlord under conditions and for pay determined solely by their former masters. Their emancipation perpetuated economic peonage while depriving them of their former rights and protections. On top of all this, peasants were required to pay an irritating tax. In theory their land was a gift from the Emperor, and the landlord was to be reimbursed by the state. Vienna, however, declined to pay and passed the obligation on to the province which, in turn, passed it on to the peasants in the form of a thirty-year tax. Which thirty-year period was never specified; in some areas the tax was still in force after 1900.

By 1861 Galicia was granted political autonomy within the multinational Austrian-Hungarian Empire, but the Polish nobility continued to push for complete independence. The peasants, represented in the newly constituted *sejm* or parliament, did not support the nobility in their claims to independence, nor did they heed their call to nationalism. Why support the nobles, their hated landlords, the very source of their distress? The peasants supported the Austrian government, but their loyalty was not rewarded. By 1866 Emperor Franz Josef had made peace with the Polish nobles and granted them full control of Galicia's internal affairs, including the peasantry, in exchange for dropping all claims to independence.

It was a woeful bargain for the peasants, for Galicia was to remain an agricultural domain and industry was to be discouraged in order not to upset the age-old *status quo*. The nobles lost no time in consolidating their position. Peasant representation in the *sejm* was eliminated. The structure of local government was revised to remove the manor from the jurisdiction of the commune or village. This had serious implications, for it was the commune that had to pay taxes, build and maintain roads and provide schools, now with no help from the lords of the manor. Despite state attempts to suppress it, the *propinacja* remained in operation and drunkenness prevailed as before. Once again, nature was not kind: cholera carried off 35,000 in 1866 and 120,000 in 1872–1873.[19]

Land remained at the root of Galicia's problems, and demand for it intensified as the population began to grow steadily after 1880. In a culture in which land was the foundation of all social as well as economic security, lack of it, or too little of it, meant total disaster. At the turn of the century, the nobility still owned 37% of all arable land (not much less than the 42% they controlled in 1848, the year the serfs were freed), and that was poorly farmed. For example, there were 45 *latifundia* of 15,000 or more acres, but as late as 1900 these did not employ scientific techniques, crop rotation, diversification or machinery. The lords preferred to lease their lands to the peasants, requiring only that rents be paid on time and in full.

Peasant holdings were always small. In 1859 two-thirds were less than fourteen acres and one-quarter were less than 2½ acres; by 1900, 84% were less than 12.5 acres, 48% were less than 5 acres, and there were 700,000 landless peasants.[20] Barely 5% of the peasant population was self-supporting and only 1% could be considered wealthy. As the population grew, peasants repeatedly divided their land to provide inheritances for sons and dowries for daughters.

> The distinctive plague of Galician agriculture was the "checkerboard" *(szachownica)*—the checker division of holdings. As a result of repeated farm division, dowry acquisitions, sales, and purchases, each peasant's land was scattered all over the village field—in lots so small that, as the saying ran, when a dog lay on a peasant's ground, the dog's tail would protrude on the neighbor's holdings.[21]

In 1859 an average of twenty individual lots were officially registered for each peasant. By 1890 the number of peasant holdings doubled, while the amount of peasant-owned land under cultivation increased by only seven percent. Since the government refused to interfere with the workings of the free market, there was no limit to the subdivisions. In fact, investigations at the time revealed that peasant plots were actually divided into twice the number officially registered. Moreover, the peasant's lots were sometimes four to five miles away from farm buildings or extended in strips a few yards wide but a mile or more in length. It was further estimated that between 250,000 and 371, 000 acres were unprofitable because of "unproductive edges" and the weird shape of lots. Obviously, sensible farming was ludicrous under these conditions.[22]

The situation tended to feed on itself. The head of the peasant family craved more land in order to survive, so he sought more patches. There were no credit facilities, so he fell prey to usury and foreclosure. His taxes were high, so he needed more land or additional work. But there was no work because there was no industry, and agriculture was surfeited with farmers. He resorted to *odrobek*—borrowing money, seed or food from the landlord in exchange for his free labor at harvest time; or he might become trapped by the portion system, an arrangement by which he received a money loan, or portion, in exchange for working for the landlord one day a week per portion—and the work represented only the interest on the loan; the capital value had to be repaid in cash. The peasant could find himself working for the landlord forever. It was the virtual reinstitutionalization of the compulsory labor of serfdom.

The peasant remained drastically in need of work to support himself and his family and to reestablish his relationship with the land. Not only had the Polish nobles, because of their bargain with the Austrian government, blocked land reform and excluded industry, but they had also failed to develop Galicia's significant natural resources. There were rich deposits of salt, potassium and potash in western Galicia near Kalisz and Stebnik. The state operated salt mines at Wieliczka but only 1,000 tons were mined annually after 1900, half of what was extracted a century earlier. Anthracite deposits were rich and abundant, especially in Silesia of Cieszyn, but Austria preferred to import coal rather than mine the Galician reserves. In the late 1870s and early 1880s large petroleum deposits were discovered in the eastern part of the province but little was done to tap them.

In 1910, 78% of the province's population was still employed in agriculture and less than 7% were engaged in industrial activity, mostly of the cottage and artisan variety. Domestic weaving, for example, had once been common but, like all incipient Galician manufactures, was wiped out or severely restricted when the railroad brought in cheaper factory-made products. Outside of the domestic artisan trades, Galicia's few industrial workers were employed in salt mines, oil refineries, saw mills, textile plants and breweries. Not until after 1910 did the Austrian-Hungarian regime attempt to tap Galicia's resources.[23] Seeing the world demand for oil as a ready source of foreign exchange, the government finally encouraged western European and Austrian capital to construct modern refineries. By 1912 oil wells were operating in 389 places in eastern Galicia. These developments came too late to provide relief for the rural proletariat. The paltry sum that could be absorbed by industry meant that most Galicians—Poles, Ukrainians and Jews, deprived of or losing their lands and livelihoods—had to seek work elsewhere, probably beyond the province. In 1902, for example, 73% of the 444,000 farmers who owned

Table 23

EMIGRATION FROM GALICIA, 1881–1910

| Years | Actual nos. | | | Per 10,000 inhabitants per annum | |
	Total (whole country)	West Galicia	East Galicia	West Galicia	East Galicia
1881–1890	− 61,421	− 74,218	+ 12,797	−34	+ 3
1891–1900	−302,826	−169,216	−133,610	−71	−29
1901–1910	−488,543	−222,397	−266,146	−86	−52
1881–1910	−852,790	−465,831	−386,959		

SOURCE: *Polish Encyclopedia* 2: 144.

less than 5 acres of land reported that they had to seek work beyond their farm, primarily as agricultural workers; of 367,000 small land-owners with 5 to 12.5 acres, 47% sought work away from their farms, again primarily as roaming agricultural workers.[24]

Migration was not new to the peoples of Galicia. It was an accustomed way of dealing with crises; famines and epidemics always saw great movements to large towns and cities, especially to Kraków and Lwów. During the hard times of the mid-nineteenth century, the Poles, concentrated in the western half of the province, went as settlers to eastern Galicia and the Bukowina, and some furtively crossed the Dnieper River into Russia. By 1870, however, internal migration was no longer a solution because there were not enough jobs in local industry and agriculture. Emigration in search of work was the only possible way of finding relief.

The 1870s was the first decade in which Galicia lost population (1,997 persons) as a result of emigration. Galicians headed for the industrial regions of Bohemia, Moravia, Silesia and lower Austria; a few started for South America and the United States. Eighty-two thousand emigrated in the 1880s and 341,000 in the 1890s. The exodus accelerated after 1900, reaching the yearly figure of nearly a half-million workmen who, in effect, supported another two million people or 25% of the total population in 1910. Each year one-half, or 250,000, of these migrant workers went to Germany; 100,000 to Hungary, Sweden, Denmark and Austria proper; and approximately 100,000 to the United States. Records show, however, that of the nearly 500,000 workers who left Galicia each year between 1905 and 1914, nearly 90% returned, including two-thirds of those who had journeyed to the

United States. Always, the yearly trek *"na Saksy"* ("to Germany," literally, "to Saxony"), accounted for the bulk of Polish emigration from Galicia. The greatest number of Polish emigres were *Sachsengänger*, those who migrated to the large estates, mines and factories of Germany, Prussia, Poland and Denmark. Others were *bandosy*, hired harvesters from the Tatras, who had been performing their specialty for generations in Congress Poland, Pomerania, Saxony and Brandenburg.

Despite the returns, the number of permanent emigration losses began to add up. In the course of three decades, 1880–1910, 850,000 Galicians—Poles, Ukrainians and Jews (it is impossible to determine the exact numbers of each)—failed to return home; more than half of them, or 490,000, were lost in the single decade 1900–1910 and were to be found, with few exceptions, in the United States and Canada.[25]

No matter where he went in search of work, the Galician peasant saved his earnings and invariably sent them home. What began as a trickle in the 1880s and early 1890s became a torrent by the eve of the war, so much so that "the earnings of emigrants formed a very important item in the credit balance" of Austrian Poland—approximately $52 million a year. Ironically, this money earned abroad brought mixed blessings to the peasant and in some ways may have worsened his condition. Always, the money was used to buy or redeem land. By 1900 demand for land was so intense that large landowners were subdividing their estates or selling them to middlemen who would resell them to eager peasants lot by lot. Between 1889 and 1902, 237,000 acres were parcelled; between 1902 and 1912 another 607,000 acres were subdivided.[26]

The problem of the checkerboard intensified and little "dwarfs" (extremely small landholdings) became more common. Gradually, the wage offerings and work opportunities of Germany, Moravia and Bohemia had to compete with those of the United States and Canada. "Increasing numbers reason, 'If we must leave home, why not go further, wherever wages may be the highest, and stay until we have earned what we need.' So the father goes himself to America, or sends his son to get money to redeem or to enlarge the farm."[27]

Russian Poland and the Congress Kingdom

In theory, Poland was restored by the Congress of Vienna in 1815, but this semireconstituted "Kingdom of Poland" was a mere fragment of its former self (one-sixth to be exact) and included only ten provinces or departments: Kalisz, Kielce, Łomża, Lublin, Piotrków, Płock, Radom, Siedlce, Suwałki and Warszawa.[28] Russia was to oversee the Kingdom's economic and political affairs; in effect, it exercised total control over the area. With the czar's conscience sufficiently appeased by the creation of the Congress Kingdom, Russia directly annexed the remaining provinces of what had once been northern and eastern Poland: Wilno, Kowno, Witebsk, Grodno, Mohylów, Mińsk, Wołyn, Kijów, Podole and Kurlandya. Russian Poland, particularly the Congress Kingdom, accounted for the majority of Polish emigration and was the major source of the Polish population in the United States.

Three conditions not found in Galicia influenced developments in nineteenth-century Congress Poland: the existence of a viable market economy; the creation of a rural proletariat as early as 1815; and state-supported industrialization. Each of these had serious implications for the peasant's future.

The market economy was organized for export, primarily of wheat and other grains but occasionally of woolen textiles and sugar beets. It was operated by the nobility on large private or state-owned estates worked by peasant labor. The peasant economy, in contrast, was notoriously uninterested in production for market. The common saying, "Matthew has harvested, Matthew has eaten," was used to mock the backwardness of the peasant but was nonetheless accurate, for what the peasant planted for himself he invariably consumed. Not until after Emancipation would the peasant become more market-oriented—vehemently so.

The primary consequence of the market economy was the gradual conversion of the peasant's compulsory labor into rent, a process which began early in the 1800s. Given the profit orientation of the market, it was more efficient for the lord to rent lands to the peasant and to pay wages, either in kind or in money, for any labor performed on the estate. Conversion to rent was very rapid on state-owned agricultural estates, an important consideration since the state was the largest landholder in the Congress Kingdom, owning more than 25% of the total area of the country, or 1.12 million acres. By 1860, 91% of all State-owned serfs were rent payers, compared with 41% of those on private estates. With compulsory labor converted to rent, the serf was able to work for himself or for whomever he chose, as long as he paid the required rent to his master.[29]

A second consequence of the market economy was the incentive to put as much land as possible into production of cash crops, primarily wheat. In adverse times, other items were substituted for cereals. When the British Corn Laws temporarily put a damper on wheat exports, the gentry turned to crops such as sugar beets; they also converted grain into alcohol, invested in sheep and encouraged manufacture of woolen textiles for export to Russia and China. These activities, however, often had adverse repercussions: alcohol production, through the *propinacja* or government monopoly, encouraged drunkenness; sheep raising required that additional pasturage be taken from the peasants, crippling their ability to raise livestock and denying them rights held in servitude for centuries. With the abolition of the Corn Laws in 1845, wheat once again became the major cash crop. The gentry continued to expand production, primarily through deforestation but also by reducing the peasant's allotment of land or by utilizing barren and fallow lands.

Reduction of peasant allotments was encouraged by the introduction of the potato in the eighteenth century which enabled the peasant to grow more food per acre than was possible with cereal crops. Taking advantage of this, landlords reduced the peasant's landholdings and put the recaptured portions into grains, beets or pasture. Deforestation was more serious because it led to confrontations over servitudes. Landlords wanted the servitudes abolished so that they could sell the timber for quick cash and put the cleared land into cultivation. This meant that the peasants were denied access to forests and thus to a miscellany of essential items—wood, kindling, fruits, berries, nuts, mushrooms, fowl and game. With the servitudes gone, they had to pay for these things or face fines and imprisonment for trespassing on someone else's property. Attempts to abolish forest servitudes inevitably led to bloodshed and minor uprisings: nevertheless, one-quarter of all forested land (1,750,000 acres) disappeared between 1865 and 1914.[30]

In addition to facilitating the conversion of compulsory peasant labor to rents and providing the incentive to cultivate as much land as possible, the market economy encouraged landlords to increase production by improving output per acre. By the 1880s new tilling techniques, better fertilizers, crop rotation and mechanical reapers, threshers and sowers were in use. Horses replaced oxen, and steam-powered machines were becoming common.

Because production for world markets required large, efficiently operated estates, parcelling, or breaking down large estates, never became as popular in Russian Poland as it was in Galicia. Only on large farms could new techniques and machinery be utilized to secure more output per acre; and only through increased output could a landlord realize a profit in an unpredictable world economy. Production for market not only hastened the peasant's emancipation by commuting his compulsory labor into rent; it also accelerated his landlessness. Without pastures and forests and with reductions in land allotments, the peasant economy was unworkable. Moreover, in the absence of parcelling, peasant holdings had to be partitioned and repartitioned, decreasing in size with each division. While the peasant population grew rapidly after 1860, the amount of peasant land grew hardly at all. The result was an upsurge in the number of landless or nearly landless peasants.

The creation of the landless or rural proletariat began as early as 1815 when many areas of Congress Poland were severely devastated by the Napoleonic Wars. The province of Płock, for example, was the scene of three major campaigns in six years, during which forests, fields and crops were ravaged beyond repair. Throughout central Poland, peasants forfeited cattle, horses, food, lodgings and sons to French and Russian armies. Of 100,000 who fought with Napoleon's Polish contingent, only 18,000 returned. New conscriptions in 1813 took away more precious labor. Peasants in areas that were once part of the Duchy of Warsaw were freed by Napoleonic decree in December 1807, but the "emancipation" was a sham. It failed to do two necessary things: it did not give the peasant the right or title to any land, merely enabling the landlord to evict him; and it did not abolish compulsory labor. Evicted serfs could only wander. Since there was little industry and little demand for unskilled labor in towns and cities, there was nowhere to go. The state absorbed many through military service and public works construction, but, as the number of landless continued to grow, these alternatives were not sufficient.

High death rates and low birth rates characterized the peasant population until 1860. With a population of four million in 1830, Congress Poland reached only five million by 1864. As in Galicia, bad harvests, potato famine, typhus and cholera killed hundreds of thousands between 1847 and 1856; in these years the population actually declined. By 1860, 40% of the agrarian population, or 1,339,000 people. were landless or were farming holdings so small that they had to work for wages on large estates.[31]

Despite large numbers of peasants sorely in need of work. Congress Poland suffered from a chronic shortage of agricultural labor, especially at harvest and haying time. Military drafts, the low birth and high death rates of previous decades, and highway and railway

Table 24
POPULATION OF THE KINGDOM OF POLAND, 1814–1913

Years	Population	Increase or decrease	
		Actual nos.	% per annum
1814	2,815,000		
1820	3,520,355	220,355	.67
1825	3,911,000	390,645	2.22
1830	3,998,000	87,000	.44
1835	4,188,112	190,112	.95
1840	4,488,009	299,897	1.43
1845	4,798,658	310,649	1.38
1850	4,810,735	12,077	.05
1855	4,673,869	− 136,866	− .57
1860	4,840,466	166,597	.71
1865	5,336,210	495,744	2.05
1870	6,078,564	742,354	2.78
1875	6,515,153	436,589	1.44
1880	7,104,864	589,711	1.81
1885	7,687,893	583,029	1.64
1890	8,256,562	568,669	1.48
1897	9,402,253	1,145,691	1.98
1904	11,588,585	2,186,332	3.32
1909	11,935,318	346,733	.60
1913	13,058,000	1,122,682	2.35

The population of the Kingdom of Poland declined in the following years:

1830–31	−370,000	(Revolution)
1847–49	− 85,774	(famine)
1852	− 39,062	
1854	− 15,246	(famine,
1855	−123,976	typhus and
(1847–1855)	−193,260	cholera)
1859	− 25,933	
1864		(numbers unknown—Revolution)
1889	− 42,000	(epidemics)
1905	−277,000	(Revolution; war mobilization)

SOURCE: *Polish Encyclopedia* 2: 146–47.

construction (where wages were poor but surpassed what could be earned by working on an estate) contributed to the shortage. Nonetheless, the psychology and conditions of the Polish peasant were major reasons for a manpower shortage in the midst of a rural proletariat of 1.3 million.

The landlord needed large numbers of reliable workers at the critical point of the harvest, for unlike other crops, wheat had to be harvested within days of maturity or all was lost. For the peasant, however, landlessness and the need to work were year-round conditions not confined to harvest time. Then, too, at harvest time he was busy with his own meager plot or that of a wealthier peasant for whom he preferred to work; he could not be rounded up en masse and delivered to large estates at a moment's notice. Finally, the peasant was not overly anxious to work for the large landowner, his former master. As Kieniewicz observes, "the average landowner did not consider the local villager a free worker with whom one should make a contract (as was done with mowers from Galicia). No, the local villager was the former serf, traditionally meant to obey, a creature not supposed to negotiate his conditions of work." Thus, each year, to assure a sufficient labor supply at harvest time, the landlords contracted with *bandosy,* experienced mowers from the Tatras of Galicia who had been performing this work for generations.[32]

Alexander II officially freed the serfs in 1864 and introduced agricultural reforms, enabling peasants to own land in their own right and giving some land to the landless. Landlords were to be compensated through the issuance of bonds worth 64 million rubles. A land tax, still in effect in 1915 (long after the 64 million rubles had been recouped), was imposed on the peasants to pay for the bonds and was often collected by military force. The Reforms of 1864 also provided for the gradual abolition of the servitudes, much to the dismay of the peasantry.

Despite taxation, loss of servitudes and too small land holdings, the conditions of the peasantry, as reflected in better diet and living conditions and higher birth and lower death rates, improved significantly. Freedom agreed with the former serfs. Their improvement was closely linked to two factors: their ability to enter the market economy, however haltingly, by consolidating and enlarging their land holdings and using improved farming methods and machinery; and their ability to find work outside of agriculture in industry and construction.

Between 1884 and 1893 the wheat growing regions of Poland were adversely affected by European importation of cheap American wheat. Prices dropped drastically and Poland actually failed to export wheat for the first time in four hundred years. By 1893 farming, especially with modern techniques and machinery, was once again profitable. The period 1907 to 1914 was particularly good for production because prices were up in all commodities. The efficient and ambitious peasant farmer benefited and was inclined to improve his advantage by buying more land.

An unfortunate side effect of better living conditions was the great upsurge in the average annual rate of natural increase after 1880; the population began to multiply rapidly. Between 1857 and 1913 the Kingdom of Poland increased its population by 179%. Comparing this figure with Galicia's 77%, Upper Silesia's 110%, Poznań's 51% and West Prussia's 52%, the enormity of the increase is apparent. Moreover, "according to the computations of the Warsaw Statistical Committee [1906], if the Kingdom of Poland kept up its rate of increase for the end of the nineteenth century it would double its population in 35 years. France would take as much as 236 years to double her numbers; Austria, 135; Germany, 98, and Russia, 65." Poland's enormous increases in population despite losses from emigration fascinated demographers in the late nineteenth and early twentieth centuries.[33]

The vast upsurge in population exacerbated the demand for land. "In 1855 there were in the whole Kingdom 95.8 inhabitants per square mile; in 1897 on every square mile of the *agricultural areas* alone (not counting forests, waste lands, etc.), there were 150.2 persons *supporting themselves by agriculture.*" In the absence of parcelling (the gentry resisted pressures to break up their estates), the amount of land owned by the peasantry increased by only 8% between the Reform of 1864 and 1890. Peasant properties, therefore, were partitioned with greater frequency, and bigger owners bought up smaller ones. The result of the rapid increase in population and subsequent partitioning of peasant properties was a substantial growth (386%) of the landless peasantry from 220,000 in 1870 to 849,000 in 1891; this was accompanied by a smaller rise (121%) in the number of peasant holdings, from 593,000 in 1870 to 717,000 in 1899. The average size of holdings was of necessity diminishing. Supposedly there were no holdings of less than six *morgi* because it was illegal to divide below this point. The peasants, however, continued to divide their properties but neglected to register them officially.[34]

The second factor contributing to improvement in the peasants' living conditions was the ability to find work outside of agriculture, in industry and related activities. Although Congress Poland's overall population increased more than 75% between 1877 and 1910, the number of industrial workers increased by 450%—from 90,767 to 400,922.[35] Unlike Austria-Hungary, Russia had definite plans for industrializing its Polish provinces. Official policy as early as 1815 was to make the Kingdom the major industrial center of the Russian Empire

and the main artery of transit between Russia and western Europe. As
we have noted, the state was the biggest land owner. Many of its holdings were mining estates in southwestern Poland where serfs, still
bound to compulsory labor, mined iron, copper and lead. The government operated large foundries in the mining areas and used serf labor to
cut wood (iron making still utilized charcoal) and to transport raw materials and finished products.

Early in the nineteenth century, through the incentives of state
loans and protective tariffs, German craftsmen and German and
English industrialists were encouraged to establish industries in Poland. It was in this way, for example, that Łódź became the foremost
textile center of the Russian Empire; founded by German Jewish
entrepreneurs, the city's textile industry was protected from Prussian
and Saxon competition by high tariffs. Additional tariffs, imposed in
the 1880s, prohibited the importation of rolled iron, forcing Polish
foundries to produce more iron and steel to meet the textile industry's
demand for new machinery. By 1900 Congress Poland was a prime sup-
plier of coal, iron and steel, granulated sugar, flax and hemp, cotton
yarns and fabric and woolen yarns and fabric, the last accounting for
43% of all woolens manufactured in the Empire. The Poles supplied
labor for these industries but not capital or technology; in 1913 more
than two-thirds of Poland's industries were controlled by foreigners
and foreign bankers.[36]

As in America, rapid urbanization accompanied Poland's industrial expansion. In 1872 there were seventeen cities with a population of 10,000 or more and two—Warszawa and Łódź—with 40,000 or
more. By 1913 there were sixty cities with 10,000 inhabitants and ten
with 40,000 or more. Warszawa increased from 175,000 in 1860 to
345,000 in 1880 and 730,000 by 1900. Of all Poland's cities, however,
Łódź represented the most notorious example of rampant growth. A
provincial city of 31,000 in 1860, this "Manchester of Russia" grew to
314,780—a ten-fold increase—by 1897, a growth, as Adna Weber remarked, "that would be regarded as phenomenal even in America."
Most remarkable of all, according to the Russian Ministry of the Interior, 25% of the residents of the Kingdom of Poland in 1913 were
urban dwellers compared with only 13% in European and Asiatic
Russia.[37]

In addition to increasing rapidly and concentrating in urban
centers, the population was redistributing itself within the Kingdom.
This redistribution was directly related to the availability and location
of employment in industry and its adjuncts. Those provinces recording

the smallest increase were the least industrialized—and also sent the largest contingents of workers to the New World; Płock, Łomża and Suwałki are good examples. The most industrialized provinces or areas had large increases in population and tended to have little or no emigration.

Of all provinces, Piotrków recorded the largest population increases between 1872 and 1913. Within its boundaries were three of Poland's four main industrial centers: Łódź, its neighboring cities of Zgierz, Pabianice, Tomaszów Rawski, Ozorków and Łask, all of which were major textile producers; the Dąbrowa coal fields with their group of urban centers specializing in heavy industry—Sosnowiec (site of Poland's largest steel mills and metal manufacturers, many of which employed more than 1,500 workers), Zawiercie and Myszków; and Częstochowa, surrounded by smaller towns such as Raków, Rudniki, Blachownia, Kamienica Polska, N. Radomsk and Kamińsk, containing many textile mills, furniture factories and blast furnaces. Poland's fourth, and largest, industrial center was in Warszawa province, with Warszawa, Żyrardów and Marki among the most important cities. Warszawa had textile mills, large metal factories, clothing works, an important sugar industry and sizable brickworks and paper mills. The linen industry alone employed 9,000 workers at Żyrardów.[38]

The men and women who crowded these cities and manned their factories were recruited from the countryside of every province of Po-

Table 25

POPULATION INCREASE OF CONGRESS POLAND BY PROVINCE
(in thousands)

Government	1872	1897	1913	Increase	
				Actual nos.	%
Piotrków	705	1,404	2,268	1,563	221.7
Warszawa	1,085	1,931	2,669	1,584	146.0
Lublin	739	1,160	1,584	845	114.3
Radom	542	815	1,149	607	111.9
Kielce	539	762	1,039	500	92.7
Kalisz	687	841	1,317	630	91.7
Siedlce	549	772	1,024	475	86.5
Płock	486	554	706	220	45.3
Łomża	493	580	650	157	31.8
Suwałki	541	583	652	111	20.5
Kingdom of Poland	6,366	9,402	13,058	6,692	105.1

SOURCE: *Polish Encyclopedia* 2: 149.

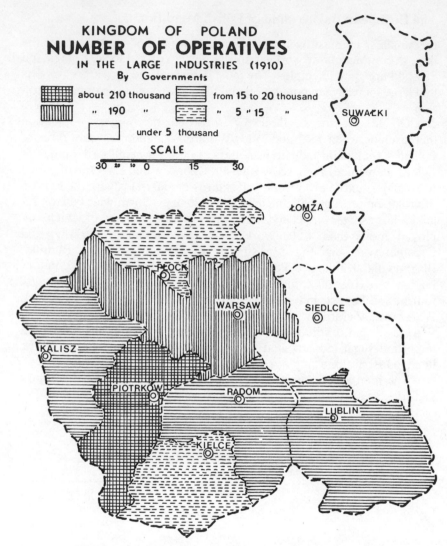

NUMBER OF OPERATIVES, KINGDOM OF POLAND, 1910

land. Heavy metal industries, oil refineries, sugar refineries, mining and unskilled construction work employed peasant labor while skilled and semiskilled crafts and factory work, especially in textile and garment manufacture, relied heavily on Jewish labor. In general, peasants went to the cities and industrial centers as seasonal or temporary workers, always intending to return to their villages. Some stayed three months, some four or five years, and many stayed indefinitely.

The high rate of natural increase which began in the 1880s and the peasant's ability to earn extra income in industry and on large estates generated the first serious pressures for parcelization in the 1890s. This pressure intensified after 1900 when peasant incomes were greatly supplemented by earnings from abroad. (After all, "in a peasant's view, purchase of land was the only conceivable way to invest his savings.") In 1890 big landholders owned almost 50% of all cultivated land; twenty years later they owned 38%. The difference—2.5 million acres—was parcelled out to smaller peasants, lesser gentry and burghers. So great was demand during this period that prices of land doubled. The Russian government, wary of the Galician experience with parcelization, established a state-owned Peasant Bank to supervise and finance sales of parcelled land. This endeavor did not spring entirely from benevolent motives: by helping the peasant to secure his coveted land, the state hoped to eliminate the ultimate source of unrest and to further political stability. By 1914 the Peasant Bank had established 26,000 new farms totalling 567,000 acres, but most of them were large operations run by well-to-do peasants and their sons. The small peasant landowner and the totally landless did not benefit much from the program. The demand for land, consequently, did not abate but grew.[39]

The greatest pressure came from the small landowner who, since Emancipation, had gradually worked to solidify his position. In 1872 22% of all peasant holdings were "dwarfs" of less than 4 acres; by 1904 this number had been reduced to 14%. On the other hand, peasant holdings in excess of 21 acres had fallen from 38% to 22% during the same period. The result was that, by 1914, 64% of all peasants, compared with 40.5% in 1872, had holdings of only 4 to 21 acres. The typical farm consisted of 5 to 7 acres, large enough to enable the peasant to limp along but never to feel secure. Even a farm of 21 acres was not enough to ensure self-sufficiency. There also remained the problem of the servitudes. As late as 1914, 57% of all forested area belonged to large private estates and 25% to the state; only 17% was in the hands of small property owners such as the peasant. The peasant, therefore, continued to pay for the privilege of using the forests of the former master.[40]

The ability to secure work away from the farm, in industry or on large estates, enabled the peasant to hold on to his meager landholdings and even to increase them. Failure to earn sufficient monies away from the farm or a season of poor crops or personal sickness could force the peasant to sell, divide or mortgage his property; the denouement, God forbid, could find him slipping into the ranks of the totally landless whose numbers, unfortunately, were growing mercilessly. By 1910 more than two million peasants were without any land at all and their living conditions left much to be desired. As Kieniewicz says, "the rural proletariat was the only segment of the population in Congress Poland that did not improve its standard of living in the entire course of the 19th century." Although great numbers of the landless worked on large estates or for wealthier peasants, a significant number, the *parobek, komornicy* and *wyrobnicy,* continued to labor under conditions differing little from those of the feudal past.[41]

Until 1900 it seemed that local industry would be able to absorb most of Poland's surplus agricultural population. It was a close race; new jobs in industry, commerce, transportation and services grew at a rate almost equal to that of the population. Well into the 1890s internal migration to areas of industry and large farm-factories was the peasant's primary response to landlessness or indebtedness. "Migration from one portion of the country to the other", the U.S. Consul General reported, "is of constant occurrence, and is caused either by lack of employment or the exhaustion of the soil", while "emigration . . . is wholly unimportant, being mostly confined to Jews. . ."[42] Although 63,000 landless and nearly landless peasants responded to Brazil's offer of free land and free transportation in the 1890s, and although a few started for the United States, the great migrations from Congress Poland did not occur until after 1900, when the Russian economy entered a self-induced depression of great severity.

The worst was yet to come, however. Because the market for manufactured goods was relatively underdeveloped at home, Polish industry had always relied on Eastern outlets in China and Asiatic Russia. The Russo-Japanese War of 1904 cut off these markets and brought further decreases in industrial production. The Revolution in Russia in 1905 brought strikes, lock-outs and greater deterioration in Polish industry. Trade ceased and production halted as orders failed to come in. Only war-related industries prospered, ones that made barbed wire, shrapnel, munitions and chocolate candy for the men at the front.

The industrial catastrophe and its accompanying upheavals had two major consequences for the peasantry: (1) substantial increases in the numbers of the rural proletariat and (2) vast upsurges in emigration. By eliminating the chief outlet of thousands of landless and indebted people and by forcing countless workers to return to the countryside where many joined the ranks of the landless, the industrial depression left emigration as the only recourse. In search of work and wages, Poles of the Congress Kingdom and other Russian provinces headed for Germany, Denmark, France, Sweden and the United States.

Official statistics for the Kingdom of Poland indicate that temporary or seasonal emigration reached enormous proportions by the eve of the First World War: 153,408 in 1904; 268,466 in 1908 and 360,142 in 1912. The great majority of these temporary migrants went to Prussia— 87.6% in 1908 and 89.5% (322,350) in 1912. At least 50% of these seasonal workers were landless and another 25% to 30% were small landholders. Most came from just those provinces, such as Łomża and Suwałki, that supported the highest portions of landless and small landowners.[43]

In addition to seasonal emigration, there was the more or less permanent emigration that lasted one year or more. This category included all those who journeyed to the United States, Canada or other areas overseas. United States immigration statistics indicate that immigration to the United States from all Polish provinces of the Russian empire—the ten provinces of the Kingdom as well as the ten provinces directly annexed by Russia—averaged 29,992 per year between 1900 and 1904; 48,433 per year between 1905 and 1909; 63,635 in 1910; 54,244 for the period July 1, 1911 to June 30, 1912; and 112,345 for July 1, 1912 to June 30, 1913. (Because these figures include the Polish provinces outside of the Kingdom, they contain substantial numbers of Russians, Bylo-Russians and Lithuanians, a smattering of Ukrainians and, most important, large numbers of Jews.) The official American estimate is that 30% of all these immigrants returned to Poland and Russia. Since these numbers include Jews, virtually none of whom returned and who, in many years, accounted for 40–60% of the total immigration to the United States from the Russian provinces of Poland, the return rate for non-Jewish groups is obviously much higher— in some years closer to 50–60%. Statistics of the Polish government support this conclusion. Depending upon the year, Polish records list permanent or net emigration (out-migrants minus returnees) at 60 to 70% of American immigration figures, indicating that 30 to 40% of overseas emigrants eventually returned. Once again, these computations of the Polish government include emigrating Jews who were not planning to return to Europe; hence, the proportions of non-Jewish returnees is actually much higher.[44]

What none of these statistical records, American or Polish, takes into account is that more Poles were intending to return to Europe but were prevented from doing so by the outbreak of the First World War in 1914; many had even booked passage or purchased ship tickets. Interviews with remaining members of the immigrant generation reveal that the intention to return was real and pervasive. Further probing reveals that fear of being drafted in Poland or having missed one's draft call at home were other negative reasons for remaining in America.

Although the numbers who left the Kingdom of Poland for overseas never matched the enormous numbers who emigrated yearly to the countries of northern and western Europe, especially Prussia, the incentive to migrate and the aim of the migrant were always the same. Quite often it was the very taste of success that prompted migration in search of work: it *was* possible to earn enough money in industry or on large agricultural estates to buy more land. With more land it *was* possible to become self-sufficient and to achieve a respectable economic and social security; it *was* possible to fulfill the imperatives inherent in the peasant's culture. The dream, always tempting, was also real: "The Polish peasant does not forsake his field. He hangs on to and even endeavors to increase his holding. He succeeds in this solely by his hard-working tenacity, his attachment to the land and the moderation of his needs."[45]

5   The Polish Experience
       in Philadelphia

Management of the [Charles Lennig] Company was controlled by John B. Lennig very largely until his death in 1920. Accounts picture him as a businessman of the "old school." He lived in the Lennig mansion until 1913 and arrived at his office at the factory regularly at fifteen after seven. Working conditions of the period of 1907 are most interesting. By this date the German element had been replaced largely by Polish employees. It was not uncommon for thirty or more immigrants to be standing at the gates seeking employment when the plant opened. Common labor worked for twelve cents an hour and averaged ten hours [a day] during the summer months. Advancement came with demonstration of ability.
                                                   —Sylvester K. Stevens[1]

By 1915 Poles had been coming to Philadelphia in search of work for at least thirty-five years; the vast majority, however, came only after 1900. Local parish records reveal that the original workers who came in the late 1870s, 1880s and 1890s were from Prussian Poland, primarily Poznań and West Prussia, but also from Silesia and East Prussia. By the turn of the century the Prussian Poles were decidedly outnumbered by compatriots from Galicia and the Kingdom of Poland. The Russian provinces of Płock, Suwałki and Łomża were especially well-represented among the later travelers to Philadelphia, so much so that by 1914 Prussian Poles had become a minority in the city.

The pioneering Prussian Poles differed in significant ways from the subsequent Austrian and Russian arrivals. They usually spoke German in addition to Polish and so invariably established the first Polish colonies, churches and parishes in German sections of the city. They were often Lutheran rather than Roman Catholic. They were literate and had had some formal schooling before their arrival because of Prussian efforts to Germanize its Polish population. More important, Prussian Poles came with skills and trades and extensive industrial exposure.

Poles from Germany were able to acquire skills and trades or at least to assume positive attitudes toward them for several reasons. The Jews had been expelled from Germany long before and the Germans themselves had replaced them as artisans and merchants. Serfdom was abolished rather early (1807) and was accompanied by a century-long campaign to push the Polish peasant off the land. Finally, the Polish provinces of Germany had undergone intensive German industrialization since the late eighteenth century. In the process, Prussian Poles shed many of their cultural distinctions between women's and men's work. Polish men from Germany were not adverse to sewing or cooking, and they were very inclined to enter trades and open shops and businesses. Despite their importance as trail blazers however, Poles from Germany always constituted less than 10% of the Polish migration to America and thus were not representative of the whole movement.

The Russian and Austrian Poles brought few if any skills with them to America. They came from areas late in abolishing serfdom and were still oriented to a "two-class" feudal society where the classless Jews performed the essential middle roles. In addition, their experience in industrial Europe was that of unskilled general laborers. Their intent was not to change occupations but to return to the one they valued so highly—farming.

The Poles' settlement and work patterns wherever they went strongly reflected their feudal past and peasant culture, their different developments under the domination of three foreign powers, and their experiences in the industrializing and urbanizing Europe of the late nineteenth century. Almost all Poles who came to America were unskilled peasant-farmers who had lost their land or were attempting to preserve what little holdings they still possessed. They intended to return to Poland and half or more of them actually did. Initially they did not work at skilled crafts or trades either in America or in Europe because they had no experience in them and because they did not aspire to these roles; those few Poles who did become weavers, tailors and cabinet makers in America were Prussian Poles whose experience under German occupation had begun to change their attitudes toward certain forms of work.

Data compiled from the *City Directory* reveals that in 1915 more than 60% of all Philadelphia's Polish workers (totalling 4,232) were engaged in unskilled occupations, either in industry or in services. Another 24% did skilled and semi-skilled industrial work. Less than 2% were professionals—business executives and managers—and less than 10% were self-employed.

Table 26

OCCUPATIONAL DISTRIBUTION OF PHILADELPHIA'S POLES, C.1915

Occupation	No.			%
Professional	57			1.3
Executive/managerial	16			0.4
Self-employed	405			9.6
Services	354	{ 230 unskilled	5.5% }	8.4
		124 skilled	2.9%	
Industry	3,389	{ 2,363 unskilled	55.8% }	80.0
		127 semi-skilled	3.0%	
		899 skilled	21.2%	
Other	11			0.3
Total	4,232*			100.0

*4,464 Polish persons were listed in the 1915 Philadelphia *City Directory*. 4,235 were men; 229 were women. 66 men and 22 women reported no occupations. 144 women were widows, also reporting no occupations. Thus, 232 persons reported no occupations, leaving 4,232 with occupations. See Appendix I for detailed listing.

The unskilled were ironworkers, steelworkers, leatherworkers and general laborers who worked in the city's chemical factories, petroleum and sugar refineries, slaughterhouses and tanneries and loaded and unloaded railroad cars and ships in Philadelphia Harbor. None of the unskilled found work in the textile or garment industries and apparently none were involved in public works construction, although general laborers occasionally worked for private construction firms.

On the whole, Philadelphia's unskilled Polish workers constituted a very transient and temporary population. The first arrivals were routed to the city by New York employment agencies at the request of local metal foundries (such as Midvale Steel Company and Disston Saw Works), tanneries, sugar refineries and chemical refineries (such as Charles Lennig Company), or they found their way to Philadelphia during periods of depression and strikes in the northeastern Pennsylvania coalfields, a short distance from the city via the Reading and Lehigh Valley Railroads. Once begun, the movement was sustained largely through a highly personal network as friends and relatives in the United States and in Poland joined other friends and relatives who had already found a niche in the city. It was a classic chain migration, vividly recorded in parish records.

Skilled Polish workers predominated in the machine shop, textile, lumber and leather industries. In the metal trades they tended to be machinists, blacksmiths and boilermakers; in the textile and garment industries they were weavers, dyers and tailors; in the lumber industry they were carpenters, cabinetmakers and woodworkers; in the leather industry they were shoemakers. Out of a total working force of 4,232, only 50 men were tailors, and they, like the majority of the carpenters, cabinetmakers, shoemakers, dyers, weavers and machinists, were Prussian Poles. The more highly skilled the industrial worker, the more likely was he to be a Pole from Poznań, West Prussia or Silesia. Most often permanent immigrants, by 1915 Prussian Poles had been here for a decade or more and thus had sufficient time to consolidate their postions.

Those Russian and Austrian Poles who managed to acquire a skill or the rudiments of one by 1915 had usually received their preparation in this country, most often in the anthracite fields of northeastern Pennsylvania or as general laborers in places like Midvale Steel Company, Disston's Saw Works or Cramp's Shipyard. Many of Philadelphia's Polish machinists and skilled factory workers got their start in the mines and mills of the state. This is supported by family histories and parish records, even though precise statistics are not available.

Generally, when we speak of the thousands employed in the mines we forget that "mining" was not a homogenous occupation or industry. Not all employees were actually "miners." There were many job classifications and titles arranged in a hierarchy of skill and status. Anthracite employees, classified as inside and outside workers, included skilled men, such as blacksmiths, mechanics and carpenters, and unskilled workers, such as breaker-boys, (mule) drivers and slate pickers.[2] Machines and tools of all sorts—locomotives, tenders, pumps, valves, pulleys, springs, engines, axles, lathes, planes, power saws—were found everywhere around the mines. Unskilled immigrants, arriving with nothing more than strength and ambition, constantly observed and were trained to work these machines and tools. The most ambitious ("those here two years or longer") were always trying to improve their position, to move up in the hierarchy.

> The most unskilled in any particular group in time becomes the least unskilled in that group; the least unskilled pass into some skilled group. Thus, there is a constant interchange of individuals from group to group and from class to class, the general tendency being a progression from the most unskilled to the most skilled. Miners are always passing out of the latter group to

Table 27

ANTHRACITE INDUSTRY: CLASSIFICATION OF EMPLOYEES, 1900

Inside employees	No.	Outside employees	No.
Miners	36,000	Mechanics	2,000
Miners' laborers	24,000	Company laborers	8,000
Platemen	750	Breaker boys	16,000
Drivers	10,000	Headmen	750
Runners	1,000	Engineers	1,200
Engineers	1,500	Firemen	3,300
Door boys	3,000	Runners	
Bratticemen		Barn-men	
Timbermen		Culm-men	18,703
Pump runners	12,562	Drivers	
Trackmen		Chute-men	
Company laborers		Clerks	
Bosses	1,300	Bosses, etc.	793

SOURCE: Peter Roberts, *The Anthracite Coal Industry* (New York: Macmillan, 1901), p. 107.

become firebosses, foremen, superintendents, or into other higher occupations, both inside and outside the industry; others are killed.[3]

Mining was a dangerous, dirty and uncomfortable business. As a temporary job it was acceptable; as a lifelong, permanent position, it was not. If death or injury (both daily occurences) didn't claim a worker, Black Lung made him useless by the age of forty. The work was grueling, and age worked against the mine laborer. Hence, the aim was to move up or out to something better. The passage upward, however, had built-in bottlenecks. Because the number of better and safer jobs was limited and great numbers were seeking them, few of the unskilled could hope to secure a better position even if they survived their "apprenticeship" and became adequately prepared.

The same situation prevailed in the steel industry. The conditions under which the unskilled steel hand worked included twelve-hour days, twenty-four-hour shifts ("the days and weeks without a day of rest"), intense heat, great danger, high accident potential, exhaustion, fatigue, death. "No man with much imagination or desire for self-improvement is willing to work seven days in the week except as a temporary expedient." As in the mining industry, iron and steel manufacture had its own hierarchy and provided training for unskilled workers eager to improve their lot.

In the open-hearth department the line of promotion runs
through common labor, metal wheelers, stock handler, cinder-
pit man, second helper and first helper, to melter foreman. In
this way the companies develop and train their own men. They
seldom hire a stranger for a position as roller or heater. Thus the
working force is pyramided and is held together by the ambition
of the men lower down; even a serious break in the ranks adjusts
itself all but automatically. [4]

Unfortunately, as in the mines, opportunities for advancement and
promotion were two few and far between.

Given these circumstances, many ex-miners and former
steelworkers who were "retired," injured or denied advancement,
found Philadelphia very attractive. Speaking some English, familar
with the ways of American industrial organization and, most important, possessing skills acquired while in the mines and mills, they
had excellent prospects of finding appropriate employment in
Philadelphia. The nature of Philadelphia's industry led the city deliberately to attract immigrants with skills, both directly from abroad,
as in the case of many British, Germans and German Poles, and in-
directly via the mines and steelmills of Pennsylvania, as in the case of
many Russian and Austrian Poles. For Russian and Austrian Poles to
have acquired a skill or craft is most revealing: it indicates that the
worker had been in the United States for some time and had decided to
remain in this country indefinitely.

The mines and mills of Pennsylvania may have served as a training
ground for the machine shops and factories of Philadelphia, but the city
also performed a reciprocal service for its hinterland. By 1880 the rural
depopulation of the northeast and its accompanying labor shortages
had become a serious concern to industrialists and entrepreneurs. Iron
and steel manufacturers and coal companies, scattered throughout
Pennsylvania in areas with no surpluses of native population, were
forced to recruit unskilled laborers in large eastern cities such as New
York and Philadelphia. As major ports of entry and termini of several
railroads, these had become assembly points for miscellaneous
persons, immigrant and nonimmigrant, in search of work. Philadelphia,
as the metropolis of a large hinterland, served as a recruitment center
for unskilled labor. From Philadelphia many Poles and other foreign
workers found their way to the mines and mills of the state before the
turn of the century. According to Pennsylvania's Commissioner of
Labor and Industry:

One means taken to secure a working force was to send an official representative to the city of New York or Philadelphia with instructions to gather together a gang of laborers and bring them back to the plant needing employees. Special inducements in the way of wages were held forth and unusual opportunities offered to all those who were willing to leave the larger cities and help out the companies in the western section of the State. Once the stream of immigrant labor was started toward the State's industrial centers, it was comparatively easy to keep it moving. Immigrant laborers who found employment in the coal fields, in the iron and steel industries, and in other industrial activities, wrote to their friends, not only in this country, but in their native country, telling them of the unusual industrial opportunities and wages, and urging them to come to the State.[5]

The Polish Experience in Perspective

Opportunities for employment were crucial in determining where the Poles went in the United States. Since they had come to America to secure work and quick wages for the farm and family back home, they chose areas that offered them the greatest chances of achieving their goal. They did not settle in places like Philadelphia that had very little to offer them.

None of Philadelphia's major industries—textiles and garment manufacture, printing and publishing and metal manufacture of the hardware and machine shop variety—employed large numbers of unskilled male laborers. Few new industries that could utilize such labor were moving into the city. While tens of thousands of Jews and Italians made their living in the needle trades, the Poles did not even try to enter this industry; perhaps the most revealing finding is that only 50 Polish men, out of a working population of more than 4,000, were employed in the garment industry (and these, as noted, were primarily Poles from Germany). The textile industry employed another 200 Polish men, a negligible number for an industry that provided the livelihood of the city's Irish, German and British immigrants and their children. Textile and clothing manufacture had a negative influence on Polish settlement; as Philadelphia's major industry, heavily staffed by women, it offered no attraction to a Polish migration composed largely of unskilled men who avoided "women's work" and sought hard, physical labor. Even though Polish women were more likely to make use of their needle, as they so often did in New York City and Chicago, they could not become a major source of labor for the garment industry unless their men could also find employment locally.

Excluded from the skilled and female labor markets of the city by lack of qualifications, the Polish laborer was confined to unskilled areas of work. There he had to compete with ready pools of unskilled Irish, Irish-Americans and blacks. The Irish and Irish-Americans (with some help from Germans and German-Americans) had established a stronghold in the private construction industry and, given their numbers, did not need additional unskilled laborers such as the Poles. Moreover, it can be argued that the Irish, acting on the values of their culture, would be loyal to their own.

In competing with the black laborer, the Pole was only moderately successful and never was able to take over those areas of Philadelphia's unskilled labor market where blacks predominated; as early as 1915 blacks outnumbered foreign-born Poles by at least eight to one, and that ratio continued to grow. Like their black counterparts, unskilled Polish workers were normally confined to the secondary labor markets of the country; the last hired, they were the first to be fired. Poles and blacks invariably worked in the same jobs, and blacks were recruited for those jobs previously held by Poles when foreign workers were no longer available, as during the first World War and again after the passage of restrictive immigration legislation in the 1920s. These tasks included tanning, rendering, soap, tallow and glue making, slaughtering and meatpacking, hauling, lifting, and domestic service, which was the mainstay of both black and Polish women.

In addition to Irish, Irish-Americans and blacks, Poles had to contend with New Immigrant competitors. More than any other group, the Italians were able to secure a place for themselves in certain areas of Philadelphia's unskilled labor market; in this sense, they were more successful in competing with Irish and blacks than were the Poles and other Slavic groups. Because of their *padroni,* a built-in brokerage network, Italians were able to monopolize unskilled activities such as railroad and public works construction which involved contracting for large numbers of men to carry out projects of limited duration. Lacking the institution of *padrone* and highly dependent on individual contacts, the Poles were at a disadvantage in entering these fields. Even in cities where Poles constituted a major or majority group (Chicago, Cleveland, Milwaukee, Buffalo), Italians continued to monopolize public functions like street cleaning, street paving, street railway and subway construction.

Employer (and employee) preferences were also influential in distributing Polish and Italian labor. Italians were considered physically unfit for certain types of work. The Industrial Commission, for example, reported that Italians shunned underground work in mines and work in the primary stages of steel manufacture because they lacked "nervous strength"; since the Commission also reported that Italians were renowned for their work with explosives and nitroglycerin, it can be safely assumed that lack of "nervous strength" was not the reason. More likely, southern Italians avoided the isolation of foundry and underground work because they were a peer group culture. In construction types of work, they could enjoy the companionship of other members of their group. The Poles were also a network people, but they never developed a strong concept of the peer group (which might also explain the nonexistence of a Polish *padrone* system). Thus, "the Polish farmer can successfully compete in factory work where hard automatic labor is necessary; but the Italian dislikes mechanical work and is better adapted to diversified pursuits where manipulation is required."[6]

In the roles of artisan and merchant, neither southern Italians nor eastern European Jews offered any competition to the Poles. While Italians and Jews traditionally performed these roles in their home societies, the Poles did not, and often had negative attitudes towards such functions. As one commentator of the time noted, "expertness in quarrying and stone cutting, as well as in plastering and moulding, has been a transmitted acquirement for more than two thousand years in Italy. . . ."[7] The southern Italian ostensibly may have been a farmer, but he was also potentially a mason, carpenter, shoemaker, tailor and cook.

The Jews were never direct competitors of the Poles because they avoided heavier manual and unskilled occupations; two-thirds or more of all Poles in the United States, but less than one-twentieth of the Jews, performed unskilled work. In effect, Poles and eastern European Jews operated in totally separate labor markets and, unlike the Italians and Jews in the garment industry, rarely met occupationally except, perhaps, as employer (Jew) v. employee (Pole).

Finally, as a major manufacturing center soliciting laborers, Philadelphia had to compete with the steel mills, coal mines, cement and glass factories of central and western Pennsylvania, industries able to employ large numbers of unskilled male laborers. It is not surprising to find that Pennsylvania had more Polish immigrants than any other state and that 70% of them lived outside of Philadelphia and Pittsburgh. This distribution not only reflects differences in opportunities and the nature of work, but also indicates the particular character of Polish immigration to America. Predominately unskilled, male and temporary, products of a highly stratified society and peasant culture, Poles came in search of quick economic gain. Just as the nature of Philadelphia's economy and skill-demanding industries worked against large-scale Polish immigration, the growing need of the state's industries for unskilled labor worked in favor of it. The Polish migrant, therefore, was more likely to seek out the central and western parts of Pennsylvania than the city of Philadelphia. For the same reasons, he was more likely to seek out cities and other regions which were the creations of new industries and new technologies. These would need unskilled men whose sole qualifications were strength, endurance and eagerness to work. The Polish stream flowed to Chicago, Cleveland, Buffalo, Detroit and Milwaukee, but not to Philadelphia.

6   The Geography
of Neighborhood

One of the notably outstanding features is that in the Port
Richmond section we have people of many different old
world extractions, truly typical of cosmopolitan America.
They live quietly, peacefully and happily with each other.

One fact that has often been commented upon is the location of the Polish-American, Irish-American and German-
American Roman Catholic churches on one of the main
thoroughfares, East Allegheny Avenue—all within a
distance of three blocks.

—Philadelphia *Bulletin*[1]

The same combination of economic, demographic and cultural factors
that influenced immigrant distribution across North America also determined the geographic arrangement of immigrant peoples within
specific areas and cities. The forces that drew the immigrants out of
their home areas in Europe—making them migrant-workers of the Atlantic Economy, attracting many of them across the ocean to the
United States and sending those directly to the industrial core—also affected their settlement in the places where they finally found work.

Avoiding the West and South, immigrant groups chose different
destinations in the large industrial centers of the North and Midwest.
As we have noted, the Poles went to Chicago, Cleveland, Milwaukee,
Buffalo, Detroit and the parts of Pennsylvania outside Philadelphia.
Eastern European Jews stayed in the older seaport cities of New York,
Philadelphia, Boston and Baltimore; less than 10% of them ventured
inland. The Italians also chose the large eastern seaport cities as well as
smaller ones in New Jersey, New York, central and northeastern
Pennsylvania. Once in a city, immigrants did not scatter randomly
around the urban landscape. Their ultimate destination was (or became) a particular ethnic neighborhood.

Thus, the final result of immigrant distribution was the ethnic
neigborhood or, as Anglo-Americans called it, "the ethnic ghetto."
The formation and location of the ethnic neighborhood followed

111

certain laws. Rather than being the forced creation of a racist or nativist society, the immigrant ghetto grew logically out of the special cultural needs of southern and eastern European peoples and the particular economic structure that they encountered in America. Furthermore, the immigrant neighborhood showed patterns and characteristics that belied the traditional image of the stagnant, homogenous ghetto. The immigrant neighborhood was never that.

Patterns of Distribution

Polish settlement in Philadelphia showed the following patterns and characteristics, which also illuminate the experience of other groups.

1. Polish settlement in Philadelphia was highly decentralized; Poles did not confine themselves to one or even to two sections of the city but settled in at least twelve distinct areas. Their dispersion, however, was a group rather than an individual matter; only 65 of 4,464 Polish persons listed in the 1915 *City Directory* could not be placed in one of these twelve enclaves.

2. Although their settlement was decentralized, their concentration within each neighborhood was intense. The Poles formed twelve highly compact clusters, settling as close to each other as possible in each location. If Poles were the dominant or largest group in the area, they often occupied most of the houses on a street, block after block. Larger clusters tended to have a definite center, a point where concentration was greatest.

3. Although they may have been the dominant group in an area (as in Port Richmond or Bridesburg), at no time did the Poles monopolize the entire physical area of a neighborhood. The relative smallness of the Polish population may have accounted for this lack of monopoly, but closer examination reveals that the same pattern held for the city's Jews and Italians, groups that, by any standard, were very large. No immigrant group in the city ever totally monopolized a particular neighborhood to the extent that it achieved isolation from members of other groups.

4. The urban *neighborhood,* defined here as a physical or geographical entity with specific (subjective) boundaries, was always shared by two or more groups; or, to be more accurate, by three or four or more groups. Each group constituted its own *community* or network of social-emotional relationships. The urban neighborhoods we are examining always housed, or were composed of, several ethnic com-

munities or social-emotional networks. *Neighborhood* and *community* were never synonomous. Diverse peoples shared the same city-space, but proximity did not lead them as a matter of course to interact with one another at the social or emotional level; rather, each group kept to its own network of affective structures. The distinction between neighborhood and community is critical, for it explains how neighborhoods could physically integrate diverse cultures and yet be "provincial" and "isolated" places. The provinciality and isolation of the immigrant resulted not from physical or spatial segregation but from the effectiveness of the many separate community networks, none of which needed or wanted to interact at the social or emotional level.

5. Unlike the bulk of Jewish or Italian settlements, most Polish settlements were not located in the oldest sections of the city, the slum areas traditionally associated with immigrants as their port-of-entry. Poles in Philadelphia tended to settle in newer or frontier sections characterized by open spaces and fluidity and newness of physical structures.

6. Each Polish settlement directly reflected the industrial structure of the neighborhood or area in which it was located. It was the availability of work that determined the location of the Polish colony, for the Poles were invariably employed in the neighborhoods where they resided.

7. Each Polish settlement had a great amount of population turnover. It was not unusual for a settlement to experience a turnover of 75% to 80% of its inhabitants in the course of a single year. This extreme mobility was most characteristic of the unskilled.

8. In light of such high population turnover, the formation and persistence of Polish communities within neighborhoods depended on (a) the establishment of an infrastructure of specifically Polish institutions such as parish, church, school, newspaper, beneficial and fraternal associations; and (b) enough occupational stratification so that a cadre of professional and self-employed persons were permanently present to provide structure and leadership for the transient members of the group.

9. For the Poles, marriage, the presence of women and children, and the ability to own a house were the most effective brakes on population turnover and were also the greatest incentives to create permanent community institutions such as church, school, newspapers, associations and so on.

10. From the Poles' perspective, the neighborhood was a self-contained entity able to satisfy all the community's needs, physical,

PHILADELPHIA'S POLISH SETTLEMENTS, 1915

1 *Southwark*. Front Street and Second Street between Catharine (800S) and Christian (900S) Streets, and the alleys and tiny streets between, were at the center of this settlement. Very rarely did Poles live west of Third Street; concentration was greatest near the Delaware River and decreased southward from Christian Street.

2 *Northern Liberties*. General boundaries were Vine Street (300N) on the south, Girard Avenue (1200N) on the north; Delaware Avenue on the east and Sixth Street on the west, with minor clustering north of Girard, as at Tilghman Street (1700N).

3 *Southern Kensington*. Front and Second Streets, 1900N to 2800N. Cumberland Street (2500N) and Waterloo Street between York (2400N) and Cambria (2900N) were the main axes.

4 *Northern Kensington*. Front Street and Second Street, Westmoreland to Tioga Streets (3300–3500N).

5 *Fairmount*. Intersection of 23rd and Callowhill Streets was the center. Poles inhabited the 2300–2400 blocks of the streets north and south of Callowhill Street and the 300N to 400N blocks of the numbered streets, 19th to 26th—and especially the tiny streets between.

6 *St. James Street*. 3200 block in West Philadelphia.

7 *Bridesburg/Frankford*. Centered on the area that ran along both sides of Frankford Creek in northeast Philadelphia. In Bridesburg Poles lived on Richmond, Salmon, Edgemont, Thompson, Mercer, Almond, Livingston, Belgrade, Miller and Gaul Streets between Juniata and Buckius Streets. In Frankford they crowded the southern part of this former borough directly adjacent to Bridesburg, residing on James, Tacony, Melrose, Stiles, Cambridge (now Milnor) and Bermuda Streets between Duncan and Bridge Streets. Of all settlements, this one had the highest Polish density; the 4700 block of Cambridge Street could be called the most Polish street in Philadelphia in 1915.

8 *Port Richmond*. Philadelphia's largest Polish settlement; Poles lived between Norris Street (2000N) and Venango Street (3600N); very rarely did they live west of Aramingo Street. Polish intensity grew toward the River. Streets such as Salmon, Tilton, Edgemont, Thompson, Mercer, Almond, Livingston and Belgrade were heavily Polish 3200N (Allegheny Avenue) to 3400N (Ontario Street). Richmond Street and Allegheny Avenue were the main axes.

9 *Manayunk* (northwest Philadelphia). Poles concentrated south of Silverwood Street between Dupont and East Streets; Cresson and Main Streets, paralleling the Schuylkill River, were the major thoroughfares. The Poles also inhabited the countless little alleys and byways that branched off these two streets.

10 *Nicetown* (north Philadelphia). The center was the intersection of Germantown and Hunting Park Avenues. In general Poles lived north of Hunting Park Avenue and west of Germantown Avenue, on Yelland, Ruffner, Blabon, Blaine, Archer, Donath, Priscilla and Alfred Streets; Dounton, Juniata, Brunner, Bonitz, Bristol, Dalkeith, Dennie, Newcomb and Blavis Streets; and the 2600 block of Deacon and Roberts Streets.

11 *Grey's Ferry* (the "Bottom"). In South-central Philadelphia, next to the Schuylkill River, Poles resided on Wharton, Sears, Earp, Reed and 36th Streets.

12 *Southwest Philadelphia*. Glenmore and Woodland Avenues between 59th and 63rd Streets.

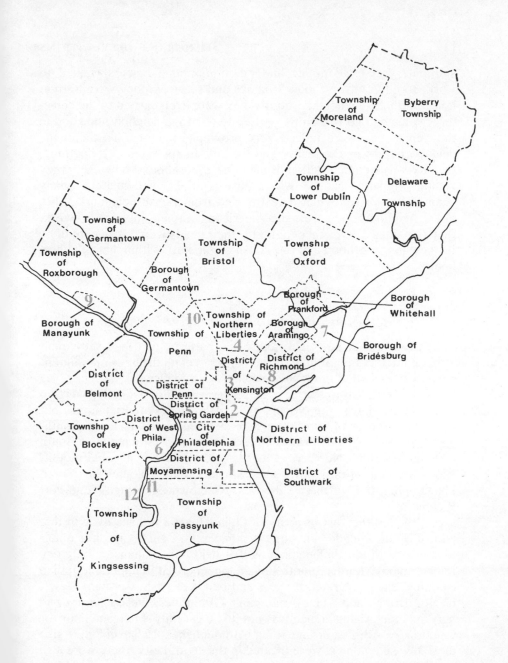

Township of Moreland

Byberry Township

Township of Lower Dublin

Delaware Township

Township of Germantown

Township of Bristol

Township of Oxford

Township of Roxborough

Borough of Germantown

Borough of Frankford

Borough of Whitehall

9

Borough of Manayunk

10

Township of Northern Liberties

Borough of Aramingo

7

Township of Penn

District of Richmond

Borough of Bridesburg

4

District of Kensington

3

District of Belmont

District of Penn

8

District of Spring Garden

2

Township of Blockley

District of West Phila.

City of Philadelphia

District of Northern Liberties

6

District of Moyamensing

1

District of Southwark

12 11

Township of Passyunk

Township of Kingsessing

spiritual, social, economic and emotional: its members walked to work, to church, to school, to shops and services; they were born at home and in some neighborhoods they were even carried to the cemetery. Poles had no reason to venture beyond the neighborhood and in this sense they were indeed very provincial persons. To them, the neighborhood was the reality and the city an abstraction. If anything, the city was a confederation of many neighborhoods—how many they couldn't be sure—each of which, just like their own, sheltered many communities. Even when they traveled from Polish neighborhood to Polish neighborhood across the American continent in search of work, they remained provincial people, for their needs were taken care of by the new neighborhood and the Polish community within that neighborhood.

The Location of Immigrant Neighborhoods

Decentralized but highly clustered patterns of urban settlement were characteristic not only of the Poles but of all the newer immigrant peoples who settled in Philadelphia between 1880 and 1920. The three largest eastern European Jewish settlements, for example, were in South Philadelphia, the Northern Liberties and Port Richmond, but there were others of substantial size in Frankford, Nicetown, Southwest and West Philadelphia. The Ukrainians had settlements in South Philadelphia, the Northern Liberties, Port Richmond, Fairmount, Nicetown and Frankford. The Slovaks had colonies in South Philadelphia, the Northern Liberties, Nicetown, Kensington and Port Richmond.

Although the vast majority of Philadelphia's Italians lived in that part of South Philadelphia directly adjacent to Center City, it is unfair to speak of South Philadelphia as if it held only Italians or only one Italian colony. Rather, South Philadelphia housed innumerable Italian colonies, each separated by seas and bands of Irish, Germans, Jews, blacks, British and Anglo-Americans. Oftentimes, these colonies had very specific origins: a man was not just from Italy, but from Sicily, or Calabria, or Abruzzi or Campania. Although most Italian colonies, like most Jewish colonies, were located in the central city, there were also smaller Italian settlements in Frankford, Port Richmond, Manayunk, Nicetown, Germantown, Chestnut Hill, Southwest Philadelphia, Greys Ferry, the Northern Liberties and West Philadelphia.

The factor most responsible for the location of immigrant settlements was work. Work brought the immigrant and the neighborhood together because it was an essential part of both experiences. The immigrant was defined by the work he performed: he came to America in search of work and livelihood but with definite preferences for certain types of work and aversions to others, as the discussion of Poles, Italians, and Jews has already shown. Work was also important in structuring the city. Most of Philadelphia's factories and industries were located where they were because of their age and type of activity. Philadelphia, it must be remembered, established its industrial structure as early as the eighteenth century, before the coming of full scale industrialization. By 1880 the city's urban core had experienced great concentration of streets, buildings and general land use as well as a general escalation in land values. Newer industries employing the latest technology and mechanization, requiring enormous transportation facilities and seeking to achieve economies of scale through bigness of operations were forced to locate on the urban frontier. Steel plants such as Midvale or Disston's, with Bessemer converters, open hearth furnaces and coking ovens requiring tons of coal and iron ore and hence miles of railroad trackage, had to locate away from congested areas of the central city; they located in Nicetown and Port Richmond. The same was true of new oil refineries, slaughterhouses, chemical plants and tanneries that needed large amounts of land on the riverfront (water was a cleanser, coolant and conduit for industrial waste) and access to railroad facilities in order to bring in raw materials and send out finished products.

Certain industries and factories epitomized the work of a particular area and thus the type of labor that would be attracted by its presence. For the Poles, these industries and factories were usually primary and basic ones. In Bridesburg/Frankford their chief employers were metal, chemical, glass, rubber and leather factories: Henry Disston and Sons, the famous saw and file maker who also manufactured its own steel; William and Harvey Rowland, manufacturers of carriage springs; American Fork and Hoe Company, manufacturers of farm tools; Miller Lock Company; Carver File Company; Fayette R. Plumb, a major tool works; Charles Lennig and Company, which became Rohm and Haas Chemical Company in 1920; Barrett Manufacturing Company, makers of coal tar products and roofing materials; Gillender and Sons, glass manufacturers; Quaker City Rubber Company; Robert H. Foerderer, leather and glue makers; and the Edwin H. Fitler Rope Company. All these establishments had large plants, labor requirements, transportation needs and capital. All used the latest technologies or machinery; all employed substantial numbers of unskilled male laborers.

In Port Richmond there was a similar diversity of industries—metals, chemicals, glass, lumber, leather and textiles as well as railroads and shipping on a massive scale. Among the more popular employers of Poles were David Lupton Sons, manufacturers of metal cornices and sheet metal products; Williamson and Bros., engine builders and machinists; Hero Manufacturing Company, makers of aluminum, brass and bronze products; William Cramp and Sons, ship and engine building company; H. W. Butterworth and Sons, manufacturers of textile machinery; Baeder, Adamson and Company, glue and gelatin makers; Berg Company, manufacturers of fertilizers, grease and tallow; John T. Lewis and Bros., manufacturers of lead, linseed oil, paints and varnishes; M. L. Shoemaker and Company, makers of fertilizers; Gill and Company, makers of glass and lamps; Atlantic Oil Refining Company; Dill and Collins Company, paper mill; McNeely, Price and Brooks, glazed kid manufacturers; Schlicter Jute and Cordage Company; the Philadelphia and Reading and Pennsylvania Railroads, complete with coal yards and terminals.

Nicetown owed its existence to the Midvale Steel Company, manufacturers of automobile and battleship steel and military ordnance. Edwin G. Budd Manufacturing Company, auto manufacturers; Link Belt Company, machinery and parts manufacturers; Niles, Bemont, Pond Company, crane manufacturers; Davis Spike Works; American Pulley Company; Blabon Oil Cloth and Linoleum Works; Felin Slaughterhouse; Emil Wahl Button Manufacturers and several railroad and coal companies were also large establishments employing unskilled Polish laborers.

In Manayunk, also, metal manufacture was primarily responsible for the Polish presence. Here it was the incomparable Pencoyd Iron Works, bridge makers to the world.

In Southwest Philadelphia and Greys Ferry, an abundance of chemical refineries and abattoirs hugging the Schuylkill River and the nation's major streetcar builder, J. B. Brill, were the chief employers of Polish labor. The Greys Ferry area was also a large river entrepôt for supplies of coal, lumber, iron and steel coming from upstate Pennsylvania; there Poles often served as stevedores and traffic handlers.

In South Philadelphia the major industries employing Poles were sugar and oil refining and shipping; in the latter industry Poles were stevedores and longshoremen.

In Fairmount and the Northern Liberties the chief employer was overwhelmingly the enormous Baldwin Locomotive Works, but there were also bakeries, breweries and miscellaneous leather and metal manufacturers. In Kensington textile companies predominated—John B. Stetson Company, the famous hat maker and John Bromley and Sons, rug makers—but various leather and metal manufacturers also employed Polish labor.

The factories that were the main employers of Poles tended to be the newest and largest ones in Philadelphia, utilizing the latest in industrialized technologies and requiring ample room for plant and transportation facilities. They were usually located in the newer or less settled areas of the city—Nicetown, Port Richmond, Bridesburg, Southwest Philadelphia and Northwest Philadelphia (Manayunk). If the Pole was not employed by a factory-type industry, he was employed by another that had just as precise a location—the shipping industry of South Philadelphia, Port Richmond and Greys Ferry.

In the early industrial city, it was imperative that workers reside as close as possible to their place of work. Walking was more than accepted; often it was the only way to get to work. While taking the trolley was technically possible, commuting to work cost both time and money. This was especially important to the unskilled worker who, it appears, worked longer hours per day (twelve or more) and also earned less. For the unskilled Polish worker, living in America temporarily and for the express purpose of earning as much as possible, spending money to commute was never given a first, let alone a second thought. The time required by commuting could be spent in more profitable ways, including sleeping. The need and the desire was to work as many hours as possible and to save as much money as possible. The intense spatial agglomeration or clustering of immigrant workers was very much a result of their need to live within walking distance of their places of work. As Edward E. Pratt observed in 1911, "the problem of congestion of population . . . seems to be closely linked with that of congestion of industries."[2]

Not all of Philadelphia's work, however, had a precise place of performance. Where the location of work was ubiquitous or constantly changing or where its sources of supply were significantly diffused, there was a greater need for laborers to settle in central locations. Italian workers, for example, were most often employed in public works construction, street paving, street cleaning, street railway construction and maintenance, or as independent artisans and truck farm laborers. Any of these activities could take them anywhere in the city and possibly beyond. Italians consequently were more likely to settle in the central city than along its fringes. Indeed, this appears to have been the preferred pattern for Italian settlement in any large northern city during this period. Here it is helpful to think of the city as an enclosed circle. The worker who lives close to the center can reach all areas of the circle, including its periphery, with equal ease. Someone who lives on the circumference of the circle, however, can reach only points in his own quarter with such ease. Central location meant access to a wider work area.

There were other activities that, because they served a scattered or decentralized market, also required a central location—meat and produce marketing; wholesaling and retailing of furniture, clothing, and so on. Once again, it is no coincidence that Philadelphia's Jews and Italians settled in central parts of the city next to the major wholesale and retail markets that employed them in large numbers. For the Jews in particular, the availability of store lofts and warehouse space, sufficiently concentrated for easy distribution of tons of textile materials and the subsequent retrieval of finished products, contributed to the existence of a vast garment industry in the central part of the city.

The rule, then, is that if work had to be performed in specific locations, immigrants formed their colonies near to their work. If work to be performed was ubiquitous or served diffused markets and suppliers, immigrants formed colonies in central locations of the city. Thus, Philadelphia's Poles had no need to seek central locations as did the Italians and Jews. Rather, they settled in newer, outlying areas of the city where specific work opportunities existed for them: factory labor employing large numbers of unskilled men. In fact, all Polish settlements were in areas annexed to the city after 1850, and only three were in areas directly adjacent to the central or original city.

The Cultural Imperatives of Clustering

The need to reside as close as possible to their places of work may have been the chief factor determining the location of immigrant settlements within the city, but it does not fully explain the intense clustering within each settlement.

In clustering tightly together in America's cities, the immigrants of southern and eastern Europe were doing what came naturally. It could even be argued that had America in 1900 been a blank slate, devoid of all physical as well as social and economic structures, southern and eastern Europeans would still have chosen to cluster tightly because of the social imperatives of their cultural systems. The peoples of southern and eastern Europe had a very different sense of society and personal identity from those of northern and western Europe—and

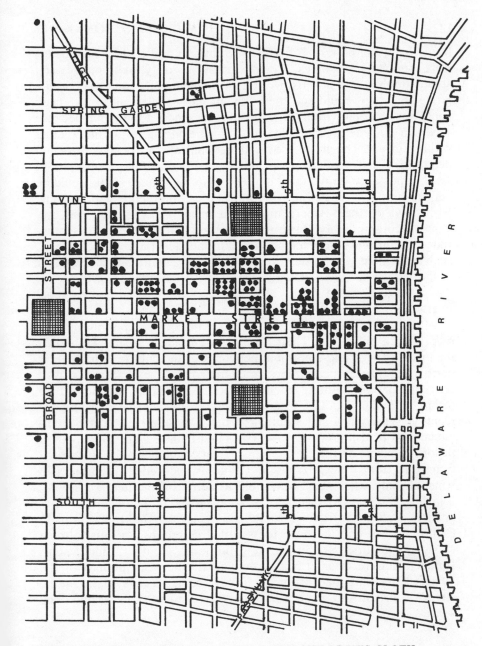

LOCATION OF WORKSHOPS, WOMEN'S AND CHILDREN'S CLOTH-
ING INDUSTRY, PHILADELPHIA, C. 1915

NOTE: Only 26 of 285 shops were not located in the very center of the city. This map accounts for all
but 36.
SOURCE: *Second Industrial Directory of Pennsylvania,* 1916 (Harrisburg, Pa., 1916), Part II, pp.
1178–1373

hence from the bulk of Americans. Southern and eastern Europeans were "network" peoples. Their identity, security, self-control, and stimulation derived not just from their membership in a group but in a group that they could see, hear, touch and smell at all times. They could not function without the constant presence of the group because a person became an individual only by belonging to and interacting within a group. The group provided mechanisms for social control and determined codes of personal behavior. For the Poles, who placed great importance on personal status within the group, status could be defined only by interacting with other Poles. Interacting with Italians, Irish, Jews or Anglo-Americans had no meaning; it was irrelevant. Agglomerated and highly clustered settlement, therefore, was essential. Indeed, in an age before telephones, automobiles, radio and television, such settlement was automatic: the world of network people, whether in the village of the Old Country or in the neighborhood of the New, was a walking world, highly dependent on oral, visual and personal interaction.[3]

Southern and eastern Europeans had been close-knit villagers for more than a millenium. Their agglomerated village system embodied the unseen social and emotional networks of the culture. Unlike their northern European and American counterparts, they had never lived on isolated or separately enclosed farms, a concept which had no meaning in their social systems. Lacking the internal capacity for identity, self-control and stimulation that characterized their Scandinavian and British predecessors, Poles and Italians were not cut out to be lone pioneers on the Great Plains; never could they exist on isolated farms far from others. Poles and Italians succeeded as farmers in America only when they were able to settle on the land *en masse,* bringing their networks with them. Poles moved into farms of the Connecticut Valley and Italians established vineyards and truck farms in California, but only because they settled as groups. In thus forming clusters, "ghettoes" or ethnic neighborhoods, southern and eastern Europeans were attempting to recreate the network pattern of the village, something that, ironic as it may seem, was easy to do on the streets of urban America but hard to do on America's farms and open spaces.

The Neighborhood's Communities

The capacity for community, for forming social and emotional networks, was ingrained in the peoples of southern and eastern Europe.

They carried this compulsion for creating community with them wherever they settled in America. It was only a matter of time before they gave more formal and visual expression to their communities by establishing parishes, churches, synagogues, schools, newspapers, fraternal and beneficial associations. The visible setting for those institutions was, of course, the neighborhood. As we have observed, neighborhood, at least in Philadelphia, never became coterminous with a single community. Philadelphia's neighborhoods contained a multiplicity of communities or social-emotional networks. One immigrant group sometimes dominated an area, that is, was the largest single group present, but no group ever monopolized an area or lived totally apart from members of other groups.

Port Richmond—or Bridesburg, Fairmount, Southwark, Greys Ferry, Nicetown (it doesn't matter which Philadelphia neighborhood is examined)—was recognized as a neighborhood with definable boundaries by all the area's inhabitants, but these inhabitants made up at least ten separate communities, each with its effective and acknowledged social-emotional boundaries, and each with its institutions of churches, schools, newspapers and associational or recreational patterns. These communities were defined by ethnicity, race, religion and social status. Port Richmond supported five Roman Catholic churches and parishes, four of which were organized along "nationality" lines— Polish, Lithuanian, German and Italian—and one that was the territorial or "Irish" church. There was also a Jewish synagogue and at least a half-dozen churches representing Episcopalians, Presbyterians, Methodists and Baptists, both black and white. As illustrated by the accompanying maps, these religious institutions were often very close to one another—across the street, next door, or down the block. This pattern, observable in any neighborhood in Philadelphia during the period, persisted until at least the Second World War. The only variations were in the number and variety of community networks contained within each neighborhood.

Given the way neighborhoods were settled—in waves and layers—cultural and structural homogeneity was virtually impossible. When Poles, Italians and eastern European Jews arrived in the late nineteenth and early twentieth centuries, they found a typical Philadelphia neighborhood inhabited by some combination of Anglo-Americans, Irish and German Catholics, German Jews, German Lutherans, Welshmen, Englishmen and, in many instances, a few blacks. Each of these groups formed its own network or community. They all coexisted, though with very little interaction at the social and emo-

LOCATION OF RELIGIOUS INSTITUTIONS, C. 1900–1920—BRIDESBURG/SOUTHERN FRANKFORD

1 St. John Cantius Roman Catholic Church and School (Polish) 2 Holy Redeemer Roman Catholic Cemetery 3 All Saints Roman Catholic Church, School and Cemetery 4 First Presbyterian Church and Burying Ground 5 St. Josaphat Byzantine Catholic Church (Ukrainian) 6 Mater Dolorosa Roman Catholic Church and School (Italian) 7 First Bridesburg Baptist Church 8 Immanuel Lutheran Church (German) 9 Bridesburg Methodist Church 10 Orthodox Street Methodist Church 11 Rehoboth Methodist Church 12 St. Thomas Methodist Church 13 St. Valentine Polish National Catholic Church 14 Emanuel Reformed Church (German) 15 First Frankford Baptist Church 16 Second Frankford Baptist Church (black) 17 White Hall Baptist Church 18 St. Stephen's Protestant Episcopal Church 19 Frankford Society of the Church of the New Jerusalem (Swedenborgian) 20 Frankford Meeting (Society of Friends) 21 Adath Zion (Jewish) 22 Campbell Chapel (Bethel African Meth-odist Episcopal) (black) 23 Frankford Avenue Presbyterian Church 24 St. Mark Protestant Episcopal Church

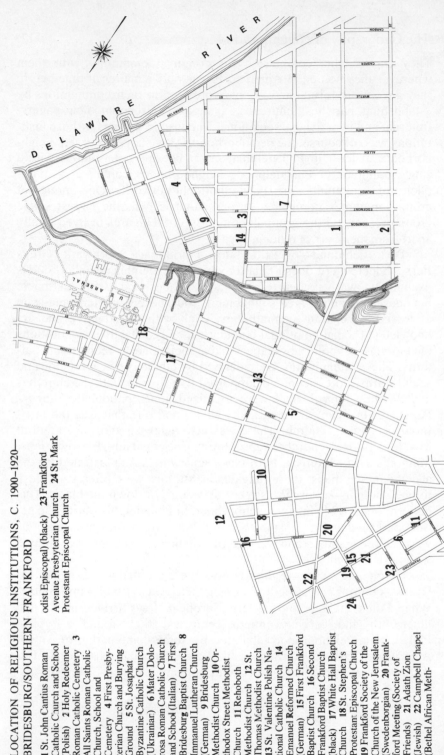

LOCATION OF RELIGIOUS INSTITUTIONS, C. 1900–1920—FAIRMOUNT (AND VICINITY)

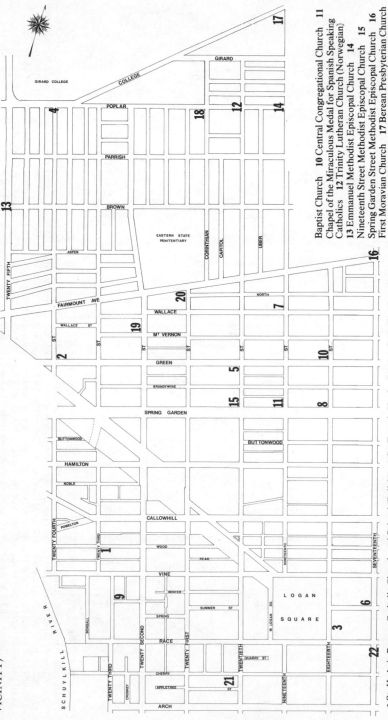

1 St. Hedwig Roman Catholic Church and School (Polish) 2 St. Francis Xavier Roman Catholic Church and School ("Irish") 3 Roman Catholic Cathedral of Sts. Peter and Paul 4 St. Nicholas Byzantine Catholic Church and School (Ukrainian) 5 Our Lady of Joy in All Sorrows Orthodox Church (Russian) 6 St. John Chrysostom Orthodox Church (autocephalus) 7 St. Andrew Roman Catholic Church and School (Lithuanian); formerly St. Matthew Protestant Episcopal Church 8 Fifth Baptist Church (includes First Swedish Chapel) 9 Immanuel Baptist Church 10 Central Congregational Church 11 Chapel of the Miraculous Medal for Spanish Speaking Catholics 12 Trinity Lutheran Church (Norwegian) 13 Emmanuel Methodist Episcopal Church 14 Nineteenth Street Methodist Episcopal Church 15 Spring Garden Street Methodist Episcopal Church 16 First Moravian Church 17 Berean Presbyterian Church (black) 18 Corinthian Avenue Presbyterian Church (German) 19 Olivet-Covenant Presbyterian Church 20 First Welsh Presbyterian Church 21 St. Clement's Protestant Episcopal Church 22 Second Church of the Covenanters (Reformed Presbyterian)

LOCATION OF RELIGIOUS INSTITUTIONS, C. 1900–1920—MANAYUNK

1 St. Josaphat Roman Catholic Church and School (Polish) 2 St. John the Baptist Roman Catholic Church, School and Cemetery ("Irish") 3 Holy Family Roman Catholic Church and School ("Irish") 4 St. Mary of the Assumption Roman Catholic Church, School and Cemetery (German) 5 St. Lucy Roman Catholic Church and School (Italian, founded 1927); formerly Mt. Zion Methodist Episcopal Church 6 Nativity of the Blessed Virgin Mary Byzantine Catholic Church (Ukrainian) 7 St. Alban's Protestant Episcopal Church 8 Wissahickon Methodist Episcopal Church 9 St. Stephen's Protestant Episcopal Church 10 St. Timothy's Protestant Episcopal Church 11 Ebenezer Methodist Episcopal Church 12 First Baptist Church of Manayunk 13 St. David's Protestant Episcopal Church and School 14 Galilee Baptist Church (black) 15 Manatawna Baptist Church 16 Mt. Vernon Baptist Church 17 Epiphany Lutheran Church (English) 18 Grace Lutheran Church (English) 19 Bethanien Lutheran Church (German) 20 Central Methodist Episcopal Church 21 Emmanuel Methodist Episcopal Church 22 First Manayunk Presbyterian Church 23 Leverington Presbyterian Church 24 Wissahickon Presbyterian Church 25 Fourth (Dutch) Reformed Church 26 Talmadge Memorial Church (Dutch Reformed) 27 Masonic Hall

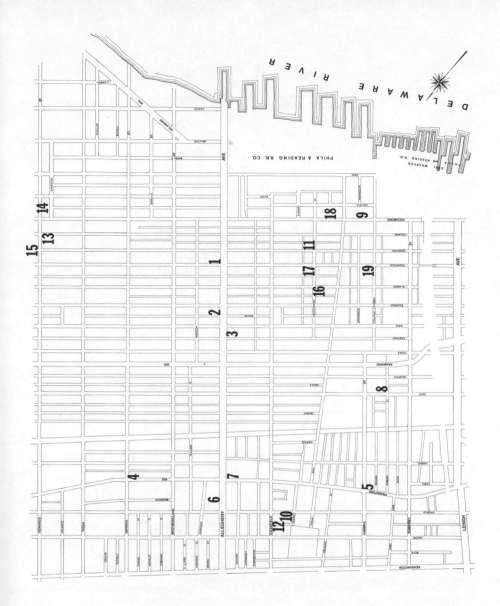

LOCATION OF RELIGIOUS
INSTITUTIONS, C. 1900–
1920—PORT RICHMOND

1 St. Adalbert Roman Catholic Church
and School (Polish)   2 Roman
Catholic Church and School of the
Nativity of the Blessed Virgin Mary
("Irish")   3 Our Lady Help of Chris-
tians Roman Catholic Church and
School (German)   4 St. John's
Reformed Church (German)   5 Trinity
Presbyterian Church   6 East Alle-
gheny Avenue Methodist Episcopal
Church   7 Allegheny Avenue Baptist
Church   8 B'nai Israel and Chevra
Thilim (Jewish)   9 Richmond Presby-
terian Church   10 St. John's
Protestant Episcopal Church   11
Richmond (Hope) Baptist Church   12
Friedens Lutheran Church (German—
Pennsylvania Ministerium)   13 St.
George Roman Catholic Church and
School (Lithuanian)   14 Bethesda Me-
morial Methodist Episcopal Church
15 St. George's Chapel (Protestant
Episcopal)   16 St. George's
Protestant Episcopal Church   17 Port
Richmond Methodist Episcopal
Church   18 Nazareth Lutheran
Church (German—Missouri Synod)
19 Mother of Divine Grace Roman
Catholic Church and School (Italian);
founded 1926

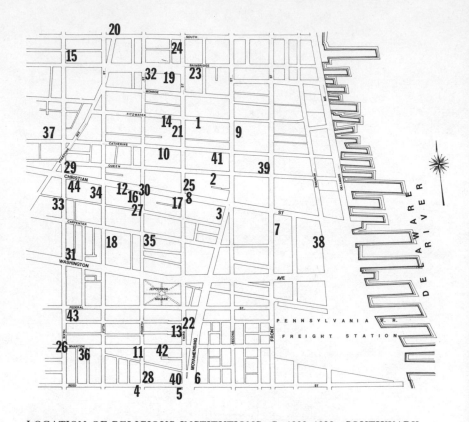

LOCATION OF RELIGIOUS INSTITUTIONS, C. 1900–1920—SOUTHWARK

1 St. Stanislaus, Bishop and Martyr, Roman Catholic Church and School (Polish); formerly, Southwark Presbyterian Church   2 St. Philip Neri Roman Catholic Church ("Irish")   3 St. Philip Neri Roman Catholic School for Boys   4 St. Alphonsus Roman Catholic Church and School (German)   5 Sacred Heart Roman Catholic Church   6 Sacred Heart Roman Catholic School   7 Polish Baptist Church (formerly, Mariner's Bethel Baptist Church)   8 Adath Israel (Jewish)   9 Ahavas Achim Anshe Nazin Nusach Hoarie (Jewish); former site of Polish Roman Catholic Church   10 Beth David (Jewish)   11 Beth Hamedrash Hagodol and Shomre Emuno Anshe Kelm (Jewish)   12 Beth Jacob Anshe Lubovitz and Shomre Shabboth (Jewish)   13 B'nai Israel (Jewish)   14 Chevra B'nai Israel Anshe Polen (Jewish)   15 B'nai Reuben Anshe Sfard (Jewish)   16 Chevra Kadisha (Jewish)   17 Chevra Kahal Adath Israel-Nusach Sfard (Jewish)   18 Chevra Poel Zedek She'eris Israel (Jewish)   19 Chevra Reim Ahuvim (Jewish)   20 Emunath Israel Oheb Sholom (Jewish)   21 First Roumanian Poras Joseph (Jewish)   22 Gates of Justice of Reisischen (Jewish)   23 Kehiloth Israel (Jewish)   24 Kesher Torah Anshe Lubliner (Jewish)   25 Kulver Chevra and Zeari Israel (Jewish)   26 Or Hachaim (Jewish)   27 Otik Mohilev (Jewish)   28 Poneviezher Lodge, No. 43 (Jewish)   29 Prushzver and Shershiver Chevra Lenath Hazedek (Jewish)   30 Rudiviler Wohliner Lodge, No. 243 (Jewish)   31 Samuel Rosenwald Lodge (Jewish)   32 Shifte Yeshuran Anshe Philadelphia (Jewish)   33 Wohliner Anshe Kupler Chevra (Jewish)   34 Zikne Israel (Jewish)   35 Emanuel Lutheran Church (German)   36 St. John Lutheran Church (German-English); also serves Lettish and Polish Lutherans   37 St. Paul's Methodist Episcopal Church   38 Gloria Dei (Old Swedes') Protestant Episcopal Church   39 Church of the Redeemer (Protestant Episcopal—Seaman's Mission)   40 St. John the Evangelist Protestant Episcopal Church   41 Trinity Protestant Episcopal Church   42 St. Casimir Roman Catholic Church and School (Lithuanian); formerly, Wharton Street Methodist Episcopal Church   43 Olivet Baptist Church   44 Mt. Zion Church and Burying Ground

tional levels—between Irish Catholics and American Protestants, for example; or German Jews and American Protestants; or American Baptists and American Episcopalians; or white American Baptists and black American Baptists.

When Poles, Italians and Jews moved in, each carrying with them their implicit sense of community, they merely added to the number of structures and networks already present. They did not enter into or identify with any of the structures or networks already established. Poles, Italians, Jews, Irish, Germans, Anglo-Americans and blacks shared the same space and identified with the same neighborhood, but they did not, as a result, feel impelled to interact socially or emotionally. Indeed, the separate cultural or ethnic networks, each with intangible boundaries eventually embodied in formal institutions, were what enabled such diverse peoples to live together as successfully as they did—for conflict was always possible.

Neighborhood conflict invariably occurred between old established groups and newer ones moving in on top of them—the sort of successive arrival best illustrated by Irish and German opposition to Poles, Italians and Jews, or German Jewish opposition to their "poor cousins" from eastern Europe. Conflict rarely occurred among groups that came to an area simultaneously, as illustrated by the lack of conflict among Italians, Jews and Poles who happened to enter a neighborhood approximately at the same time.

When new groups with latent networks and institutions moved into an area already inhabited by groups with matured institutions and networks, it appears that conflict between newcomers and older residents was normal until a new balance was worked out. It was always more difficult for a new group to move into areas with established structures and values, especially if that group's values and structures differed greatly from existing ones. Groups arriving simultaneously engaged in little or no conflict at the neighborhood level because each faced the same problems and confronted the same existing structures and institutions. Each intent on making the new neighborhood meet its implicit requirements, the new groups found themselves in confrontation with previously established groups rather than with each other. To the "insiders," there was little difference between Poles and Jews and Italians; they were all "outsiders" trying to get in. The outsiders, consequently, had little time to compete with one another, as their chief preoccupation was with the insiders—the Irish, Germans and Anglo-Americans who had preceded them in the neighborhood.

The Poles shared specific relationships with the other groups in their neighborhood, with those who were there before them, primarily the Irish and Germans, and those who arrived with them, Jews, other Slavs and Italians. In 1870 the Germans were one of Philadelphia's largest immigrant groups, second in number only to the Irish. Because of the Germans, Poles from Poznań, Silesia and West Prussia were able to make inroads within the city and form the kernel of future Polish settlements. German language skills and contacts enabled them to find housing with German landlords and to secure jobs with German employers, especially in sugar and oil refineries and chemical and textile plants. The first Polish colonies in Philadelphia put down roots among the Germans of Southwark, the Northern Liberties, Bridesburg and Manayunk. These first Poles attended local German Catholic churches until they were ready to form parishes of their own; this was the case in South Philadelphia, Port Richmond, Bridesburg, Kensington and the Northern Liberties.

Relations between Poles and Germans, however, were usually neither cordial nor even peaceful. Conflict within the neighborhood over housing and church use was common. Encouraged to emigrate because of Bismarck's *Kulturkampf,* Prussian Poles were not well disposed toward their German neighbors. Discrimination against them by German landlords and employers appeared as the American version of the *Kulturkampf*. Because of such discrimination, Philadelphia's Poles were often compelled to pass themselves off as Germans (as they had done in Germany) in order to find jobs, to secure lodgings or to buy land to build a church. The record of Polish-German interaction in Buffalo, Milwaukee and Chicago reveals the same kind of tensions.

In varying degrees, the Irish were present in every neighborhood where the Poles settled. In fact, the Poles often associated the Irish and Irish ways with being American—a perfect illustration of the effects of successive v. simultaneous arrival in a neighborhood, for never did the Poles mistake Italians or Jews for "Americans." Although they shared the same neighborhoods and often worked in the same factories or industries (where the Irishman frequently was the Pole's "boss"), it was the Church that remained the greatest scene of Polish-Irish interaction and conflict; the official territorial parish of each neighborhood was invariably controlled by the Irish.

While Roman Catholicism may have appeared monolithic to other religious bodies, the immigrants realized only too well that each group had its unique historical relationship to the Church as well as its own cultural style. As in Ireland, the Church in Poland was responsible for holding together a beseiged and divided nation and preserving its language, literature and culture. The Poles, consequently, identified strongly with their Church and could not conceive of letting a foreign element represent them in it or exercise control over it. A local parish without a Polish priest, or a church hierarchy containing only Irishmen, was an abomination.

This clash of cultural needs and preconceptions was not fully appreciated nor articulated as such at the time. The Irish version of Roman Catholicism was permeated with puritanical Jansenism while the Polish form was not. The Irish God was a God of unremitting justice and eternal punishment; God the Almighty Father was the archetypal representative. The Polish God was a God of forgiveness and mercy; and the Blessed Virgin Mary softened the sternness of the Father. Failure to perceive these differences as historical and cultural resulted in virtual battles between the Irish hierarchy and the Polish faithful. An Irish bishop remarked in 1903 that "it is well known that the Poles have a deep religious sense; that they are attached to their faith; that they are industrious, generous and courageous. But it is also evident that they are hot-tempered, as a rule, and their lack of familiarity with the ways of Americans renders them often suspicious, where there is otherwise no reason for distrust." [4]

Although they were also Roman Catholic in faith, the Italians' attitude toward religion, especially that of the men, was extremely nonchalant, even indifferent. No bulwark of the Italian peasant, the Church in Italy had been a chief antagonist. The Irish established church schools to protect their children from the American or Protestant schools; the Poles established church schools to protect their children from both the Protestants and the Irish; the Italians, during their early years in Philadelphia, were content to send their children to the local public school. Only after the Second World War did "Americanized" or "Hibernicized" Italian-American Catholics begin to patronize parochial schools in increasing numbers. [5]

Thus, although they often shared the same neighborhoods in the city, Italians and Poles largely avoided conflict because their social networks and institutions, established simultaneously, kept them sufficiently segregated. In the workplace there was also little cause for conflict because these two groups usually performed different types of work in different industries. Even in the same factory Polish and Italian workers had different jobs; at the gigantic Midvale Steel complex in North Philadelphia, for example, Poles were employed as furnace tenders, smelters, steel rollers and general metalworkers, and Italians worked with railway cars, railway beds, coal and slag.

Wherever Poles were found in the city, so were Ukrainians, Lithuanians, Russians, Slovaks, Croatians, Serbs, Slovenes and Hungarians. Slavic peoples always settled near each other, often on the same streets or even in the same buildings, because they were drawn to the area by the same types of work and were employed in the same industries. The larger American world had great difficulty in differentiating the various Slavic peoples and tended to lump them together under a common name of "Slav," "Hunky" or "Polack." This was not entirely unjustified, at least from the outsider's point of view, since languages, although distinct, were not always mutually incomprehensible, and customs, manners, values and religion were often the same.

In many instances, the proximity of Slavic settlements represented Old World relationships transplanted to the New. In Galicia and Russian Poland, Poles, Ukrainians, Lithuanians, Russians, Jews and even Moslems and Tartars shared the same villages in much the same way that a myriad of peoples shared the same neighborhood in the American city. Through the course of centuries, these peoples had worked out a way of life in which they coexisted in a common space or village but yet went their separate ways; each, in other words, adhered to its own social network. The practice of sharing territory with a diversity of peoples followed the Poles to America. Coexistence was possible in both places precisely because unseen networks were recognized and respected.

The Poles' settlement patterns in relation to their Jewish contemporaries is the most interesting and lucid example of Old World traits transplanted; it is also a vivid illustration of adaptation to new circumstances by duplication of previous experience. Eastern European Jews had always lived in the midst of or adjacent to the Poles. In America, Galician Jews tended to settle near Poles from Galicia, Jews from Suwałki and Płock near Poles from Suwałki and Płock, Jews from Lublin near Poles from Lublin, and so on. This arrangement was not coincidental, for it occurred in every Polish settlement in Philadelphia and in every major city of the nation where Poles and Jews were found.

Although each group may have harbored misgivings about the other, there were positive elements which prompted them to become next-door neighbors. Louis Wirth in his classic study of Chicago Jewry noted of the Jews and Poles who lived together on Chicago's Northwest Side: "These two immigrant groups, having lived side by side in Poland and Galicia, are used to each other's business methods. They have accommodated themselves one to another, and this accommodation persists in America." The Chicago Jews opened shops on

Milwaukee Avenue and Division Street "because they know that the Poles are the predominant population in these neighborhoods." In addition, "Poles come from all over the city to trade on Maxwell Street because they know that they can find the familiar stands owned by Jews."[6] These same conditions prevailed in Philadelphia. Accustomed to Old World trade patterns, Jews and Poles soon reestablished them in every Polish neighborhood. Jewish settlements in Slavic areas were invariably linear and always extended along major arteries of commerce and transit. In Port Richmond Jewish merchants settled along Richmond Street; in Manayunk, along Cresson and Main Streets; in Fairmount, along Ridge Avenue; in Bridesburg and Frankford, along Frankford Avenue; in Nicetown, along Germantown and Hunting Park Avenues.

This tacit alliance between the two groups, however, was based on more than mutual toleration for the sake of commerce: language was important and so were common experiences. "The Jews are versatile; they speak Yiddish among themselves, and Polish, Russian, Lithuanian, Hungarian, Bohemian and what not, to their customers."[7] The Poles and Jews also shared a common country and could not help exchanging information concerning methods, routes and ultimate destinations. In most Polish provinces, especially those of Galicia and Russia, the Jews were the first to emigrate, often with government approval or encouragement. As forerunners, they paved the way for others, Jews and Gentile alike. In later years, Jews and Poles sailed for America on the same ships.

Jews and Poles settled next to each other in the New World because the presence of the other was one of the few Old World realities that continued to make sense: Jews and Poles simply duplicated their age-old roles. By maintaining separate social networks and institutions, Poles and Jews were able to share the same neighborhoods quite peacefully; in these early years structural collision between the two groups was slight, if it occurred it all.

Geographic Mobility and the Early Industrial Economy

Philadelphia's Polish settlements had extremely transient populations. Poles were constantly moving in and out of the city and from neighborhood to neighborhood within the city, so much so that there was little persistence or continuity in the population of an area from one year to the next. This mobility was especially characteristic of unskilled workers who constituted the majority of Poles in each settlement. What appeared to the outsider as a tightly-knit, stagnant ghetto ("all immigrants look alike") was in reality no such thing. The scenery and even the cast of characters may have stayed the same, but the actors were constantly changing. Only a small essential core remained intact from year to year, providing a semblance of structure; and even here it was often the roles of this core group more than the individuals themselves that remained the same. If the Polish experience in Philadelphia is at all typical, fluidity and transiency, not stagnancy and immobility, were the chief characteristics of large, urban immigrant neighborhoods.

The forces creating such extreme geographic mobility are not difficult to identify. Certain characteristics of the early industrial economy made it very different from the industrial economy of the mid-twentieth century: constant unemployment for large numbers of workers; partial or irregular employment of still larger numbers; low or insufficient wages; regular recurrences of recessions, depressions, layoffs and shut-downs; nonexistence of health, old age, unemployment and death benefits (no retirement pensions, Blue Cross/Blue Shield, Social Security, severance pay, unemployment compensation, Aid to Families with Dependent Children, and so on); lack of a sense of responsibility of corporations toward their employees; poor to horrendous working conditions that subjected the laborer to accidents, injury, disability and death. The name of the game was survival. Workers never knew when they would lose their jobs, break a leg or contract tuberculosis. To survive it was essential to work, but work was just what workers had the least control over. For that reason, it remained their constant preoccupation. Just as lack of work had forced them out of their homelands to come to America, lack of work in America, or a specific part of America, compelled them to move again—and again.

The most abhorrent aspects of the early industrial economy were unemployment, irregular or partial employment, and low wages. Although these maladies picked no favorites, foreign laborers suffered the most, as they formed the bulk of the unskilled and were considered expendable by employers. A study undertaken in 1914 by the Pennsylvania Department of Labor and Industry's Division of Immigration and Unemployment (even the name indicates how closely linked were the two entities) revealed that between June 1913 and June 1914 "practically one fourth [113,239] of the men who ought normally to be employed have been compelled to shift their occupation, or have been thrown out of employment. . . ." The industries most responsible for this situation were metal products manufacture, textiles, including garment manufacture, and mining—the very ones that, except for textiles, relied heavily on foreign labor.

The report assigned various causes to unemployment: employment is governed by production and hence there must always be alternating periods of high and low labor demand; certain industries (construction, farming) are seasonal; lack of communication within the labor market allows certain areas to be in need of labor while others have too much; industrial and vocational training, especially among the young, is inadequate, leaving individuals to scramble for whatever jobs are available.[8]

Another study, conducted in 1915 by the Metropolitan Life Insurance Company, surveyed 78,058 policy-holding families in Philadelphia. The 78,058 families contained 137,244 wage earners (or 18% of all wage earners in the city.) More than 10% of these wage earners were unemployed at the time of the survey and almost 20% were working part time. Metropolitan Life concluded that in March 1915, 79,000 persons were unemployed and 150,000 were working part time. The textile, clothing, building and metal industries (especially electric and steam railway equipment and ships) were the chief culprits: one-fifth of their workers had been out of work for more than six months. In reporting its findings to the mayor, the insurance company concluded that "unemployment is permanent, if not steadily increasing," warning that "when we ordinarily assume that men and women who are willing and able to work are minus a job only in times of unusual and widespread industrial depression, such as we experienced during the last winter—we lose sight of the fact that there is always, even in the most prosperous times, a large amount of unemployment and part time employment for these same workers." The report also noted that "foreigners" were a large percentage in many of the industries experiencing the high rates of unemployment.[9]

In 1916 Pennsylvania employed 612,144 foreigners, but in 1920 the state employed only 449,034—a decrease of 163,110 persons. Viewed from the county level, the fluctuations are even greater. Philadelphia, for example, employed 72,923 foreign laborers in 1916, 93,670 in 1918, but only 59,537 in 1920. Luzerne County, a major mining area, employed 48,781 foreigners in 1916, but the number steadily declined to 37,195 by 1920; Schuylkill County, another big anthracite area, employed 24,124 foreigners in 1916 but only 13,852 in 1920. Northampton County employed 20,056 foreign laborers in 1916 and 23,392 in 1918 but only 11,723 in 1920—half the number employed two years earlier. Alle-

gheny County offered work to 96,668 foreigners in 1916, 109,070 in
1918, 85,630 in 1919 and 89,738 in 1920. And so on, county by county
across the state (Table 28).

One can only wonder what became of all of these people—the
163,110 foreign men and women who lived and worked in Pennsylvania
in 1916 but were unaccounted for by 1920. Either they all died (which is
unlikely), migrated to another state or county in search of work (which
is a possibility), or were unemployed (which is also a possibility). No
matter what their fate, however, the fact remains that industry in Pennsylvania, typical of the nation, was erratic in its demand for labor and
thereby contributed both to the mobility of the population and its
unemployment. The constant fluctuations elicited this comment from
the Metropolitan Life Insurance Company:

> In industrial concerns employees are continuously coming and
> going. The number hired and fired is out of all proportion to the
> number employed. The average concern hires as many new
> persons during a year as it employs regularly. Such an excessive
> hiring and firing is costly to employers, has a degenerate effect
> on employees, and is one of the basic causes of unemploy-
> ment.[10]

Whatever the pernicious effects of extended periods of total unemployment, partial or irregular employment was equally prevalent and
debilitating. Before the First World War the normal work week was
six days. A few places and industries were introducing the half-holiday
on Saturday, but that practice was not widespread. A fully employed
worker expected to work at least 312 days a year, Sundays and
Christmas off. To work less meant a reduction in income neither an-
ticipated nor desired by the worker. In the period 1914–1920, however,
not once did Pennsylvania's industries average more than 287 days of
work (in 1916). Again, the impact is more revealing at the local level,
county by county or industry by industry (Tables 29 and 30).

In 1915 Philadelphia's industries were in operation an average of
281 days. The only firms operating 360 days or more were public
services—gas, water, electricity, telephone. The building and contracting industries, which employed a large part of the city's Italians and
Irish, were the least busy. Paving and road construction, for example,
was in process for only 220 days of the year. Brick, cement and stone
work averaged 240 days, railway construction, 251 days.

According to both the Pennsylvania Unemployment Study and the
Metropolitan survey, those most affected by irregularity of employ-

Table 28

FOREIGNERS EMPLOYED IN PENNSYLVANIA AND SELECTED COUNTIES, 1915–1920

Area	1915	1916	1917	1918	1919	1920
Pennsylvania	516,481	612,144	545,154	546,609	451,011	449,034
Allegheny Co.	103,973	96,668	98,631	109,070	85,630	89,738
Beaver Co.	5,815	12,836	12,692	9,505	9,852	11,387
Bucks Co.	1,567	1,271	1,157	4,657	3,034	1,277
Cambria Co.	21,331	20,615	21,676	19,008	17,332	17,783
Chester Co.	2,492	4,018	4,427	4,204	2,368	3,127
Dauphin Co.	7,112	4,130	4,945	4,182	3,696	3,632
Delaware Co.	4,150	6,735	6,640	10,157	11,032	9,546
Fayette Co.	23,124	22,345	22,680	22,687	20,503	17,263
Indiana Co.	3,596	10,557	11,482	8,359	7,026	7,204
Jefferson Co.	3,244	7,126	3,145	3,329	3,019	2,849
Lackawanna Co.	32,834	29,903	23,228	29,598	27,676	25,785
Lehigh Co.	6,776	7,935	6,948	6,248	5,255	5,562
Luzerne Co.	48,039	48,781	41,486	42,235	39,849	37,195
Mercer Co.	5,676	7,587	6,762	8,980	5,510	5,953
Northampton Co.	16,740	20,056	14,638	23,392	14,001	11,723
Northumberland Co.	8,955	8,543	5,930	5,696	6,275	5,775
Philadelphia Co.	80,208	72,923	72,739	93,670	59,197	59,537
Schuylkill Co.	20,140	24,124	17,240	15,822	16,154	13,852
Westmoreland Co.	30,983	31,353	30,008	26,812	25,801	26,287

SOURCE: Commonwealth of Pennsylvania, Department of Labor and Industry, Office of Information and Statistics, 1915–1920.

Table 29

PENNSYLVANIA'S INDUSTRIES: AVERAGE DAYS IN OPERATION, 1915–1920

Industry	1915	1916	1917	1918	1919	1920
Building and contracting	265	269	265	270	269	268
Chemicals and allied products	303	297	292	304	290	290
Clay, glass and stone	278	279	270	255	245	252
Clothing manufacture	283	233	282	290	267	253
Food and kindred products	281	230	284	302	295	292
Leather and rubber	292	290	294	297	284	278
Liquors and beverages	261	279	283	290	276	278
Lumber and its remanufacture	276	282	282	284	280	278
Paper and printing industries	289	296	292	297	296	294
Textiles	275	290	287	284	273	253
Laundries	281	284	286	280	281	252
Metals and metal products	287	296	290	300	263	290
Mines and quarries	232	262	255	240	205	230
Public service	324	344	326	358	351	352
Tobacco and tobacco products	276	261	278	278	265	253
Miscellaneous	286	292	291	260	289	292
All industries	281	287	285	285	275	278

SOURCE: Commonwealth of Pennsylvania, Department of Labor and Industry, Office of Information and Statistics, 1915–1920.

Table 30

AVERAGE NUMBER OF DAYS WORKED, ALL INDUSTRIES, FOR
PENNSYLVANIA AND SELECTED COUNTIES, 1914–1920

Area	1914*	1915	1916	1917	1918	1919	1920
Pennsylvania		281	287	285	285	275	278
Allegheny Co.	279	287	297	291	294	281	280
Bucks Co.	268	279	287	276	230	285	287
Cambria Co.	293	289	305	306	302	253	257
Carbon Co.	273	290	288	307	286	300	278
Chester Co.	283	292	300	285	287	295	291
Clarion Co.	289	285	288	268	278	254	273
Clearfield Co.	272	285	288	283	290	230	252
Dauphin Co.	283	295	293	300	292	288	282
Delaware Co.	275	292	292	293	291	287	282
Fayette Co.	277	276	287	277	287	246	266
Huntingdon Co.	265	278	284	272	258	232	256
Indiana Co.	260	264	281	280	281	252	272
Jefferson Co.	273	286	293	286	293	240	267
Lackawanna Co.	281	286	295	284	293	282	271
Lehigh Co.	279	285	285	291	286	284	280
Luzerne Co.	268	277	285	283	278	268	272
Mercer Co.	250	287	300	285	288	280	279
Northampton Co.	275	288	287	286	295	288	284
Northumberland Co.	260	281	289	272	283	278	269
Philadelphia Co.	286	289	295	291	293	289	282
Schuylkill Co.	266	285	289	293	286	277	255
Washington Co.	284	291	293	290	285	264	273
Westmoreland Co.	276	288	314	288	278	261	272

*Mining industries not included in these averages.

SOURCE: Commonwealth of Pennsylvania, Department of Labor and Industry Office
of Information and Statistics, 1914–1920.

ment were the unskilled, untrained and uneducated. Most often these
workers were foreign-born and were the first to lose their jobs. In times
of recession and economic lag, the skilled worker fared better if only
because, as the Metropolitan agent put it, "the influence of irregularity
in work is offset for the skilled mechanics by a higher rate of wage.
This, however, does not apply to the unskilled men, who are the
hardest hit. . . ."[11]

Low or insufficient wages, another hallmark of the early industrial
economy, also had negative implications for the immigrant. Even if a
man were gainfully employed for 312 days a year—which was most unlikely—his earnings were insufficient to support himself plus a family.
The average daily wage in Pennsylvania in 1915 was $2.22; in 1916, it

Table 31

AVERAGE DAILY WAGE IN PENNSYLVANIA BY INDUSTRY, 1916–1919

Industry	1916		1917		1918		1919	
	M	F	M	F	M	F	M	F
Building and contracting	$2.39	$1.23	$2.75	$1.45	$3.64	$1.75	$3.76	$ .77(?)
Chemicals and allied products	2.67	1.18	3.07	1.32	3.92	1.65	4.58	2.13
Clay, glass and stone products	2.52	1.25	3.05	1.54	4.06	1.82	4.64	2.10
Clothing manufacture	2.39	1.30	2.80	1.45	3.41	1.75	4.19	2.11
Food and kindred products	2.44	1.23	2.74	1.28	3.33	1.46	3.89	1.82
Leather and rubber goods	2.27	1.30	2.61	1.46	3.27	1.72	4.09	2.15
Liquors and beverages	3.27	1.06	3.47	1.09	4.14	1.49	4.51	1.88
Lumber and its remanufacture	2.11	1.17	2.52	1.29	3.09	1.59	3.55	1.95
Paper and printing industries	2.53	1.19	3.01	1.37	3.57	1.69	4.23	2.01
Textiles	2.15	1.30	2.55	1.46	3.31	1.87	4.02	2.36
Laundries	2.61	1.13	2.86	1.26	3.64	1.53	4.01	1.79
Metal and metal products	2.94	1.33	3.66	1.74	4.67	2.20	5.61	2.55
Mines and quarries	2.79	1.73	3.97	1.75	5.78	1.49	6.44	2.81
Public service	2.56	.96	3.07	1.44	3.97	1.71	4.08	3.31
Tobacco and its products	1.81	1.41	2.26	1.71	2.55	1.89	3.00	2.26
Miscellaneous industries	2.37	1.13	3.10	1.37	5.41	1.84	4.83	2.10
Total average	$2.76	$1.27	$3.40	$1.48	$4.59	$1.85	$4.84	$2.19

SOURCE: Commonwealth of Pennsylvania, Department of Labor and Industry, Office of Information and Statistics, 1915–1920.

was $2.76 (Table 31). If a man worked 300 days a year, he would not earn more than $825. Pennsylvania's Department of Labor and Industry considered $900.00 per year per family of five to be the poverty line. Apparently, virtually all immigrant wage earners and their families in Pennsylvania lived in poverty, at least if the worker were married and attempting to support his family by working full time in one of Pennsylvania's industries. If he were unmarried, or traveling alone without wife and children to support, however, he could manage, by living cheaply, to save substantial sums of money to send to the family in Poland or Italy—as long as work remained available and he remained healthy.

The usual response to unemployment, irregular employment and low wages was to find another job. In periods of permanent or prolonged unemployment, the worker often had to move in order to find work. This was much easier for the single or unattached foreign migrant-laborer than for the immigrant or native-born American worker with wife and children. The geographic mobility of the foreign-born migrant-laborer was astounding. Just as he had migrated from place to place in his homeland, he migrated from place to place in America, always in search of work. Parish records, city directories, interviews with immigrants and the numbers in Table 28 testify to this intense mobility.

In some Polish settlements in Philadelphia less than 20% of those living in the city in 1905 were present in 1910 or 1914. Some Polish settlements added thousands of members every year only to lose twice as many at a later date. What happened to the 11,000 foreign workers, most of them Slavic and Italian, who worked in Luzerne County in 1916 but were not employed there in 1920; or the 26,000 who were employed in Allegheny County in 1918 but were gone by 1920; or the 34,000 working in Philadelphia in 1918 who were not working there in 1920? Since not all of these persons could have died, disappeared or been content to remain unemployed for very long, they must have sought work elsewhere. Either they migrated within the industrial core of the United States or they returned to Europe.

Community Creation

Hypermobility of the immigrant population had serious repercussions for the formation of stable and permanent communities. It could be argued that so much turnover in the population would make it almost impossible for immigrants to form stable, permanent communities—and yet they obviously did. Community creation and stability were made possible by the establishment of an institutional infrastructure that, no matter how often and how drastically the population changed, remained intact and operating. Very early upon entering an area, the immigrants established a parish, church or synagogue, a school, a newspaper (or two) and a multiplicity of social and beneficial organizations. In this way the unskilled Polish worker could move from Nicetown to Manayunk to Port Richmond or from Bridesburg to Wilkes-Barre to Chicago without experiencing any serious dislocations. These institutions were always present and constituted the cement of the community. They provided stability and permanence in the midst of constant fluidity and transiency of populations.

For the Poles, the parish was the paramount institution; it either encompassed or gave rise to all others. In the course of Polish history, it was the Church that was primarily responsible for preserving the Polish people as a nation. The Church united the people, gave them an identity, preserved their language and their culture and helped them to resist the constant attempts to Russianize and Germanize them. The Polish upperclasses, educated and cosmopolitan, normally remained aloof or indifferent to the Church, but the peasants identified very strongly with the Catholicism that was an integral part of their daily life and culture. Given the role of the Church in Poland, it was only natural that it should take on added importance in America where threats to Polish identity were even greater than those faced in the homeland. By 1915 six Polish settlements in Philadelphia had established parish organizations complete with schools, and a seventh would follow in 1927. They were St. Laurentius in Kensington (1882), St. Stanislaus in Southwark (1891), St. John Cantius in Bridesburg (1892), St. Josaphat in Manayunk (1898), St. Ladislaus in Nicetown (1906), St. Adalbert in Port Richmond (1904), St. Hedwig in Fairmount (1907), and St. Mary of Częstochowa in Southwest Philadelphia (1927).

There could be no true Polish community in Poland or in America without a parish, a church building and a priest. In addition to religious services, the parish organized dances, picnics, theatrical performances and lectures, and even subscribed to newspapers. It was the center of information for all newcomers; through the pulpit, the press and the school, it kept the people informed about activities and opportunities. As a basic social organization invested with great moral power, it attempted to serve as a mechanism of social control. In its final form the parish was a peculiar Polish adaptation to the strangeness of America. Not wholly Polish but definitely not all American, it aimed to satisfy the peasants' desire for social response and their need for recognition from members of their group—elements, as we have seen, that were at the root of Polish peasant culture. So strong were the bonds of the parish that in time its name became synonymous with the territory or neighborhood in which it was located.

At the center of every parish was the priest, the first leader of the Poles in America. In the New World as in the Old, the Poles turned to the priest for guidance and information. Most often the priest organized the parish and put up the church building. He also encouraged the immigrants to form associations, encouraged the establishment of newspapers and settled clashes between employers and immigrant employees. The priest was interpreter and mediator between America and the Polish newcomers. No one was better suited for the task because no other individual initially possessed the authority or commanded the respect—and fear—of the people. Philadelphia, like Buffalo, Chicago, Milwaukee or New Britain, had its share of "immigrant pastors" who attempted to build mighty fiefdoms in which they could control the peasant masses.[12]

The parish, then, was more than a religious or spiritual association. Purely religious needs could be satisfied by the local Irish or German Catholic church, but the Poles preferred to build their own churches because they could not conceive of a church organization containing no Poles but only Irishmen and Germans.

In addition to the parish with its church and school, Philadelphia's Polish settlements supported three indigenous newspapers and many beneficial and fraternal associations. The *Gwiazda, Patryota* and *Przyjaciel Ludu* kept the various communities informed of happenings in the U.S.A. and in the homeland and provided features, informational articles and short stories. The Polish associations ranged from social clubs that dotted every neighborhood to neighborhood-based insurance societies such as the Polish Beneficial Association of St. John Cantius in Bridesburg, to national insurance associations such as the Polish National Alliance and the Polish Roman Catholic Union with its branches in most Polish neighborhoods. Among immigrant groups, the Slavs were unique in their ability to form large, nationwide self-help organizations to provide life insurance and protection against ill health. In time, these beneficial societies became the major link in a national Polish community or "Polonia."

Community creation in the midst of hypermobility was also made possible by the presence within each Polish neighborhood of a cadre of professional and self-employed persons. Comprising 10% to 20% of the

Poles in each community, these people were permanent residents who performed certain roles, including staffing and operating the community's institutions. Community creation depended upon some degree of occupational stratification and permanence for a core group of people.

Professionals comprised less than 1% of Philadelphia's Polish population in 1915. Included in this category were thirteen priests who staffed the six Roman Catholic churches, one Polish National Catholic church (St. Valentine's in Frankford), and a boy's college (preparatory high school); one publisher and three newspaper editors who were responsible for the *Gwiazda, Patryota* and *Przyjaciel Ludu;* a "librarian" who operated the city's only Polish library; a secretary (chief administrator) of a large beneficial association; and a handful of physicians and teachers. The clergymen, newspaper people, librarian and secretary were the most important leaders of Philadelphia's Polish communities: they were permanent residents serving a Polish constituency. They were the only ones in the city whose leadership roles transcended neighborhood boundaries: the Church, the newspapers and the city-wide beneficial associations joined the various territorial communities into a larger network.

Equally important for community creation and stability were the self-employed. The self-employed had lived in America, especially in Philadelphia, longer than any other occupational group, except the professionals. They tended to be permanent settlers who had made the important decision to remain in America. Tavern keepers and "sellers of liquors," for example, were required by a Pennsylvania law of 1887 to be native-born or fully naturalized citizens. Philadelphia's twenty-eight Polish liquor dealers, therefore, were U.S. citizens with strong ties to their American neighborhoods. Self-employed operators such as liquor dealers, tavern keepers, undertakers and real estate and insurance agents, because they often required public licenses or dealt with semilegal matters, were automatic links to the larger non-Polish world of the city and thus, more often than not, became the Polish communities' first politicians and political leaders.

Like the tavern keepers, grocers, meat shop and bakery proprietors were self-employed types who played key roles in the formation of community, primarily by conveying information and staffing the community's institutions. In an era without supermarkets and refrigerators, meat, fruit, vegetables and bread were bought daily or often several times daily. Rare was the neighborhood that did not have a small grocery store or meat market on every corner or at least every

Table 32

POLISH OCCUPATIONAL DISTRIBUTION BY AREA OF SETTLEMENT

Occupation	A	B	C	D	E	F	G	H	I	J	K	L
Professional	0.9	1.0	0.9	0.0	2.5	0.0	1.4	1.3	1.2	0.6	0.0	10.6
Executive/managerial	0.9	1.0	0.0	0.0	0.0	0.0	0.2	0.0	0.1	0.6	1.4	2.1
Self-employed	13.4	8.4	5.5	2.6	9.0	0.0	9.7	10.6	10.6	8.5	4.1	8.5
Services (skilled and unskilled)	11.3	9.4	10.1	3.9	9.8	0.0	8.0	5.3	8.5	7.4	2.7	23.4
Skilled and semi-skilled	19.8	39.5	60.6	82.9	39.3	28.0	26.0	21.7	27.4	35.0	43.2	55.3
Unskilled	53.4	40.5	22.0	10.5	39.3	68.0	54.5	61.1	52.0	47.6	47.3	0.0
Other	0.0	0.3	0.0	0.0	0.0	4.0	0.3	0.0	0.1	0.2	1.4	0.0

KEY: A = Southwark; B = Northern Liberties; C = Southern Kensington; D = Northern Kensington; E = Fairmount; F = St. James Street; G = Bridesburg; H = Manayunk; I = Port Richmond; J = Nicetown; K = Southwest Philadelphia; L = other.

NOTE: Columns do not equal 100% due to rounding.

other corner. In view of the nature of the work—shopkeeping and pro-
prietary business—it is not surprising that virtually all of these early
self-employed people were German Poles who came to America with
positive attitudes toward these roles, an orientation not at first shared
by their compatriots from Russian and Austrian Poland.[13]

The importance of the self-employed cannot be underestimated,
for they were a ready index of the maturity and viability of the immigrant community. The greater their variety, the more developed and
permanent was the community. The first to appear were usually
grocers, meat dealers and bakers, followed, if conditions and size
permitted, by clothing, shoe, furnishings and variety stores. Florists,
hardware and paint stores and pharmacies made a third tier. The last to
appear were small manufacturers such as the wagon builders in
Manayunk, a pretzel manufacturer in Bridesburg and a harness maker
in Port Richmond.

The same principle operated in community services: saloons were
the first to appear everywhere, but it was the larger and more
industrially diversified centers that established the *Gwiazda* and
Patryota and supported the real estate agents, undertakers, insurance
and steamship agents. Not all neighborhoods supported the same
diversity of self-employed. By 1915 a recognized hierarchy had
developed among the Polish communities of the city. With a large and
densely settled population located in the midst of diversified industries,
many of them new, utilizing the latest technologies and hence employing large numbers of unskilled workers, Port Richmond was emerging
as the leader. The Polish newspapers and the headquarters or main
branches of the major Polish associations were located there. This
neighborhood also supported the most diversified assortment of shops
and services. Someone needing a Polish physician, lawyer or steamship agent and not finding one in his own neighborhood, could find one
in Port Richmond. This hierarchical arrangement of Polish settlements
in terms of shops and services contributed to the insularity of the
Polish people; it helped to make Philadelphia a conglomeration of
smaller towns or mini-cities within a larger urban matrix. This intra-
urban hierarchy enabled Philadelphia's Polish neighborhoods to
provide their constituents with a wider range of goods and services
than would otherwise have been possible. Individual concentrations
could not always support the minimum threshold required for certain
goods and services.

The presence of public service personnel and skilled workers sig-
nified additional occupational stratification and was another indicator

of a community's stability and permanence. Such occupations as trolley conductor, trolley motorman, army officer, porter, waiter, policeman, mailman, telephone operator, postal clerk and train engineer required long-term residence in the city or at least some familiarity with the English language and the American environment. Because they earned higher wages than did unskilled workers, and because their work appears to have been more predictable but limited in location, the skilled worker was not as geographically mobile as the unskilled worker. On the whole, skilled Polish workers, like the self-employed and those in public service occupations, had lived in Philadelphia longer than unskilled workers. And as might be expected, most public service and skilled workers were German Poles or the American-born children of Polish fathers.

In contrast to the skilled or service worker, the nearly 2,000 unskilled laborers (fully one-half of Philadelphia's working Polish population) listed in the 1915 *City Directory* tended to be the newest residents of the city and had lived at their listed addresses the shortest period of time; streets with high percentages of laborers were areas of recent settlement. Of all categories of workers, the unskilled were the most likely not to be in the same house or in Philadelphia the following year. For young, unmarried men who had come precisely to find work, moving was the natural and accepted way of finding it when it was lacking in a particular locale.

The extreme mobility of the Poles, especially the unskilled, should not be thought to signify the breakdown of traditional cultural systems or structures.[14] Rather, the very transience of the immigrants, particularly the Slavs and Italians, tends to confirm the strong hold traditional systems and cultures continued to have on their members. Why, after all, did 50 to 75% of them return to Europe? The ties to the homeland, to the traditional culture, must have been very strong to compel such a high rate of return. Italians and Slavs were impelled to migrate by the very strength of their social and cultural networks. They went out only in order to return with resources to preserve and strengthen the traditional system. That more returned home than remained, that more moved about than stayed in the same neighborhood, indicates that they never lost sight of their original motive for coming and that they were following the imperatives of their cultural system: to find work, to earn money, to return home, to save the traditional way of life. And, as we have seen, when Poles and Italians did move across the American continent, they moved from one Polish or Italian neighborhood to another. The creation of a permanent institutional infrastructure in each place to receive and support the migrant testifies to the hold of ethnicity, not to the lack of it, in America.

Constraints on Mobility

Three conditions worked to lessen the great mobility of Polish workers and, in the process, facilitated the creation of permanent communities: (1) the presence of women, which led to marriage, children and the need for institutions such as church and school; (2) the ability of women to find work, for in an economy of erratic male employment, two incomes were better than one; and a working wife could reduce the need to move in times of economic adversity; and (3) property acquisition; owning a house was an imperative in Slavic culture and offered a modicum of economic as well as social security.

Communities were formed by persons with steady jobs who did not constantly disappear in search of work. It was thus marriage, with prospects of children, that became the most decisive factor in converting the Polish man from a migrant-laborer to a permanent resident; it forced him to see his future here and not in Poland. Marriage also curtailed his peripatetic existence: a wife and children needed arrangements other than workmen's camps and boarding houses. Steady, settled work came to be preferred to the quick dollar when there were others to think about. Marriage and family strongly encouraged the establishment and persistence of communities.

Unlike the Jews or the Irish, Italians, Poles and other Slavic peoples did not usually emigrate as families. Polish parish records reveal that the vast majority of Poles in Philadelphia were single men between the ages of nineteen and thirty. The records also show that marriage was very popular with them and that they did, in fact, marry young Polish women between the ages of seventeen and twenty-three. Where did they find these young Polish women?

Since the greater proportion of all Polish men returned to Europe, not all Polish men in America were looking for wives. For those who remained, there were in general two ways of finding a wife. The young man could acquire a wife directly from Poland; or he could meet his future wife in America. Each approach predominated in certain areas, depending on local conditions and the extent to which the individual was still controlled or influenced by his family. In the first situation, the parents of the man would select the girl, or the son would have known of her previously or learned about her from friends. He would then write to her and, after a period of correspondence, would ask her to join him in America. In this arrangement the couple knew each other slightly or not at all; they relied on the opinion of the group, either that of the family or of the new matrix of friends that temporarily replaced the family in America.

Not all women waited for the invitation of prospective husbands before leaving Poland. By 1915 there was a substantial stream of young women coming as migrant-laborers. After 1907 the number of single women migrants increased. Lured by prospects of work (the chance to earn money for a dowry) and marriage (it was believed that it was easy to get married in America and that Polish-American husbands were to be preferred), most of these single girls joined relatives, usually brothers or young uncles, who had been in America for some time. They found work in textile, garment and paper box factories, or, more often, in the "service"—cleaning, ironing and cooking. Since the idea of a single girl working in a factory was never fully accepted by the Polish community, and given the honored place of marriage in the Polish social system, unmarried Polish girls in America did not remain unmarried for very long.[15]

The motivations for marriage may have been primarily cultural or personal, but the impulse was furthered by the peculiarities of the early industrial economy. Polish conventional wisdom held that without marriage men would not save but would waste their time and money on drink, women and other nasty pursuits. Be that as it may, it was easier for a working man to survive in America married than single. There was security in the added earnings of a wife and children. These earnings could keep a man fed and sheltered when out of work, sick or injured. A wife and children may have been a drain on earnings during times of employment, but they were definitely a lifesaver when employment failed. The family was an economic necessity. During hard times it responded to the crisis as a unit so that each of its members could survive. The principle of familial solidarity allowed no distinctions and provided for no exceptions.

Ready sources of employment for women, no matter how poor the remuneration, were crucial to the formation of strong immigrant communities and neighborhoods. This was especially true for immigrants such as the Poles and Italians who were primarily unskilled laborers, but it applied to all poor immigrants in general—families of Italian street workers who were employed for only part of the year, families of Polish coal miners, families of Jewish peddlers and garment workers. Women enabled the immigrants to adapt to the irregularities of the early industrial economy by bringing additional income to the family.

They did this in three ways: by participating directly in the industrial workforce in the factory or at home; by self-employment; and by performing a miscellany of needed services that never made anyone's list of gainful occupations.

In 1915 approximately 14% of Pennsylvania's industrial labor force consisted of women who worked in the manufacture of clothing, textiles, food products, leather and rubber goods, paper, tobacco and metal products. Immigrants constituted anywhere from 10% to 75% of all women employed in various branches of these industries. If American-born children were included, the percentages would have been much higher. According to the Pennsylvania Department of Labor and Industry:

> Prior to the coming of immigrants from eastern and southern Europe, women in Pennsylvania industry did not play a great part. Women of English, Welsh, Scotch, and German descent did not find industrial employment particularly attractive. Upon the coming of the recent immigrants, however, many of them with large families and small means, female members of the family sought employment to eke out a living. Pursuits presenting the most immediate opportunities naturally were the manufacturing and mechanical occupations. Comparatively few women are engaged in agricultural and allied occupations, but the number engaged in cigar and tobacco manufacturing, in textile manufacturing and as dressmakers, sewers and sewing machine operators is great. We find no less than 3,858 engaged in cigar and tobacco factories, over 1,300 in knitting mills and over 6,600 as sewers and sewing-machine operators in factories. Approximately 4,800 are engaged as dressmakers and seamstresses not in factory employment. It is interesting to note that several hundred women of foreign origin are engaged as laborers in blast furnaces and rolling mills, shoe factories, and other industries where employment is unpleasant and very heavy. About 4,000 native-born of foreign or mixed parentage are also engaged in manufacturing and mechanical pursuits. A striking proportion of the women of foreign origin engaged in industrial pursuits are semi-skilled operatives. On the whole, the woman of foreign birth is willing to accept employment at a lesser wage than the man.[16]

The exact numbers employed in "industrial homework"—a hybrid situation that enabled the worker to earn money by doing industrial work at home—cannot be determined for certain. A survey taken in cooperation with the Pennsylvania Department of Labor and Industry reported an average of 12,394 industrial homeworkers for 1916, not counting 5,000 persons making army clothes.[17] The total number of persons employed in homework in any one year, however, may have approached ten times that sum. Ninety-six percent of home-workers were women, 71% were married and 25% were foreign-born, more than 50% of whom were Italian. Philadelphia contained the largest single concentration of homeworkers, but smaller cities and towns in the heavy industrial areas of the state also housed significant numbers.[18]

The textile, garment and tobacco industries employed the bulk of homeworkers, but these industrious women also manufactured paper bags, books, brushes, cough drops, candy eggs, flags, gas mantles, hair goods, leather gloves, hooks, eyes, patent fasteners, jewelry, silverware, lampshades, razor blades, sanitary rubber goods, corsets, sheets, pillow cases, spectacle cases, suspenders, garters, toiletries, toys and sporting goods. The work itself was routine and monotonous and required little skill. Never did the homeworker actually "manufacture" an entire shirt, flag or toy. Basic work was completed in the factory; women at home performed such tasks as stringing and wiring tags; assembling valentines, Christmas bells, Halloween decorations and paper party hats; sewing rags together for carpets; covering baseballs; mending machine-made laces and curtains; or sewing safety-pins, hooks and eyes, pins and needles to cards.[19]

The labor available for these tasks was totally elastic. Italian women in Philadelphia, for example, complained that there was never enough work to keep willing hands busy. In fact, the plentiful labor supply appears to have delayed the introduction of machinery and factory methods; "the manufacturers both of tags and of hooks and eyes have machines in the factory to perform the process done by hand in the homes, yet the cheap labor supply makes handwork profitable."[20]

In addition to industrial work at home or in the factory, immigrant women were self-employed shopkeepers and budding entrepreneurs. Women operated groceries, bakeries, confectionaries, dry goods, variety and tobacco stores, restaurants, saloons and laundries. They peddled wares, from old shoes to lace trimmings; hawked fruits and vegetables and sold newspapers. They manufactured calendars, canvass shopping bags and pretzels; crocheted bootees, scarves and hats and canned home-grown fruits and vegetables for sale. Shopkeeping was especially popular among Jewish women, and Italian and Jewish women were more likely to be peddlers and hawkers than were Polish women. Nevertheless, in the largest neighborhoods, Polish women operated groceries, bakeries, confectionaries, laundries and restaurants. For all groups, commercial proceeds were usually used to supplement the husband's income. If a woman were widowed, deserted or divorced, or if her husband were incapacitated, her commercial and business earnings would constitute the primary income of the family.

Immigrant women also performed a host of essential services: cooking, cleaning, washing, ironing, catering christenings, weddings and funerals, seamstressing, midwifery, keeping lodgers and feeding boarders. Among Polish women "domestic service" and keeping lodgers and boarders were the most popular. Before they were married Polish girls would work in textile, clothing, tobacco, boot, shoe and paper box factories, or they would hire themselves out as domestics. After they were married or after the birth of the first child, they were less likely to work in factories because of family and household responsibilities and domestic service, plus the care of lodgers, became their mainstay.[21] Although they did work for wealthier families and individuals, Polish women preferred the higher pay and security of cleaning offices, hotels, businesses, hospitals, schools, churches and department stores. If the worker did not go out to clean an office or a home, she took in laundry and ironing. This latter arrangement was common in areas where there were large numbers of migrant-laborers without wives. Slavic women were always assured of employment because of their reliability and because of their willingness to work for very little pay, often driving out their black and Irish competition in the process. During hard times entire Polish familes were known to have survived on women's earnings from domestic work.

In domestic trades, the Polish woman had no competition from her comtemporaries, the Italians and Jews. Jewish women preferred to do garment work at home or in the factory or to operate small businesses. Italian sexual mores placed great emphasis on chaperonage and, according to John MacDonald, Italian women in the United States "avoided work as domestic servants since it was regarded as a threat to their chastity, a very serious consideration in the southern Italian view."[22] Before marriage, Italian women preferred to work in textile, garment or other factories where women would be the only workers and where sisters, mothers, daughters and other female relatives could serve as chaperones. After marriage and the birth of children, Italian women forsook the factory and, as we have seen, did needle work or other piecework at home.

No matter what the source—factory work, homework, self-employment, domestic service—supplemental income reduced the need of the family to move about in search of work. Unless families were allowed to stay put for some time, strong community ties could not form. Strong ethnic communities and neighborhoods tended to take root in areas where it was possible to establish a symbiotic relationship between male and female employment or male and female industries. Philadelphia, with an economy based on the traditional women's industries of textile and garment manufacture, was fortunate in this respect. These industries, together with myriad opportunities for shopkeeping, peddling and domestic service, made it relatively easy for women to find work—and hence for communities to develop.

The availability of inexpensive housing, especially the opportunity to own a home, was another important factor reducing the mobility of immigrant populations. Home ownership rooted people to the neighborhood and thus increased the stability of the community. In 1915 nine-tenths of Philadelphia's dwellings were single family brick row houses, fourteen to twenty feet wide, usually two or three, but sometimes four, stories high. Because of the rowhouse, Philadelphia was spared many of the problems of tenements and apartment buildings that plagued New York and Chicago.[23]

Despite unflattering comments concerning the monotony and ugliness of the rowhouse, that structure did more to make Philadelphia a "City of Homes" and to root people to the city than any other single factor. As contemporary social workers and city inspectors came to realize, the rowhouse was a most effective force in converting the Italian or Pole from a migrant-worker to a permanent resident: the opportunity to own property was most persuasive. If achieving this goal in Poland or Italy proved difficult, the best alternative was to own property in America. For the Pole, ownership of property determined social status within the community. According to the Philadelphia Real Estate Survey of 1934, about 66% of the dwellings in the Polish sections of Port Richmond and Manayunk were owner-occupied, as were 73% of those in the Polish sections of Frankford and 70% of those in Bridesburg. While it is more difficult to extract the data for Polish sections in Nicetown, Kensington, Fairmount and Southwark, the Real Estate Survey indicates that more than 50% of all dwellings in Nicetown and Kensington were owner-occupied, while parish surveys reveal that 75% or more of the Poles in these areas owned their homes.[24]

The cheapness of the rowhouse ($1,200–$2,000), its availability and the Philadelphia mode of financing via two mortgages made home ownership a real possibility for the workingman. Because of the rowhouse, it was easy for a family to acquire ample living space and privacy, complete with separate entrance, and at the same time enjoy the company of others in the high density neighborhood that such construction encouraged. By providing an environment of constant exposure to members of the group, the rowhouse reinforced the common bonds of the people. The result was a paradox. The rowhouse rooted the immigrants to America and at the same time inhibited their broader Americanization.

The Provincial City

In their neighborhoods, the Poles walked to work, to the grocery store, to the butcher shop and bakery. They walked to church and to school. They walked to visit friends and relatives (unless they lived in another Polish neighborhood, in which case they took the trolley). Their children were born at home, and when they died in Nicetown, Bridesburg, Port Richmond or Manayunk, they were not too far from the cemetery. Because all their needs could be satisfied within their immediate environment, they had little reason to venture outside. The beauty of the neighborhood was its self-sufficiency. To Polish immigrants, their neighborhood was detached from other neighborhoods and from the rest of the city. They identified with their neighborhood because it physically represented a system of relationships of which they were individually a part. When the parish marriage, death or baptismal register requested their place of residence, they usually gave the name of their neighborhood; when the Polish newspaper referred to them, it was also by their territorial or parish origins.

The immigrants' provincial identity merely extended their Old World experience. Long before they came to America, they were provincial people. The concept of the state or even the province was largely unarticulated or too abstract. The local area (*okolica,* as the Poles called it), was the reality, and the local area meant the village and the parish. Once in America the Poles merely substituted one area of identity for another. Instead of defining themselves as members of St. Joseph parish which encompassed the village of Chorodyszcie, they now were members of St. Adalbert parish which encompassed the area of Port Richmond—or St. Stanislaus parish which encompassed the area of South Philadelphia. When registering as a member of a Polish parish in America, or when making arrangements for a marriage or baptism, Poles were always asked their place of birth and baptism.

Their answer usually was the name of their village and parish. It was often the more knowledgeable priest who supplied the name of the province or sector where the village was located. (One priest kept a detailed map of "Poland" on hand for just such purposes.) The Poles seem not to have learned of their larger "Polishness" until after their arrival in America; it was here they confronted the counter-reality of an Anglo-American macroculture and a multiplicity of nationalities.

The provinciality of the Polish community in America was reinforced by the diverse origins of its people. All might have seemed "Polish" to their American hosts and fellow migrant-laborers from elsewhere in Europe, but there were subtle differences noticed by the Poles themselves. There were discrepancies in language—vocabulary and pronunciations were not the same. There were variations in food and eating habits—one group used fruits in making deserts, another preferred cheese and a third favored rice. Some were beer drinkers while others preferred vodka. In music and dance some had their polkas, others their mazurkas and still others their obereks and krakowiaks. In religion, too, different groups had specific devotions to Mary and the Saints.

Each settlement was an amalgam of various Polish villages and provinces. The Bridesburg settlement, for example, always retained a generous representation of German Poles, but Galicians and, especially, Poles from the Russian provinces of Płock, Warszawa and Łomża greatly outnumbered them in 1915. Poles from Płock, Suwałki and Łomża made up the majority of those in Kensington and the Northern Liberties, although Prussian Poles, Galicians and Poles from Warszawa and Kalisz were also numerous. Manayunk was predominantly a Galician preserve, with Russian Poles from Grodno, Suwałki, Płock, and to a lesser extent, from Radom and Łomża, rounding out the community's numbers. Port Richmond, like Manayunk, was a Galician stronghold, but there were ample representatives from Poznań, Łomża and Płock, and some from Lublin, Kalisz and Wilno, Poles from Lwów, Galicia, formed a tight and homogenous group in the Fairmount community and were balanced by Poles from Suwałki, Płock and Lublin. Nicetown's origins were strong and simple: almost all were Lublinites and Galicians. No two Polish settlements had the same mix of specific origins.[25]

Within each neighborhood there was often some differentiation. Galicians might monopolize the western portion of a colony, Russian Poles from Suwałki might occupy the central part, and German Poles from Poznań might predominate in the eastern section. Or, Galicians from Nowy Sącz might maintain a block for themselves, while Lublinites would occupy another two or three blocks, and Poles from Warszawa still another block. As is vividly revealed in parish records, once a nucleus was established, a chain migration began, attracting fellow villagers directly from Poland or those who were already in the United States or both. The commonality of origins reinforced the bonds of the community.

Summary

The immigrant neighborhood was an institutionally complete and self-contained entity.[26] The presence of congenial work was the impetus for its creation and location, for it was the need to reside as close as possible to the place of work that brought the immigrants to the neighborhood. If the work had precise locations, they settled next to it. If the work was ubiquitous, they settled in neighborhoods in central portions of the city; centrality of location gave them the greatest accessibility to jobs.

The creation of an institutional infrastructure in the form of churches, schools, newspapers and associations; the development of a cadre of professionals and self-employed persons to staff these institutions; the location of shops and services within the neighborhood; the development of a hierarchical relationship among the many immigrant neighborhoods in shops and services; and the "network" culture of the eastern and southern European immigrants themselves—all contributed to the self-sufficiency and provinciality of the neighborhood.

This self-sufficiency and provinciality extended beyond economic and commercial needs and encompassed social and emotional ones as well. Because the neighborhood was the physical locus for their system of social and emotional networks, immigrant workers identified with the neighborhood rather than with the city as a whole. The city remained an abstraction, the neighborhood was a reality. It was the neighborhood, not the city, which provided immigrants with their identity, security and stimulation. Philadelphia, one of the nation's largest cities, was for them a very provincial place—not because of any geographic or physical isolation, but because of the networks that the immigrants themselves created.

Conclusion

Immigrant Destinations—
The Legacy

It's nice to come into Little Italy and groove on the garlic,
but there is a lot about the German Towns or the Little
Italy's of America that represent its unseen heart. The family
structure, the ethnic organizations, political clubs, the relationship between school, church, and lending institutions
form the community. It is not bricks, mortar, or European
recipes, but how people live with each other and the institutions they create that form the neighborhood. The Com-
muter Romantics relish the surface but don't perceive the
substance.

—Barbara Mikulski[1]

The preceding pages have presented a model for understanding the
movement of immigrants across the American continent in the years of
the greatest migration, 1880–1920. The distribution of immigrant peoples resulted from the interaction of three major variables—economic,
demographic and cultural—an interaction that, in effect, was a syner-
gistic process, for each variable reacted to and combined with the
others to produce patterns of great complexity. Untangling and sorting
out the various interactions is no simple task, but the importance of the
relationships is clear.

Massive opportunities for work, matched by a desperate need for
work on the part of surplus European and Asian populations, were the
main forces of the process. Work was differentiated by location, by industry, by degree of skill required within and between industries,
by sex, by methods of hiring, by size of required workforce, by
permanence or limited duration, and so on. The immigrants, depending
on their intentions in migrating and their previous experiences, reacted
to all these shades of difference as well as to competitors such as the
children and grandchildren of earlier arrivals, surplus rural Americans
both black and white, and other immigrants.

Although work has been presented here as the most important
variable, the essential one in determining the distribution of immigrant

159

populations both nationally, throughout the Industrial Core, and locally, within the city itself, it is not sufficient to explain all that happened. Each immigrant group responded differently to similar or identical work offerings; some accepted them, some rejected them and some simply preferred others. The response patterns are too strong to be dismissed as mere coincidence. Why were Jews overwhelmingly concentrated in the garment industry and absent in mines and steel mills? Why did Italians, especially southern Italians, tend to monopolize public works and railroad construction in northern parts of the country? And why were Poles and other Slavs the primary workers in coal mines, steel mills and slaughterhouses, but not in construction, garment manufacture or shopkeeping? This phenomenon—functional or occupational differentiation—was not only a creation of economic forces but was very much an outcome of the cultural and structural conditions and the goals and horizons of each group—the ethnic factor if you will. Immigrant destinations, in other words, were a function of ethnic as well as economic and demographic considerations; and once again, it was the interaction of the three that determined ultimate destinations.

The Ground Floor and Its Passing

The functional differentiation that accompanied immigrant distribution has important implications for our study. The peoples of the New Immigration came to America because this country offered work, sometimes sporadically, sometimes abundantly. They came at the very time that America's economic structure was expanding to form a solid secondary sector concentrated in manufacturing and industry. They participated in this process from its beginning. Because they entered the industrial system on the ground floor, each group was able to establish its own economic niche—the Jews in garment manufacture and retail trade, the Italians in construction, and the Poles in mining and steel manufacture. In another sense, the ground floor was the only area they were permitted to occupy. When coming to work in America, the immigrants took on an "entrance status," the condition for being allowed to enter, work and stay. Their history in this country begins with their assumption of this status, one that varied from group to group but was never very high in the eyes of the larger Anglo-American society.[2]

The New Immigrants and their descendants who gained upward mobility generally did so within these special tracks and on occasion used those tracks as springboards to cast future members into new areas of the economy, such as the professions. Thus, functional differentiation rather than functional integration characterized the work of these immigrants and their children. In effect, the peoples of the New Immigration had worked out a way of coping that, at least during the period of heavy industrialization, enabled them to avoid intense competition and intergroup rivalry among themselves. The competition and rivalry came in their relationships with groups of the Old Immigration, the Irish and Germans in paricular, with native Americans both black and white. To a large extent, each group of the New Immigration worked its way up not by crossing over but by staying on its own trajectory. In this way competition could be minimized and economic rewards maximized. While this analysis is based on the reading of historical data, its implications are only beginning to be studied by sociologists and political scientists. According to one sociologist, William Newman, the major European immigrant groups attained some parity of resources and achieved a degree of political and social assimilation not by invading the existing economic structure but by constructing their own parallel institutions. Irish domination of several trade unions and some civil service occupations, Jewish pre-eminence in garment manufacturing and retailing and Greek and Chinese domination of some parts of the retail food industry—all represented the creation of structures parallel to those found by the immigrants. Thus, Newman believes, structural assimilation may be a very poor measure of overall assimilation. The most assimilated minority groups in American Society are those who were best able to create their own resource structures alongside those of the established society:

> the prevailing pattern is one of a division of labor between
> groups in the economy. It may indeed be the case that groups at-
> tain resource parity and a common investment in the social
> system, not through sharing the same institutional structures
> (structural assimilation), but through a complex pattern of inter-
> related and interdependent differentiation.[3]

Because the fluidity and newness of the early industrial period are gone forever, it is increasingly difficult for new groups to gain a place for themselves within the industrial system or to establish an economic niche within industry uniquely their own that they can use as a base for future mobility. The economic system is now limited in its ability to employ new groups because the secondary or industrial sector is no longer growing rapidly and providing a pool of available jobs. In effect, the ground floor is closed. The tertiary or service sector has replaced it and the entry point has moved several stories up. The entrance qualifications of many of the new migrants—blacks from the South, Puerto Ricans and Chicanos—do not meet the requirements of most of the new jobs appearing in the economy, primarily in the tertiary sector. Still largely unskilled or semi-skilled, possessing work qualifications similar to foreign workers of the late nineteenth and early twentieth centuries, the new migrants confront a job market where education and skill are now minimum, not maximum, requirements. The work qualifications of turn-of-the-century immigrants and their children meshed nicely with those of the expanding industrial sector; the work qualifications of today's migrants are generally out of gear with the expanding tertiary sector. Apparently, this situation will continue until either the entrance qualifications of the recent migrants are raised to meet the minimum requirements of the tertiary sector, or until enough new unskilled tasks are found in industry and elsewhere to supply work for those who need it.

Their Own Histories

Regional variation in settlement patterns is a second aspect of immigrant distribution with implications for this study. The immigrant experience is largely a Northern, not a Southern, one and is one of the primary historical differences between the two regions. The South's history is irrevocably entwined with the black experience, but the North's history, especially its urban industrial history, is very much tied up with the progress of the immigrant. While the role of the black in the South has been noted, the role of immigrants in the North and their impact on the larger society has rarely received much attention. It is too easy and too simple to assume that Europe's immigrant peoples and their descendants "melted" smoothly into one white majority. It is also too easy and too simple to use visibility of race as the primary cleavage of pluralism in American society. More detailed study of the Northern industrial core would reveal that the bases of pluralism growing out of the immigrant experience are not yet fully comprehended. While all whites may look alike, they do not necessarily share the same histories, structures and cultures in American society. As we have seen, the immigrants were very adept at creating structures to maintain their identities, even as they and their children went on to become "Americanized." The functional differentiation that they achieved in the economy, for example, not only served to maintain a pluralism of ethnic structures but actually facilitated upward social movement and political assimilation, for it was these various economic tracks that provided the resources, primarily financial, for the movement upward.

Moreover, the ethnic pluralism that characterizes the North is based on more than economic or functional differentiation or the formation of parallel social structures. A form of cultural pluralism, heretofore unrecognized, continues to persist. The material culture of the immigrants may largely have been lost or abandoned but nonmaterial or intangible forms continue to survive, even to thrive. These are passed on through child rearing and family practice, with the process taken for granted by the people involved. These "hidden dimensions" of culture, as the anthropologist Edward Hall calls them,[4] take the form of different values and attitudes toward things such as work, sex, family, child rearing, pain, property, education and the elderly (among others), and have for too long been unnoticed by a society whose scribes have summarily assumed that the Melting Pot accurately described the American experience, and by a society that, preoccupied with the black-white cleavage, forgot that other bases of pluralism continue to affect values and perceptions.

In addition to differing from the conventional American in their structures and non-material forms of culture, the New Immigrants and their children differed in history as well. They entered the American experience through the industrial economy. Although a few individuals of each group may have been present in earlier times, as groups the peoples of the New Immigration did not participate in the founding of the United States or partake in the war that reunited North and South. Their historical connection to America begins much later and is fused with the nation's Industrial Revolution. These peoples who came to America have long and rich histories of their own. Any attempt to deny them these histories or to replace them with the history of the America that preceded them is misguided. Can a people really assume a history that is not theirs or discard one that is? The black movement of the 1960s and 70s has taught us that the answer is no. Should it be any different for the descendants of America's immigrant peoples simply because they happen to be "white" and hence "invisible"? Perhaps many of the misunderstandings and misconceptions that surround ethnic Americans as they move beyond the third generation and beyond the working class stem precisely from the national inability to appreciate not only the hidden dimensions and invisible structures that remain but also the historical differences that are irrevocable. Here is the heart of the American dilemma of trying to create a "nation of nations."

A third implication of this study concerns the treatment and presentation of immigrants in the general literature and the common image of the immigrant experience in the popular mind. As this book has attempted to demonstrate, the immigrant experience was not monolithic. It varied from group to group according to its reasons for making the great move. Perhaps the greatest blow to the traditional perception is the realization that not all immigrants came with the intention of staying. Many, and for some groups most, actually returned to European or Asian homelands, and it is this transient or temporary immigration that distinguishes the New Immigration from the Old. It was the very strength, not weakness, of the immigrants' social and cultural systems that enabled them to move, to stay, or to return. Emma Lazarus' image of "wretched refuse," which has endured for generations, seriously needs revision. It does a grave injustice to a major aspect of American history—and European, too, for the historical ramifications of the great migrations of the late nineteenth and early twentieth centuries cannot be fully appreciated unless the movement is seen with its European as well as its American context.

The Ethnic Neighborhood

The final product of immigrant distribution was the formation of ethnic neighborhoods, many of which continue to characterize the cities, large and small, of America's Industrial Core. In its maturity, the ethnic neighborhood represented a balance of work, geography and ethnicity. If these three ingredients continued in harmony over time, the neighborhood remained stable. If one or more weakened, the neighborhood entered a period of stagnation or decline.

Work was the original impetus for the creation and location of the neighborhood. If jobs remained steady and plentiful, the people could remain together. If the number or type of jobs changed, the neighborhood's residents would be forced to adapt or to leave. As many neighborhoods lost jobs to improved technology and machinery and to the movement of jobs out of the neighborhood to suburbs and other parts of the country, they were hard pressed to remain stable. To do so, the other variables, geography and ethnicity, had to be strong enough to compensate. Sometimes they were, but sometimes they were not.

The geography of the equation refers to the physical environment and housing of the neighborhood. Often the immigrants first found housing in the slums of the city, areas where shabby buildings meant cheap rent. Such sections were often located in the older, central portions of the city. Southern Italians and eastern European Jews were usually the ones who made use of these areas, inheriting them from Irish and German predecessors. In Philadelphia, at least, the majority of Poles and other Slavs did not settle in the oldest slum areas. Their work tended to take them into newer or frontier areas of the city where the more modern industries were located. In the Port Richmond and Bridesburg sections of Philadelphia, for example, the Poles were often the first residents to occupy newly constructed workingmen's houses built by savvy contractors who foresaw the local demand; or they occupied company housing provided by local industries such as the Midvale Steel Company in Nicetown. So strong was their desire for work that the Poles arrived first in many areas of Philadelphia and their housing came later. The Poles, it must be remembered, were primarily migrant workers, young, male and unattached, most of whom were transient. They were interested in saving, not spending, money, and they had less need to be fastidious about housing than did permanent immigrants or those with wives and children. Boarding and lodging houses, basements, shacks and tent camps were very common arrangements in areas where work opportunities had expanded faster than housing supplies.

In time, Poles and southern Italians who chose to remain began to improve the housing in their neighborhoods. It was very typical of network peoples to improve conditions where they were so that the network could remain intact rather than to move piecemeal or unilaterally to areas of better housing. Unlike the eastern European Jews who soon left their original areas of settlement for areas of better housing and better schooling, the Italians and Poles remained where they had first arrived. South Philadelphia, for example, once contained as many Jews as Italians (if not more), but the area today shows no evidence of ever having been a Jewish ghetto, so complete was the out-migration. Meanwhile, the Italians in South Philadelphia and the Poles in Bridesburg and Port Richmond (and Nicetown and Manayunk) stayed on and on. Over the years, using their savings and often doing much of the work themselves, they made permanent improvements to their homes, installing indoor plumbing, electricity, gas or oil heat. When the housing or physical environment of the neighborhood deteriorated beyond the ability of residents to maintain it, something which has become increasingly common in many cities because of financial institutions' loan patterns, expressway construction and urban renewal, an important prop of the neighborhood trilogy was lost and the future of the neighborhood imperiled.

In addition to a change in the work structure or physical environment, the neighborhood could also experience a change in its ethnic composition—either internally, externally or both. If jobs remained steady in number and in kind, the ethnic composition of the neighborhood could remain stable only if adequate numbers of the second and third generation were willing to perform these jobs. As one generation yielded to the next, however, many sons and especially grandsons were not as willing to perform jobs that had satisfied their fathers and grandfathers. Unskilled day labor or working in a sweat shop or factory may have been fine for the first generation, but the second and third generations, feeling the pressures of American culture, often wanted something better. If local job opportunities exceeded the number of available workers, new, alien groups would be attracted and the ethnic composition of the neighborhood would undergo drastic change. The newcomers, often differing in race, culture and values from the ethnic Europeans, would find themselves in the same position as the immigrants of two generations before—outsiders attempting to move into areas with established institutions, structures and values.

For many Italians and Poles, their children and grandchildren, the neighborhood became increasingly important because it was the physical entity embodying their community, their system of social and emotional relationships. Their homes became extensions of themselves, and the neighborhood became the physical extension of their homes. The neighborhood was a personalized, almost internalized, thing. Any threat to it was a threat to them. This is a concept that is perhaps difficult for many Americans (and city planners) to grasp, but it is part of the personal fiber of peoples whose culture is network rather than atomistic. In the Old Country the Poles referred to this concept of community-neighborhood, the merging of invisible social and emotional systems with a geographic territory, as the *okolica*. The word has no accurate equivalent in English, but the idea nonetheless came to America and lives on, with or without a name. It remains a vast hidden dimension very characteristic of those American cities, especially in the North, that still house large ethnic populations. The ethnic neighborhood was the final destination of the immigrants and their children, spiritually as well as physically.

Appendixes

Appendix A

PHILADELPHIA: COMPOSITION OF FOREIGN-BORN POPULATION, 1870–1920

	1870 No.	1870 %	1880 No.	1880 %	1890 No.	1890 %	1900 No.	1900 %	1910 No.	1910 %	1920 No.	1920 %
Austria*	519	0.28	686	0.33	2,003	0.74	5,154	1.80	19,860	5.60	13,387	3.30
Bohemia	101	†	215	0.10	189	†	270	0.10			2,240‡	0.60
Belgium	117	†	191	†	365	0.13			478	0.12	517	0.10
British America	1,488	0.81	2,354	1.15	2,684	0.95						
Canada: French							294	0.10	301	†	209	0.10
Canada: British							2,989	1.00	3,735	0.97	4,035	1.00
Denmark	192	0.10	354	0.17	704	0.26	934	0.30	1,119	0.29	1,131	0.30
France	2,479	1.35	2,588	1.26	2,550	0.94	2,521	0.90	2,659	0.69	3,886	1.00
Germany§	50,746	27.60	55,169	27.30	74,971	27.80	71,319	24.20	61,480	15.98	39,766	9.90
Greece			14	†	31	†			589	0.15	1,814	0.50
Great Britain & Ireland	123,408	67.20	134,522	65.80								
England	(22,034)‖		26,315	12.90	38,926	14.40	36,752	12.40	36,564	9.50	30,886	7.70
Scotland			5,696	2.78	8,772	3.25	8,479	2.90	9,177	2.38	8,425	2.10
Wales			680	0.33	935	0.34	1,033	0.40	1,033	0.26	973	0.20
Ireland	(96,698)		101,808	49.82	110,935	41.16	98,427	33.30	83,196	21.62	64,590	16.10
Holland	390	0.20	505	0.24	260	†	258	0.10	349	†	480	0.10
Hungary	52	†	192	†	1,354	0.50	2,785	0.90	12,495	3.25	11,513	2.90
Italy	516	0.28	1,656	0.81	6,799	2.50	17,830	6.00	45,308	11.77	63,723	15.90
Norway	53	†	195	†	1,500	0.55	692	0.20	1,144	0.29	1,255	0.30
Poland#	146	†	577	0.28	2,189	0.81	7,554	2.55			31,112	7.80
Austria							970	0.30				
Germany							1,728	0.60				
Russia							4,163	1.40				
not spec.							693	0.20				
Roumania									4,413	1.14	5,645	1.40

168

	No.	%	No.	%	No.	%	No.	%	No.	%	No.	%
Russia**	94	†	276	0.13	7,879	2.90	28,951	9.80	90,697	23.57	95,744	23.90
Spain	107	†	103	†	136	†			200	†	648	0.20
Sweden	225	0.12	613	0.29	1,626	0.61	2,143	0.70	2,429	0.63	2,651	0.70
Switzerland	1,791	0.97	1,916	0.93	1,710	0.63	1,707	0.60	2,013	0.52	1,889	0.50
Total city population	674,022		847,170		1,046,964		1,293,697		1,549,008		1,823,779	
foreign-born population	183,624	100.00	204,335	100.00	269,480	100.00	295,340	100.00	384,707	100.00	400,744	100.00

*In 1870, 1880, 1890 and 1910, "Austria" includes Galician Poles; in 1910 it includes Bohemia.

†Less than 0.1%.

‡These persons are called "Czechs" in the 1920 Census.

§In 1870, 1880, 1890 and 1910 "Germany" includes some German Poles.

‖Figures in parentheses are those of the Rev. Stephen Byrne, O.S.D., taken from his *Irish Emigration to the United States: What It Has Been and What It Is* (New York: The Catholic Publication Society, 1873), p. 162.

#In 1870, 1880 and 1890 "Poland" includes only those persons from Congress Poland or the Kingdom of Poland as set up at Vienna in 1815. Austrian Poles, German Poles and those Russian Poles living outside of the boundaries of the Congress Kingdom are not included, but are listed under "Austria," "Germany," and "Russia." In 1910 all Poles are included in the figures for "Austria," "Germany," and "Russia." In 1920 Poland is defined as reconstituted at Versailles, 1919.

**In 1870, 1880, 1890 and 1910 "Russia" includes Poles from Russian-administered territories.

SOURCE: United States Census.

Appendix B

TOTAL POPULATION, FOREIGN-BORN POPULATION, PERCENTAGE OF FOREIGN-BORN, AND IMMIGRANT GROWTH RATES FOR 15 U.S. CITIES, 1870 TO 1920

	1870			1880			1870–1880
	Total population	Foreign-born population	% foreign-born	Total population	Foreign-born population	% foreign-born	Immigrant growth rate
Baltimore	267,354	56,484	21.12	332,313	56,136	16.89	-0.61
Boston*	250,526	87,986	35.12	362,839	114,796	31.64	30.47
Buffalo	117,714	46,237	39.27	155,134	51,268	33.02	10.88
Chicago	298,977	144,557	48.35	503,185	204,859	40.71	41.71
Cincinnati	216,239	79,612	36.81	255,139	71,659	28.09	-9.98
Cleveland	92,829	38,815	41.81	160,146	59,409	37.10	53.00
Detroit	79,577	35,381	44.46	116,340	45,645	39.23	29.00
Milwaukee	71,440	33,773	47.27	115,587	46,073	39.86	36.41
Minneapolis			34.01	46,887	15,013	32.01	
New York†	942,292	419,094	44.47	1,206,299	478,670	39.68	13.80
Newark	105,059	35,884	34.15	136,508	40,330	29.54	12.38
Philadelphia	674,022	183,624	27.24	847,170	204,335	24.12	11.27
Pittsburgh‡	86,076	27,822	32.32	156,389	44,605	28.52	60.30
Providence	68,904	17,177	24.92	104,857	28,075	26.77	63.40
St. Louis	310,864	112,249	36.10	350,518	105,013	29.96	-6.40

170

Appendix B (continued)

	1890				1880–1890	1900				1890–1900
	Total population	Foreign-born population	% foreign-born	% foreign stock	Immigrant growth rate	Total population	Foreign-born population	% foreign born	% foreign stock	Immigrant growth rate
Baltimore	434,439	69,003	15.88	41.6	22.90	508,957	68,600	13.47	38.0	0.58
Boston	448,477	158,172	35.26	67.8	37.78	560,892	197,129	35.14	71.7	24.60
Buffalo	255,664	89,485	35.00	77.3	74.50	352,387	104,252	29.58	73.7	16.53
Chicago	1,099,850	450,666	40.97	78.4	119.98	1,698,575	587,112	34.56	77.3	30.27
Cincinnati	296,908	71,408	24.05	69.0	0.00	325,902	57,961	17.78	60.7	–18.83
Cleveland	261,353	97,095	37.15	75.2	63.40	381,768	124,631	32.64	75.4	28.35
Detroit	205,876	81,709	39.68	77.5	79.00	285,704	96,503	33.77	77.1	18.10
Milwaukee	204,468	79,576	38.91	86.5	72.70	285,315	88,991	31.19	82.7	11.83
Minneapolis	164,738	60,558	36.76	66.4	303.79	202,718	61,021	30.10	69.0	0.76
New York	1,515,301	639,943	42.23	77.2	33.69	3,437,202	1,270,080	36.95	76.6	
Newark	181,830	55,571	30.56	67.0	37.80	246,070	71,363	29.00	68.1	28.40
Philadelphia	1,046,964	269,480	25.73	56.6	31.88	1,293,697	295,340	22.82	54.7	9.60
Pittsburgh	238,617	73,289	30.71	65.9	64.30	321,616	84,878	25.60	62.8	15.81
Providence	132,146	40,364	30.54		43.79	175,547	55,855	31.80		38.40
St. Louis	451,770	114,876	25.42	67.7	9.39	575,238	111,356	19.35	60.9	–3.06

171

Appendix B (continued)

	1910				1900–1910	1920				1910–1920
	Total population	Foreign-born population	% foreign-born	% foreign stock	Immigrant growth rate	Total population	Foreign-born population	% foreign born	% foreign stock	Immigrant growth rate
Baltimore	558,485	77,662	13.90	37.9	13.20	733,826	84,809	11.55	33.6	9.20
Boston	670,585	243,365	36.29	74.2	23.46	748,060	242,619	32.43	73.3	-0.30
Buffalo	423,715	118,689	28.01	71.3	13.85	506,775	121,824	24.03	66.5	2.64
Chicago	2,185,283	783,428	35.85	77.5	33.43	2,701,705	808,558	29.92	72.0	3.20
Cincinnati	363,591	56,859	15.64	52.0	-1.90	401,247	42,921	10.69	41.0	24.50
Cleveland	560,663	196,190	34.99	74.8	57.41	796,841	240,173	30.14	69.0	22.42
Detroit	465,766	157,534	33.82	74.0	63.24	993,678	290,884	29.27	64.2	84.65
Milwaukee	373,857	111,529	29.83	78.6	25.33	457,147	110,160	24.09	70.9	-1.23
Minneapolis	301,408	86,099	28.57	67.2	41.10	380,582	88,248	23.18	63.9	2.50
New York	3,766,883	1,944,357	40.79	78.6	53.09	5,620,048	2,028,160	36.08	76.4	4.31
Newark	347,469	111,007	31.95	69.9	55.55	414,525	117,549	28.35	68.5	5.89
Philadelphia	1,549,008	384,707	24.83	56.8	30.26	1,823,779	400,744	21.97	54.2	4.17
Pittsburgh	533,905	140,942	26.39	62.2	22.70	588,343	120,792	20.53	56.7	14.29
Providence	224,326	76,303	34.00		36.60	237,595	69,895	29.41		-8.39
St. Louis	687,029	126,233	18.37	54.2	13.36	772,897	103,626	13.40	44.4	17.90

*Boston. 1920 figure includes population of Hyde Park, annexed to Boston after 1910. Combined population: 1910, 686,092; 1900, 574,136; 1890, 458,670; 1880, 369,927; 1870, 254,662.

†New York. 1870 figure is for Manhattan only; 1880 and 1890 figures are for Manhattan, parts of other boroughs, but not Brooklyn, which is reported separately until 1900; 1900, 1910 and 1920 figures include the population of five boroughs: Bronx, Brooklyn, Manhattan, Queens and Richmond.

‡Pittsburgh. 1910 and 1920 figures include population of Allegheny which had been annexed after 1890. Population of Allegheny 1890, 105,287; 1880, 78,682; 1870, 53,180.

NOTE: The above changes have been taken into account when determining the immigration growth rates; the same territory is used for each computation.

SOURCE: U. S. Census.

Appendix C

IMMIGRATION AND RACIAL PATTERNS FOR 15 U.S. CITIES, 1880–1920

By ranking the fifteen cities in the survey by deciles for each of twelve selected variables, we can more readily see the ways in which Philadelphia either resembled or differed from its contemporaries. Please refer to the accompanying table.

1. Philadelphia's *total growth rate, 1880 to 1890,* was very low. This was true of all the old cities as well as the three semi-southern cities. In contrast, the new cities of the Midwest grew very rapidly.

In the decade *1900 to 1910* Philadelphia's growth rate was also low. Only Baltimore and Cincinnati failed to increase to the same extent as Philadelphia. All other cities, except for Pittsburgh and St. Louis, which paralleled the Philadelphia experience, grew more rapidly (factors IIIa, IIIb).

2. In comparison with other cities Philadelphia's *percentage of foreign-born inhabitants* was small. The city's pattern resembled that of the semi-southern cities of Cincinnati and St. Louis (factors Ia, Ib).

3. The *rate of increase of Philadelphia's foreign-born population* was low. Once again, this was true of all the older cities of the East. In the 1880s total city growth and immigrant growth rates generally paralleled each other, but this trend was somewhat modified in the decade 1900 to 1910. Although Philadelphia's rate of immigrant growth was low for this period, it was greater than that of Baltimore, Boston, Buffalo, Cincinnati, Pittsburgh and St. Louis, equal to that of Milwaukee, and less than that of Chicago, Cleveland, Detroit and Minneapolis, newer cities of the nation; it was also less than that of New York City, Newark and Providence, older cities of the East (factors IIa, IIb).

4. Boston, New York and Providence, cities that ranked very low in overall population increase 1880 to 1890 (factor IIIa), ranked very high in factor IVa, *"Percentage of total population increase due to immigration."* Cities with high or intermediate rankings in total city growth also held intermediate rankings with respect to this factor. Philadelphia was outranked by all the older cities except Newark and by all the newer cities except Pittsburgh; these two exceptions, Newark and Pittsburgh, paralleled Philadelphia. In contributions to total city growth, only three cities, those of the semi-South, were less influenced by immigrants than Philadelphia.

In the decade *1900 to 1910* immigration made its greatest contributions to the total city growth of Boston, Chicago, Cleveland, New York City and Providence. Philadelphia and Newark were next in rank. Thus, Philadelphia ranked low in overall growth, but ranked high in the percentage of increase due to immigration. The same was true of Boston. Once again, the growth of the semi-southern cities was least influenced by immigration. In sum, while the newer cities registered higher percentages of foreign-born, higher total city growth rates and higher immigrant growth rates than the Eastern cities or those of the

173

semi-South, the older cities of the East relied upon immigration as a source of population increase to the same or greater extent than the newer cities. Had it not been for the immigrants, the older cities would have ceased to grow; decentralization and suburbanization were more advanced here than in the newer cities of the west.

5. *In 1880 Philadelphia was an Irish city.* Only Boston and Providence had larger proportions of foreign-born Irish. The Irish were concentrated in the cities of the East. In contrast, *the Germans were strong in the Midwest* and especially so in the semi-southern cities of Baltimore, St. Louis and Cincinnati. The higher a city's rank in factor VI, "Percentage of foreign-born who are Irish, 1880," the lower was its rank in factor V, "percentage of foreign-born who are German, 1880." The opposite was also true: the higher the rank in German concentration, the lower the rank in Irish concentration. Generally, there was an inverse relationship between these two groups of the Old Immigration—at least in settlement patterns. Only three cities—New York, Newark and Pittsburgh—had intermediate rankings for both groups.

6. In 1920 only Providence, Newark and New York City had larger *percentages of Italians* than Philadelphia (factor VII) while Boston held the same ranking. The cities of the Midwest and the semi-South ranked low in Italian concentration. The Italians showed a preference for the older cities of the East as opposed to the newer ones of the west.

7. *Philadelphia's concentration of Russians was very high,* ranking with New York and outranked only by Baltimore. These cities—Baltimore, New York and Philadelphia—were the three major ports of entry for the Jewish (Russian) people. That they disembarked there helps to explain why these cities rank so high on the Jewish factor. While economically more mobile than other immigrant peoples, the Jews were not as geographically mobile (see chap. 5). As in the Italian case, the newer cities had relatively small proportions of foreign-born Russians (factor IX).

8. In contrast to the Russian and Italian pattern, the newer cities ranked high in *"Percentage of foreign-born who are Polish, 1920)"* (factor VIII). Buffalo, Detroit, Milwaukee, Chicago and Cleveland, in that order, ahd the largest percentages of foreign-born Poles. Obviously, the Polish movement was to the newer cities of America, particularly to those which ranked high or relatively so on the German factor in 1880. Philadelphia's rank as a Polish city was comparatively low.

9. The *"Percentage of foreign-born who are Irish, 1920"* and *"Percentage of foreign-born who are German, 1920"* (factors X and XI) indicate which cities continued to maintain strong concentrations of peoples of the "Old" Immigration. Boston, Providence and Philadelphia were still Irish cities as of 1920. The Germans were strong in Cincinnati, Milwaukee and St. Louis, but not in Philadelphia.

10. Philadelphia and Pittsburgh held unique positions in *"Percentage Non-White"* (factor XII). Their proportions of non-whites were larger than

those of all the Eastern cities and all the new cities of the West. Philadelphia's rank was the same as that of Cincinnati and/or St. Louis for the 1880 to 1920 period. Philadelphia had the largest percentage of black residents of all northern cities, both old and new. Pittsburgh's ranking is best explained by the same variables that accounted for Philadelphia's situation: proximity to a hinterland of black labor willing to migrate short distances and to work in low status jobs for low pay.

IMMIGRATION AND RACIAL PATTERNS FOR 15 U.S. CITIES (ranked on a scale of one to ten)

City	Ia	IIa	IIIa	IVa	Ib	IIb	IIIb	IVb	V	VI	VII	VIII	IX	X	XI	XIIa	XIIb	XIIc
Baltimore	0	0	0	2	0	2	0	3	3	3	3	4	9	4	2	9	9	9
Boston	7	1	0	9	8	3	1	8	0	9	5	0	4	0	9	1	1	1
Buffalo	7	2	2	7	5	2	1	4	7	2	4	9	0	3	2	0	0	0
Chicago	9	3	4	7	8	5	3	8	5	2	2	6	3	3	2	0	1	2
Cincinnati	3	0	0	0	0	0	0	0	9	2	2	0	1	9	3	2	3	4
Cleveland	8	2	2	7	7	9	6	8	5	2	2	5	1	2	1	0	0	2
Detroit	9	2	2	7	7	9	9	6	5	1	1	7	1	2	0	0	0	2
Milwaukee	8	2	2	7	5	4	3	5	9	0	1	7	0	8	0	0	0	0
Minneapolis	7	9	9	7	5	6	7	5	1	0	0	1	0	1	0	0	0	0
New York	9	1	0	9	9	8	5	9	4	6	6	1	8	1	3	0	1	1
Newark	5	1	0	6	6	8	5	7	6	4	8	3	5	2	2	1	1	2
Philadelphia	3	1	0	6	4	4	1	7	3	7	5	2	8	1	6	2	3	4
Pittsburgh	5	2	1	6	4	3	1	6	4	5	4	4	2	2	4	2	2	4
Providence	5	1	0	8	7	5	3	8	0	9	9	0	1	0	7	1	1	1
St. Louis	3	0	0	1	1	2	1	3	7	3	2	0	3	6	3	3	3	5

KEY (and distribution range of percentages): Ia = % foreign-born 1890 (15.9%–42.2%); IIa = % foreign-born increase 1880–1890 (0%–303.4%); IIIa = % total population increase 1880–1890 (16.4%–251.4%); IVa = % total increase due to immigration 1880–1890 (0%–52.2%); Ib = % foreign-born 1910 (13.9%–40.8%); IIb = %foreign-born increase 1900–1910 (-1.9%–63.2%); IIIb = % total population increase 1900–1910 (9.7%–63%); IVb = % total increase due to immigration 1900–1910 (-3%–50.7%); V = % of foreign-born who are German 1880 (3.9%–68.3%); VI = % of foreign-born who are Irish 1880 (7.9%–60.3%); VII = % of foreign-born who are Italian 1920 (0.9%–27.5%); VIII = % of foreign-born who are Polish 1920 (2.8%–25.8%); IX = % of foreign-born who are Russian 1920 (6.4%–27.4%); X = % of foreign-born who are German 1920 (2%–41.5%); XI = % of foreign-born who are Irish 1920 (1.3%–23.5%); XIIa = % non-white 1890 (0.2%–15.4%); XIIb = % non-white 1910 (0.3%–15.5%); XIIc = % non-white 1920 (0.5%–14.8%).

NOTE: Factors V and VI, "% of foreign-born who are German 1880" and "% of foreign-born who are Irish 1880," are used as indicators of the relative distribution of old immigrant groups within and among America's cities; the Irish and the Germans were the two major components of the Old Immigration. Their geographical patterns were established well before 1880 and before the arrival of masses of eastern and southern Europeans.

Factors VII, VIII and IX, "% of foreign-born who are Italian, Polish and Russian, 1920," are used to indicate the distributions of the newer immigrant groups within and among America's cities. The Russians, Italians and Poles were the largest contributors to the New Immigration.

1920 was chosen because 1905 to 1915 was the period of heavy immigration for these newer groups and by this year the geographical direction of each group had stabilized. 1920 is used also because, for the first time, meaningful (but not perfect) statistics are available for the Polish population of the United States which heretofore had been recorded under Austria, Germany and Russia.

Appendix D
DISTRIBUTION OF POLISH IMMIGRANTS IN THE UNITED STATES

Destination of Polish Immigrants during the Decade Ended June 30, 1908

Pennsylvania	209,697	Nebraska	1,205
New York	159,849	Maine	1,094
Illinois	92,532	Washington	1,061
Massachusetts	64,377	North Dakota	794
New Jersey	62,972	Kansas	644
Connecticut	34,285	Colorado	535
Ohio	25,870	California	385
Michigan	25,733	Iowa	381
Wisconsin	12,864	Virginia	341
Maryland	9,831	Wyoming	257
Rhode Island	5,672	Montana	193
Indiana	5,069	South Dakota	141
Missouri	4,604	Louisiana	138
West Virginia	4,563	Tennessee	103
Minnesota	4,175	Oregon	93
Delaware	3,817	Alabama	54
New Hampshire	3,795	Utah	21
Vermont	3,350	Arizona	20
Texas	1,812		

SOURCE: Compiled from Emily Greene Balch, *Our Slavic Fellow Citizens* (New York: Charities Publication Committee, 1910), p. 256.

Distribution of Polish Immigrants and Their Children, 1907–1908

Pennsylvania	422,790	Washington	4,480
Illinois	388,745	Colorado	4,100
New York	355,725	Iowa	3,755
Wisconsin	197,945	South Dakota	3,360
Michigan	160,830	Kentucky	3,340
Massachusetts	128,515	Maine	3,215
Ohio	96,110	Oklahoma	2,780
New Jersey	92,785	Oregon	2,656
Minnesota	88,805	Tennessee	2,610
Connecticut	61,490	Arkansas	2,575
Indiana	41,335	Montana	2,065
Missouri	21,400	Indian Territory	1,995
Maryland	19,415	Vermont	1,795
Nebraska	18,770	Georgia	945
Texas	18,740	Alabama	865
Rhode Island	10,310	Louisiana	840
Delaware	8,630	South Carolina	815
California	6,600	Mississippi	650
North Dakota	6,270	North Carolina	375
Kansas	5,455	Florida	210
New Hampshire	5,320	Total	1,199,411

SOURCE: Kruszka's estimate in Polish *Press,* March 2, 1907, as in Balch, p. 263.

Appendix D (continued)

Distribution of Polish Immigrants and Their Children, 1908

Pennsylvania	525,000	West Virginia	25,000
New York	500,000	Delaware	20,000
Illinois	450,000	North Dakota	15,000
Massachusetts	300,000	Kansas	8,000
Wisconsin	250,000	California	8,000
Michigan	250,000	Washington	7,000
New Jersey	200,000	Colorado	6,000
Minnesota	140,000	Iowa	6,000
Connecticut	125,000	Oklahoma	6,000
Ohio	125,000	Oregon	6,000
Indiana	70,000	Vermont	6,000
Missouri	60,000	South Dakota	5,000
Maryland	50,000	Kentucky	5,000
Nebraska	50,000	Montana	5,000
Rhode Island	40,000	Tennessee	5,000
Maine	35,000	Other States	5,000
Texas	25,000	Total (including Canada):	
			c. 4,000,000

SOURCE: Anonymous estimate in Polish *Press,* December 15, 1908; (see Balch, p. 263).

NOTE: Pennsylvania is ranked highest in all estimates, and the overwhelming majority of Polish immigrants are located in the North Atlantic and Great Lakes regions. In the Census of 1910, 1,707,640 persons gave Polish as the language used in daily intercourse. Of this number, 163,000 were in the six New England states, and 1,083,535 in the area surrounding the Great Lakes—Pennsylvania, New York, New Jersey, Ohio, Michigan, Indiana, Illinois, Wisconsin and Minnesota. The remaining 461,104 were south and west of the Ohio and Missouri Rivers. The 1910 survey of the Polish National League of America lists 3,063,000 Polish speaking persons (in comparison with the census figure of 1,707,640); of these, 407,000 are in the six New England states; 1,930,000 in the Great Lakes area, and the remaining 1,326,000 south and west of the Missouri and Ohio Rivers. See Julian Korski-Grove, "The Polish Group in the United States," *Annuals of the American Academy of Political and Social Science* 93 (January 1921): 154. In 1910 the Poles constituted 10% of the population of Michigan, 12% of Wisconsin and 6% of Minnesota and North Dakota. The South as a whole attracted very few Poles (Korski-Grove, pp. 155–56).

Appendix E

PHILADELPHIA'S WAGE EARNERS, 1915, BY RACE, SEX, AND NATIONALITY, ARRANGED BY INDUSTRY

Summary of industries	Total No.	Total %	American No.	American %	Foreign No.	Foreign %	Black No.	Black %
1. Building & contracting	15,396	4.9	10,947	71.1	2,893	18.8	1,556	10.1
2. Chemicals & allied products	11,785	3.8	7,965	67.6	3,188	27.0	632	5.4
3. Clay, glass & stone products	4,972	1.6	3,153	63.4	1,438	28.9	381	7.7
4. Clothing manufacture	65,517	20.9	40,030	61.1	25,148	38.4	339	0.5
5. Food & kindred products	14,592	4.7	9,130	62.6	5,073	34.8	389	2.6
6. Leather & rubber products	11,655	3.7	7,249	62.2	4,340	37.2	66	0.6
7. Liquors & beverages	2,140	0.7	1,808	84.5	313	14.6	19	0.9
8. Lumber & its remanufacture	8,619	2.7	5,586	64.8	2,863	33.2	170	2.0
9. Paper & printing	21,391	6.8	18,746	87.6	2,174	10.2	471	2.2
10. Textiles	38,459	12.3	30,605	79.6	7,700	20.0	154	0.4
11. Laundry work	3,404	1.1	2,888	84.8	375	11.0	141	4.1
12. Metals & metal manufacture	53,494	17.0	40,366	75.5	12,060	22.5	1,068	2.0
13. Mines & quarries	447	0.1	253	56.6	93	20.8	101	22.6
14. Public service	33,709	10.7	28,890	85.7	4,259	12.6	560	1.7
15. Tobacco & its products	5,852	1.9	2,774	47.4	2,817	48.1	261	4.5
16. Miscellaneous	22,351	7.1	15,926	71.2	5,474	24.5	951	4.3
Totals	313,783	100.0	226,316	72.1	80,208	25.6	7,259	2.3

Appendix E (continued)

Nature of industry	Average days in operation	Average no. employees	American		Foreign		Black		Male		Female	
			No.	%	No.	%	No.	%	No.	%	No.	%
1. *Building and contracting (4.9%)*												
Brick, cement and stone work	240	1,399	831	59.4	292	20.9	276	19.7	1,398		1	
Building construction	280	6,702	4,512	67.3	1,347	20.1	843	12.6	6,698		4	
Electrical construction	291	600	596	99.3	4	0.7			598		2	
Painting and decorating	266	1,088	1,007	92.6	72	6.6	9	0.8	1,072		16	
Paving and road construction	220	1,882	843	44.8	691	36.7	348	18.5	1,882			
Plumbing and heating	294	1,382	1,341	97.0	33	2.4	8	0.6	1,374		8	
Railway construction	251	585	197	33.6	328	56.0	60	10.2	585			
Roofing and sheet metal work	280	1,340	1,259	94.0	69	5.1	12	0.9	1,339		1	
Structural iron work (erecting)	285	418	361	86.4	57	13.6			418			
Totals		15,396	10,947	71.1	2,893	18.8	1,556	10.18	15,364	99.8	32	.2
2. *Chemicals and allied products (3.8%)*												
Alcohol	157	21	10		11				21			
Charcoal	310	26	26						26			
Chemicals	264	913	695	76.1	182	19.9	36	3.9	755		158	
Cleansing and polishing preparations	282	362	256	70.7	102	28.2	4	1.1	264		98	
Dyestuffs and extracts	231	10	10						10			
Fertilizers	228	605	249	41.2	284	46.9	72	11.9	605			
Flavoring preparations	254	28	26		2				26		2	
Glue and gelatin	288	81	7	8.6	74	91.4			81			
Grease and tallow	293	698	297	42.5	184	26.4	217	31.1	680		18	
Ink, printing	303	143	95	66.4	19	13.3	29	20.3	143			
Ink, writing	259	9	9						5		4	

Product	Code	Total	No.	%	No.	%	No.	%	No.	%	No.	%
Mucilage and paste	303	78	73	93.6			5		57		21	
Oils, crude	289											
Oils, linseed	356	6	5		1				6			
Oils, lubricating	303	173	152	87.9	14		7		173			
Oils, refined, kerosene, etc.	325	3,593	2,456	68.4	1,107	30.8	30	0.8	3,578		15	
Oils, not specified	308	384	214	55.7	95	24.7	75	19.5	380		4	
Paints and varnishes	295	969	687	70.9	236	24.4	46	4.7	934		35	
Patent and proprietary medicine	295	1,121	1,069	95.4	18	1.6	34	3.0	561		560	50.0
Soap	270	759	668	88.0	48	6.3	43	5.7	663		96	
Sulphuric, nitric & mixed acid	331	1,689	852	50.5	803	47.6	32	1.9	1,561		126	
Tar	300	2	1		1				2			
Toilet preparations	303	97	93		2		2		29		68	
Wood alcohol & acetate of lime	313	20	15		5				20			
Totals		11,785	7,965	67.6	3,188	27.0	632	5.4	10,580	89.8	1,205	10.2
3. Clay, glass and stone products (1.6%)												
Artificial stone	270	36	24		12				36			
Brick	236	1,104	620	56.2	266	24.1	218	19.7	1,104			
Crucibles	282	82	31	37.8	34	41.5	17	20.7	82			
Emery & other abrasive wheels	282	99	55	55.6	44	44.4			99			
Glass bottles	283	573	527	92.0	44	7.7	2	0.3	484		89	
Glass, cut	271	94	89	94.7	5	5.3			79		15	
Glass, decorative	301	646	469	72.6	175	27.1	2	0.3	601		45	
Glass, plate	300	8							8			
Glass, window	300	8	7		1				8			
Grindstone	307						8					
Lamps and chimneys	300	321	222	69.2	99	30.8			289		32	
Lime	312	306	55	18.0	226	73.9	25	8.1	806			

Appendix E (continued)

Nature of industry	Average days in operation	Average no. employees	American No.	American %	Foreign No.	Foreign %	Black No.	Black %	Male No.	Male %	Female No.	Female %
Mantels and tile	302	28	24		4				28			
Marble & granite work	285	869	668	76.9	195	22.4	6	0.7	869			
Mirrors	301	105	80		25				105			
Paving materials	267	284	85	29.9	97	34.2	102	35.9	284			
Pottery, terra cotta and fine clay products	314	384	181	47.1	203	52.9			384			
Wall plaster	305	25	16		8		1		25			
Totals		4,972	3,153	63.4	1,438	28.9	381	7.7	4,791	96.4	181	3.6
4. Clothing manufacture (20.9%)												
Clothing, men's	271	4,506	2,349	52.1	2,107	46.8	50	0.1	2,767		1,739	38.6
Clothing, women's & children	279	15,097	6,955	46.1	8,052	53.3	90	0.6	5,686		9,411	62.3
Corsets	308	83	57	68.7	25	30.0	1		28		55	66.3
Fur goods	245	194	136	70.1	49	25.3	9	4.6	116		78	40.2
Furnishing goods, not spec.	302	359	316	88.0	43	12.0			98		261	72.7
Gloves, other than leather	299	110	97	88.2	13	11.8			22		88	80.0
Hats and caps, other than straw	271	5,900	4,714	79.9	1,182	20.0	4	0.1	4,414		1,486	25.2
Hats, straw	218	58	58	100.0					26		32	55.2
Hosiery and knit goods	281	22,945	13,260	57.8	9,645	42.0	40	0.2	6,855		16,090	70.1
Ladies' skirts	281	726	367	50.6	347	47.8	12	16.5	389		337	46.4
Millinery	273	5,552	5,036	90.7	438	7.9	78	1.4	1,755		3,797	68.4
Neckwear	293	610	525	86.1	85	13.9			318		292	47.9
Overalls	276	88	69	78.4	19	21.6			27		61	69.3
Shirts	276	3,244	2,201	67.8	1,028	31.7	15	0.5	917		2,327	71.7

Industry	No.											
Shirt waists	293	3,718	1,872	50.3	1,809	48.7	37	1.0	495		3,223	86.7
Suspenders	302	192	57	29.7	135	70.3			78		114	59.4
Underwear	278	2,135	1,961	91.9	171	8.0	3	0.1	252		1,883	88.2
Totals		65,517	40,030	61.1	25,148	38.4	339	0.5	24,243	37.0	41,274	63.0

5. Food and kindred products (4.7%)

Industry	No.											
Baking powder	306	5	5						4		1	
Bread & other bakery products	314	5,351	3,532	66.0	1,661	31.0	158	3.0	4,273		1,078	20.1
Butter, cheese & condensed milk	281	355	282	79.4	62	17.5	11	3.1	343		12	
Canned and preserved goods	258	431	315	73.1	110	25.5	6	1.4	282		149	34.6
Chocolate and cocoa products	254	314	276	87.9	38	12.1			262		52	16.6
Coffee & spices, roasting, etc.	282	375	371	99.0	2	0.5	2	0.5	208		167	44.5
Confectionary	272	2,922	2,179	74.6	704	24.1	39	1.3	1,211		1,711	58.6
Cordials and syrups	207	2	1		1				2			
Flour & grist mill products	303	219	138	63.0	52	23.7	29	13.2	215		4	
Ice cream	321	555	360	64.9	120	21.6	75	13.5	449		106	
Ice	296	641	321	50.1	307	47.9	13	2.0	641			
Molasses	309	36	24		12				36			
Slaughtering and meat packing	292	1,464	790	54.0	625	42.7	49	3.3	1,423		41	
Sugar refining	295	1,896	518	27.3	1,371	72.3	7	0.4	1,781		115	
Vinegar and cider	337	26	18		8				26			
Totals		14,592	9,130	62.6	5,073	34.8	389	2.6	11,156	76.5	3,436	23.5

6. Leather and rubber goods (3.7%)

Industry	No.											
Belting and hose	304	421	301	71.5	87	20.7	33	7.8	339		82	19.5
Boots and shoes	287	3,703	2,633	71.1	1,061	28.7	9	0.2	2,472		1,231	33.2
Hides and skins	268											
Leather, sole	305	121	52	43.0	69	57.0						
Leather, tanned, curried and finished	289	4,653	2,515	54.1	2,133	45.8	5	0.1	4,313		340	7.3
Leather goods	289	1,491	1,248	83.7	240	16.1	3	0.2	844		647	43.4
Rubber goods, not spec.	302	529	245	46.3	273	51.6	11	2.1	510		19	

Appendix E (continued)

Nature of industry	Average days in operation	Average no. employees	American No.	American %	Foreign No.	Foreign %	Black No.	Black %	Male No.	Male %	Female No.	Female %
Trunks and suit cases	300	737	255	34.6	477	64.7	5	6.7	699		38	
Totals		11,655	7,249	62.2	4,340	37.2	66	0.6	9,298	79.8	2,357	20.2
7. Liquors and beverages (0.7%)												
Carbonated beverages	292	282	247	87.6	24		11		267		15	
Liquors, distilled	211	91	79	86.8	10		2		84		7	
Liquors, malt	303	1,708	1,428	83.6	277	16.2	3	0.2	1,704		4	
Table waters	305	59	54	91.5	2		3		54		5	
Totals		2,140	1,808	84.5	313	14.6	19	0.9	2,109	98.6	31	1.4
8. Lumber & its remanufacture (2.7%)												
Barrels, kegs & tanks	292	304	228	75.0	73	24.0	3	1.0	304			
Beds and cots	302	9	9	100.0					9			
Billiard tables and supplies	300	9										
Bobbins and spools	256	218	89	40.8	129	59.2			218			
Boxes, cigar	265	69	69	100.0					30	43.5	39	56.5
Boxes, packing	294	871	780	89.6	80	9.2	11	1.2	870		1	
Carriages, wagons and parts	296	619	475	76.7	142	22.9	2	0.3	619			
Children's carriages, sleds, etc.	253	332	228	68.7	103	31.0	1	0.3	318		14	
Cooperage, etc.	298	100	50	50.0	48	48.0	2	2.0	100			
Furniture	298	2,773	1,318	47.5	1,423	51.3	32	1.2	2,741		32	
Lasts	303	82	82	100.0					82			
Lumber & timber products	302	128	102	79.7	16	12.5	10	7.8	128			
Models and patterns, not paper	297	87	80	92.0	6	7.0	1	1.0	87			
Planing mill products	299	2,435	1,691	69.4	639	26.2	105	4.3	2,330		105	

Code	Industry										
352	Refrigerators and ice boxes	215	142	66.0	72	33.5	1	0.5	215			
307	Washing machines and ringers	1	1						1			
294	Wood, turned and carved	357	223	62.5	132	37.0	2	0.5	351		6	
272	Wood novelties	19	19	100.0					19			
	Totals	8,619	5,586	64.8	2,863	33.2	170	2.0	8,422	97.7	197	2.3

9. Paper & printing industries (6.8%)

Code	Industry										
301	Bags, paper	39	37		2				17		22	
296	Boxes, fancy and paper	3,488	2,950	84.6	459	13.2	79	2.2	1,014	29.1	2,474	70.9
304	Cardcutting and designing	237	200	84.4	35	14.8	2	0.8	178	75.1	59	24.9
295	Electroplating, engraving and diesinking	751	747	99.5	4	0.5			511	68.0	240	32.0
299	Labels and tags	302	264	87.4	25	8.3	13	4.3	147	48.7	155	51.3
293	Paper goods, not specified	1,479	954	64.5	492	33.2	33	2.2	1,053	71.2	426	28.8
314	Photo engraving	463	433	93.5	24	5.2	6	1.3	445	96.1	18	3.9
297	Printing and publishing	11,935	11,217	94.0	399	3.3	319	2.7	9,602	80.5	2,333	19.5
150	Pulp goods	609	234	38.4	372	61.1	3	0.5	527	86.5	82	13.5
306	Roofing paper	501	228	45.5	270	53.9	3	0.6	501	100.0		
283	Sand and emery paper & cloth	65	54	83.0	11	17.0			65	100.0		
302	Stationery goods, not spec.	769	746	97.0	20	2.6	3	0.4	283	36.8	486	63.2
274	Stereotyping & electrotyping	230	218	94.8	2	0.9	10	4.3	225	97.8	5	2.2
301	Wall paper	523	464	88.7	59	11.3			444	84.9	79	15.1
	Totals	21,391	18,746	87.6	2,174	10.2	471	2.2	15,012	70.2	6,379	29.8

10. Textiles (12.3%)

Code	Industry										
298	Bags, other than paper	253	253	100.0					62	35.9	191	64.1
286	Blankets, flannels, etc.	987	771	78.1	199	20.2	17	1.7	711	72.0	276	28.0
291	Braids, tapes & bindings	1,997	1,833	91.8	163	8.1	1	0.1	538	26.9	1,459	73.1
278	Carpets and rugs	4,761	4,143	87.0	618	13.0			3,070	64.5	1,691	35.5
251	Cordage & twine, jute and linen goods	1,505	671	44.6	822	54.6	12	0.8	815	54.2	690	45.8
288	Cotton goods	1,983	1,735	87.5	248	12.5			1,043	52.6	940	47.4
294	Curtains	416	352	84.6	63	15.1	1	0.2	184	44.2	232	55.8

Appendix E (continued)

Nature of industry	Average days in operation	Average no. employees	American		Foreign		Black		Male		Female	
			No.	%	No.	%	No.	%	No.	%	No.	%
Dyeing & finishing textiles	283	3,199	2,559	80.0	628	19.6	12	0.4	2,900	90.6	299	9.4
Haircloth	285	310	290	93.5	20	6.5			160	51.6	150	48.4
Hammocks	190	125	125	100.0					71	63.4	54	36.6
Handkerchiefs & embroideries	294	1,634	1,368	83.7	263	16.1	3	0.2	651	39.8	983	60.2
Horse blankets & robes	289	323	262	81.1	61	18.9			198	61.3	125	38.7
Shoddy	301	134	79	59.0	55	41.0			99	73.9	35	26.1
Silk & silk goods & throwsters	390	3,334	2,722	81.6	611	18.3	1	0.1	1,713	51.4	1,621	48.6
Thread	286	288	227	78.8	61	21.2			57	19.8	231	80.2
Towels	267	658	639	97.1	19	2.9			233	35.4	425	64.6
Waste	279	464	375	80.8	88	19.0	1	0.2	366	78.9	98	21.1
Wool pulling	299	133	31	23.3	101	75.9	1	0.8	127	95.5	6	4.5
Woolen, worsted & felt goods	286	6,712	5,498	81.9	1,214	18.1			3,502	52.2	3,210	47.8
Yarns	259	9,243	6,672	72.2	2,466	26.7	105	1.1	3,865	41.8	5,378	58.2
Totals		38,459	30,605	79.6	7,700	20.0	154	0.4	20,365	53.0	10,894	47.0
11. *Laundry work* (1.1%)												
Totals	270	3,404	2,888	84.8	375	11.0	141	4.1	1,281	37.7	2,123	62.3
12. *Metals & metal products* (17.0%)												
Agricultural implements and machinery	246	392	382	97.4	9	2.3	1	0.3	387		5	
Aluminum and products	263											
Automobiles and parts	293	2,672	2,040	76.3	623	23.3	9	0.4	2,635		37	
Axes and edge tools	284	49	49	100.0					49			
Axles	297	22	19	86.4	3	13.6			22			

Babbit metal and solder	299	133	119	89.5	13	9.8	1	0.7	133		
Bars, lead and lead sheets	229	90	30	33.3	40	44.4	20	22.2	90		
Bars, iron and steel	266	1,403	818	58.3	584	41.6	1	0.1	1,403		
Beds and bedsprings	303	282	191	67.7	89	31.6	2	0.7	265	17	
Bicycles, motorcycles and parts	290	14	8		6				14		
Boilers, tanks and stacks	300	460	294	63.9	159	34.6	7	1.5	460		
Bolts, nuts and rivets	258	579	279	48.2	300	51.8			576	3	
Brass and bronze products	288	1,234	846	68.6	377	30.5	11	0.9	1,215	19	
Cars and car wheels	306	2,062	1,475	71.5	571	27.7	16	0.8	2,042	20	
Castings, iron and steel	276	1,642	1,163	70.8	457	27.8	22	1.3	1,580	62	
Chains	290	72	6	8.3	64	88.9	2	2.8	72		
Cornices, ceilings, ventilators/etc.	292	210	165	78.6	43	20.5	2	0.9	210		
Cutlery	283	6	5				1		6		
Elevators and hoists	315	565	493	87.2	68	12.0	4	0.8	565		
Engines, gas and gasoline	292	55	41	74.5	13	23.6	1		55		
Engines, railroads	308	7,626	5,452	71.5	2,174	28.5			7,626		
Ferro alloys	300	16	15	94.0	1				16		
Files	289	1,235	819	66.3	416	33.7			996	239	19.4
Fire escapes	305	55	38	69.1	17	30.9			55		
Fire arms and ammunition	303	200	180	90.0	20	10.0			200		
Fixtures, gas and electric lamps and reflectors	305	775	552	71.2	216	27.9	7	0.9	697		
Forgings, iron and steel	276	4,492	2,347	52.2	1,445	32.2	700	15.6	4,490	2	
Frogs and switches	309	20	18		2				20		
Hardware and specialties	285	2,283	1,679	73.5	598	26.2	6		2,073	210	
Iron and steel work, ornamental	291	104	58	55.8	44	42.3	2		104		
Instruments, professional and scientific	288	926	808	87.2	111	12.0	7	0.8	878	48	
Machinery and parts	291	5,961	4,896	82.1	1,025	17.2	40	0.7	5,889	72	
Machine repair shops	290	506	490	96.8	16	3.2			502	4	
Machine tools	303	1,459	1,256	86.1	180	12.3	23	1.6	1,452	7	

Appendix E (continued)

Nature of industry	Average days in operation	Average no. employees	American No.	%	Foreign No.	%	Black No.	%	Male No.	%	Female No.	%
Meters	301	400	399	99.8			1	0.2	387		13	
Motors, dynamos, generators, etc.	300	10	9		1				10			
Nails and spikes	225	7	7						7			
Needles, pins, hooks and eyes	303	341	232	68.0	108	31.7	1		85	25.0	256	75.0
Piling, rolled sheet	300	3	3						3			
Pipes and tubing	301	301	253	84.0	5	1.7	43	14.3	301			
Plumbers supplies and steam fittings	280	747	696	93.2	44	5.9	7	0.9	713		34	
Pulleys, hangers & bearings	300	2,246	1,916	85.3	321	14.3	9	0.6	2,158		88	
Pumps and valves	301	352	337	95.7	12		3		347		5	
Radiators	302	3	2		1		3		3			
Railroad supplies	271	632	582	92.0	50	8.0			632			
Safes, vaults and locks	287	169	131	77.5	38	22.5			169			
Saws	255	1,723	1,699	98.6	24	1.4			1,648		75	
Scales	307	137	62	45.2	75	54.8			137			
Scrap iron and steel	286	82	30	36.6	42	51.2	10	12.2	79		3	
Shafting, cold, rolled, drawn and turned	306	7	7						7			
Shapes, structural	251	377	206	54.6	135	35.80	36	9.5	377			
Shapes, other than iron & steel	303	817	719	88.0	97	12.0	1		817			
Sheets		61	56	91.8	5				61			
Shovels		91	84	92.3	7		2		91			
Silverware and plated ware		134	128	95.5	4				131		3	
Smelting and refining	287	17	4		10		3		17			
Springs	248	110	70	63.6	40	36.4			110			

Stoves, heaters and ranges	293	799	689	86.2	106	13.2	4		798		1	
Supplies, electrical	313	2,238	1,674	74.8	552	24.7	12	0.5	1,999		239	
Tin and terne plate	307	7	7						7			
Tinners' and roofers' supplies	299	151	116	76.8	35	23.2			151			
Typefounding	391	258	245	95.0	5	1.9	8	3.1	229		29	
Typewriters	300	5	3		2				5			
Ware, tin and stamped	284	927	592	63.9	329	35.5	6	0.6	780		147	
Ware, enamel and galvanized	288	148	82	55.4	66	44.6			148			
Watches, clocks, jewelry, etc.	290	698	633	90.7	64	9.2	1		610		88	
Wire products	286	821	687	83.7	134	16.3			662		159	
Garages making repairs	322	1,075	975	90.7	64	6.0	36	3.3	1,070		5	
Totals		53,494	40,366	75.5	12,060	22.5	1,068	2.0	51,526	96.3	1,968	3.7
13. Mines and quarries (0.1%)												
Clay	304	38	13				25		38			
Slate, other than roofing	304	10	4		6				10			
Stone	235	15	2		9		4		15			
Stone, cut	282	375	227	60.5	76	20.3	72	19.2	375			
Stone, crushed	292	9	7		2				9			
Coal, bituminous	300											
Totals		447	253	56.6	93	20.8	101	22.6	447	100.0		
14. Public service (10.7%)												
Repair shops	334	6,048	3,305	54.6	2,674	44.2	69	1.1	6,026		22	
Auto transit companies	365	137	111	81.0	14	10.2	12	8.8	137			
Canal and navigation companies	233	122	122	100.0					122			
Electric light, heat & power companies	357	1,837	1,545	84.1	252	13.7	40	2.2	1,836		1	
Gas companies	365	2,206	2,206	100.0					2,206			
Gas and electric companies	365	76	65	85.5	10	13.1	1	1.3	76			
Pipe line companies	365	14	14	100.0					14			
Municipal sewage treatment	365	7	5		2				7			

Appendix E (continued)

Nature of industry	Average days in operation	Average no. employees	American		Foreign		Black		Male		Female	
			No.	%	No.	%	No.	%	No.	%	No.	%
Steam heating companies	305	30	25		5				30			
Steam railroads	340	6,753	5,150	76.3	1,172	17.3	431	6.4	6,743		10	
Electric railway companies	351	9,308	9,271	99.6	35		2		9,239		69	
Telephone companies	360	7,132	7,039	98.7	91		2		3,010	42.2	4,122	57.8
Turnpike companies	365	14	14	100.0					8			
Water companies	365	25	18		6		1		25			
Totals		33,709	28,890	85.7	4,259	12.6	560	1.7	29,479	87.5	4,230	12.5
15. *Tobacco & its products* (1.9%)												
Chewing tobacco	300	1	1						1			
Cigars	282	5,781	2,753	47.6	2,767	47.9	261	4.5	1,508	26.1	4,273	73.9
Cigarettes	309	70	20	28.6	50	71.4			43	61.4	27	38.6
Totals		5,852	2,774	47.4	2,817	48.1	261	4.5	1,552	26.5	4,300	73.5
16. *Miscellaneous* (7.1%)												
Artificial flowers, feathers and plumes	292	727	597	82.1	129	17.7	1		76		651	
Awnings, tents and sails	268	81	81	100.0					61		20	
Asbestos products	305	14	14	100.0					14			
Baskets, rattan and willow ware	265	38	17	44.7	20	52.6	1		38			
Brooms	290	57	52		4		1		57			
Brushes	289	237	169	71.3	62	26.1	6		200		37	
Buttons	305	617	385	62.4	229	37.1	3		315		302	48.9
Caskets & undertakers' supplies	303	74	61		11		2		51		23	
Coke	15	50	40		10				50			

Industry												
Cork cutting	275	43	33		10				23		20	
Curled hair	291	359	116	32.3	242	67.4	1		293		66	
Engineering service	287	128	107	83.6	15	11.7	6		127		1	
Fancy articles & specialties	271	223	185	83.0	38	17.0			163		60	
Flags, banners, regalias, emblems, etc.	287	31	29		2				16		15	
Gold and silver leaf & foil	272	279	279	100.0					134	48.0	145	52.0
Hair work	308	114	91	79.8	21	18.4	2		59		55	
Hand stamps, stencils & brands	307	163	159	97.5	3		1		129		34	
Junk, paper, rags, etc.	294	59	16		38	64.0	5		38		21	
Laboratory service	302	73	61		11		1		55		18	
Mats and matting	168	191	191	100.0					109		82	
Mattresses and bedding	290	593	456	76.9	131	22.1	6		360	60.7	233	39.3
Musical instruments, not spec.	303	17	12		5				16		1	
Nursery products	330	128	66		53	41.4	9	0.7	128			
Oil cloth and linoleum	305	975	696	71.4	272	27.9	7		969		6	
Optical goods	305	514	496	96.5	13		5		369	71.8	145	28.2
Packing, steam, etc.	266	122	109	89.3	12		1		95		27	
Pens and pencils	299	123	117	95.1	6				58		65	
Photographic apparatus & supplies	299	457	438	95.8	18		1		360		97	
Pianos and organs	297	234	207	88.5	17		10		226		8	
Pipes, tobacco	300	153	110	71.9	43	28.1			146		7	
Plants and flowers	316	395	355	89.9	36		4		382		13	
Signs	300	207	195	94.2	10		2		197		10	
Soda water apparatus	274	192	167	87.0	22		3		190		2	
Sporting and athletic goods	295	701	676	96.4	24		1		394		307	
Surgical appliances and artificial limbs	302	428	392	91.6	35		1		268		160	
Teeth	299	594	572	96.3	18		4		274		320	
Toys and games	259	433	258	59.6	174	40.2	1		314		119	
Umbrellas and parasols	283	150	149	99.3	1				44		106	
Upholstering	302	203	144	70.9	52	25.6	7		169		34	

Appendix E (continued)

Nature of industry	Average days in operation	Average no. employees	American No.	%	Foreign No.	%	Black No.	%	Male No.	%	Female No.	%
Window shades and fixtures	294	118	102	86.4	15	12.7	1		95		23	
Miscellaneous industries	277	12,056	7,526	62.5	3,672	30.4	858	7.1	10,414		1,642	
Totals		22,351	15,926	71.2	5,474	24.5	951	4.3	17,476		4,875	
All industries: Totals (100.0%)		313,783	226,316	72.1	80,208	25.6	7,259	2.3	223,101	71.1	90,682	28.9

Appendix F

PENNSYLVANIA'S WAGE EARNERS, 1915, BY RACE, NATIONALITY AND SEX, ARRANGED BY INDUSTRY

Summary of industries	No. of establishments	Days in operation	American		Foreign		Black		Male		Female		Total
			No.	%	No.	%	No.	%	No.	%	No.	%	
1. Building and contracting	2,787	265	32,141	64.3	14,101	28.2	3,715	7.4	49,842	99.8	115	0.2	49,957
2. Chemicals and allied products	769	303	21,684	67.3	9,139	28.3	1,402	4.4	29,825	92.6	2,400	7.4	32,225
3. Clay, glass and stone products	882	278	35,610	58.7	23,337	38.5	1,724	2.8	57,973	95.6	2,698	4.4	60,671
4. Clothing manufacture	1,423	283	74,995	77.7	21,044	21.8	435	0.5	29,889	31.0	66,585	69.0	96,474
5. Food and kindred products	2,876	281	29,607	74.4	9,391	23.6	790	2.0	29,731	74.7	10,057	25.3	39,788
6. Leather and rubber goods	435	292	24,090	73.7	8,372	25.7	213	0.6	26,047	79.7	6,628	20.3	32,675
7. Liquors and beverages	614	261	7,998	87.2	1,141	12.4	36	0.4	8,996	98.0	179	2.0	9,175
8. Lumber and its remanufacture	1,267	276	28,046	82.5	5,635	16.6	305	0.9	32,728	96.3	1,258	3.7	33,986
9. Paper and printing industries	2,000	289	39,702	89.3	4,058	9.1	680	1.5	33,326	75.0	11,114	25.0	44,440
10. Textiles	927	275	82,860	80.2	20,284	19.6	146	0.1	47,684	46.2	55,606	53.8	103,290
11. Laundries	338	281	8,778	90.9	687	7.1	197	2.0	3,210	33.2	6,452	66.8	9,662
12. Metals and metal products	3,092	287	231,048	62.9	131,192	35.7	5,092	1.4	360,019	98.0	7,313	2.0	367,332
13. Mines and quarries	1,232	232	119,658	35.3	217,367	64.1	2,211	0.6	339,179	99.9	57	0.1	339,236
14. Public service	1,639	324	184,787	82.7	36,787	16.5	1,828	0.8	214,534	96.0	8,868	4.0	223,402
15. Tobacco and its products	948	276	24,855	71.6	9,433	27.2	419	1.2	12,121	35.0	22,586	65.0	34,707
16. Miscellaneous	1,130	286	21,388	81.7	4,513	17.2	267	1.0	19,774	75.6	6,394	24.4	26,168
Totals	22,359	281	967,247	64.3	516,481	34.4	19,460	1.3	1,294,878	86.1	208,310	13.9	1,503,188

Appendix F (continued)

Nature of industry	No. of establish-ments	Days in opera-tion	American No.	American %	Foreign No.	Foreign %	Black No.	Black %	Male No.	Male %	Female No.	Female %	Total
1. Building & contracting													
Brick, cement, stone work	192	231	1,964	58.9	739	22.2	630	18.9	3,330		3		3,333
Building construction	762	274	10,035	76.5	2,075	15.8	1,013	7.7	13,114		9		13,123
Electrical construction	174	292	1,219	99.1	10		1		1,222		8		1,230
Painting and decorating	109	297	1,207	92.3	90	6.9	10		1,282		25		1,307
Paving, road construction	66	208	1,550	33.0	2,516	53.7	623	13.3	4,689				4,689
Plumbing and heating	841	299	4,437	95.1	181	3.9	50		4,640		28		4,668
Railway construction	13	247	1,159	59.3	735	37.6	60		1,954				1,954
Roofing, sheet metal work	344	279	2,088	93.1	120	5.3	35		2,239		4		2,243
Structural iron work	17	271	811	72.5	277	24.8	30		1,115		3		1,118
Misc. contracting	269	253	7671	47.0	7,358	45.2	1,263	7.8	16,257		35		16,292
Totals	2,787	265	32,141	64.3	14,101	28.2	3,715	7.4	49,842	99.8	115	0.2	49,957
2. Chemicals, allied products													
Alcohol	2	313	10		11				21				21
Charcoal	4	314	41		10				51				51
Chemicals	44	300	3,197	54.7	2,469	42.3	175	3.0	5,267		574		5,841
Cleansing, polishing preparations	51	303	343	75.0	106	23.2	8		334		123		457
Dyestuffs & extracts	9	275	203	66.8	3		98	32.2	300		4		304
Fertilizers	27	283	405	49.7	303	37.2	107	13.1	815				815
Fireworks	1	305	1						1				1
Flavoring preparations	16	300	52		4				41		15		56
Glue & gelatin	5	304	103	26.3	286	73.0	3		369		23		392
Graphite, graphite refining	7	300	34		19		12		65				65
Grease & tallow	38	305	554	39.5	326	23.3	522	37.2	1,384		18		1,402
Ink-printing	8	303	95		19		29		143				143

Ink-writing	5	302	13						6		7		13
Malt & yeast	1	312	4						3		1		4
Matches	2	240	157						74		83		157
Mucilage & paste	7	303	73				5		57		21		78
Oils, crude	68	339	1,369	99.9	2				1,370		1		1,371
Oils, linseed	1	356	5		1				6				6
Oils, lubricating	15	396	188		16		7		210		1		211
Oils, refined-kerosene	63	332	4,758	72.8	1,621	24.8	160	2.4	6,513		26		6,539
Oils, not specified	23	303	408	67.4	121	20.0	76	12.6	597		8		605
Paints & varnishes	104	294	1,463	65.6	711	31.9	57	2.5	2,150		81		2,231
Patent & proprietary medicines	80	284	1,493	95.6	30		38		874	56.0	687	44.0	1,561
Powder, other explosives	44	228	2,755	78.1	764	21.7	8		3,188	91.4	339	9.6	3,527
Soap	43	291	938	89.3	68	6.5	44	4.2	914	87.0	136	13.0	1,050
Sulphuric, nitric & mixed acids	14	307	1,398	48.4	1,446	50.1	44		2,762		126		2,888
Tar	1	342	1		1				2				2
Toilet preparations	14	307	112		2		2		33	28.8	83	71.2	116
Wood alcohol, acetate of lime	45	341	976	63.7	557	36.30			1,533				1,533
Chemicals, unclassified	27	316	535	68.2	243	30.0	7		742		43		785
Totals	769	303	21,684	67.3	9,139	28.3	1,402	4.4	29,825	92.6	2,400	7.4	32,225

3. Clay, glass & stone products

Artificial stone	42	219	199	73.2	58	21.3	15	5.5	272				272
Brick	210	234	6,716	64.0	3,232	30.8	541	5.2	10,478		11		10,489
Cement	19	320	2,525	31.0	5,592	68.7	22		8,132		7		8,139
Crucibles	4	278	42	36.8	55	48.2	17	15.0	114				114
Emery, other abrasive wheels	6	297	94	65.3	50	34.7			133		11		144
Glass bottles	45	267	5,167	77.4	1,397	20.9	108		6,270		402		6,672
Glass, cut	37	257	2,825	87.7	395	12.2	3		2,779	86.2	444	13.8	3,223
Glass, decorative	53	295	1,199	80.9	278	18.6	5		1,210	81.6	272	18.4	1,482
Glass, plate	11	243	1,525	36.2	2,664	63.3	22		4,181		30		4,211
Glass, tableware	16	281	2,698	80.9	625	18.6	10		2,728	77.8	605	22.2	3,333

Appendix F (continued)

Nature of industry	No. of establish-ments	Days in opera-tion	American No.	American %	Foreign No.	Foreign %	Black No.	Black %	Male No.	Male %	Female No.	Female %	Total
Glass, window	22	300	3,517	61.0	2,138	37.1	112	2.0	5,765		2		5,767
Grindstones	3	304	13		18				31				31
Lamps and chimneys	12	278	1,403	53.2	1,224	46.4	12		2,078	78.8	561	21.2	2,639
Lime	42	289	1,187	39.2	1,590	52.5	249	8.2	3,026				3,026
Mantles and tile	24	301	334	54.7	265	43.4	12		524		87		611
Marble & granite work	229	282	1,277	80.5	297	18.7	13		1,583		4		1,587
Mirrors	9	275	176		35				204		7		211
Paving materials	12	252	274	44.3	238	38.4	108	17.4	620				620
Pottery, terra cotta & fire clay products	66	301	4,191	54.0	3,137	40.44	429	5.5	7,512		245		7,757
Wall plaster	14	277	155	68.9	34	15.1	36	16.0	2		3		225
Clay, glass & stone products, unclass.	6	289	93	78.8	15	12.7	10	8.5	111		7		118
Totals	882	278	35,610	58.7	23,337	38.5	1,724	2.8	57,973	95.6	2,698	4.4	60,671
4. Clothing manufacture													
Clothing, men	200	291	4,699	63.0	2,693	36.1	62		3,585	48.1	3,869	51.9	7,454
Clothing, women, children	233	281	7,967	48.7	8,271	50.6	117		5,830	35.6	10,525	64.4	16,355
Corsets	6	302	475	93.5	32		1		75	14.8	433	85.2	508
Fur goods	39	242	197	71.9	61	22.3	16	5.8	161	58.8	113	41.2	274
Furnishing goods, not spec.	8	290	467	89.1	57	10.9			106	20.2	418	79.8	524
Gloves, other than leather	17	288	1,116	98.6	16				222	19.6	910	80.4	1,132
Hats, caps, other than straw	60	269	5,820	81.0	1,357	18.9	4		5,344	74.4	1,837	25.6	7,181
Hats, straw	3	288	58						26		32		58
Hosiery & knit goods	296	264	28,434	90.4	2,974	9.4	48		7,397	23.5	24,059	76.5	31,456
Ladies skirts	31	336	455	54.6	367	44.0	12		413	49.5	421	50.5	834
Millinery	47	279	5,172	90.9	442	7.8	78	1.3	1,794	31.5	3,898	68.5	5,692
Neckwear	20	295	589	87.3	86	12.7			355	52.6	320	47.4	675

Overalls	21	256	628	85.0	110	15.0			114	15.5	624	84.5	738
Shirts	147	265	7,473	80.3	1,816	19.5	15		1,721	18.5	7,583	81.5	9,304
Shirt waists	53	292	1,923	51.0	1,809	48.0	37	1.0	495	13.1	3,274	86.9	3,769
Suspenders	9	279	72	34.8	135	65.2			83	40.0	124	60.0	207
Underwear	132	282	8,664	93.3	617	6.6	4		1,649	17.8	7,636	82.2	9,285
Clothing manufacture, misc.	101	301	786	76.4	201	19.6	41		519	50.5	509	49.5	1,028
Totals	1,423	283	74,995	77.7	21,044	21.8	435	0.5	29,889	31.0	66,585	69.0	96,474
5. Food & kindred products													
Baking powder	5	332	11		1				8		4		12
Bread, bakery products	1,611	307	10,648	77.9	2,733	20.0	293		11,055	80.8	2,619	19.2	13,674
Butter, cheese, condensed milk	165	327	1,703	90.3	159	8.4	24		1,756		130		1,886
Canned, preserved goods	59	208	2,290	68.1	1,048	31.2	23		1,736	51.7	1,625	48.3	3,361
Chocolate, cocoa products	6	281	1,510	86.9	222	12.8	6		1,092	62.8	646	37.2	1,738
Coffee, spices, roasting, etc.	21	289	436	98.9	3		2		251	56.9	190	43.1	441
Confectionary	184	267	5,347	79.6	1,300	19.4	66		2,564	38.2	4,149	61.8	6,713
Cordials & syrups	1	155	1		1				2				2
Flour, grist mill products	393	363	1,780	93.4	79	4.1	46	2.4	1,888		17		1,905
Glucose & starch	2	225	11						6		5		11
Ice	137	272	1,615	69.7	602	26.0	101	4.3	2,290		28		2,318
Ice Cream	6	308	1,406	78.8	255	14.3	123	6.9	1,508	84.5	276	15.5	1,784
Molasses			104	84.6	18	14.6	1		82	66.7	41	33.3	123
Slaughtering, meat packing	80	286	2,016	55.2	1,562	42.8	74	2.0	3,545		107		3,652
Sugar refining	3	297	518	27.3	1,371	72.3	7		1,781		115		1,896
Vinegar & cider	10	285	44		15				58		1		59
Food & kindred products misc.	13	266	167	78.4	22	10.3	24	11.3	109	51.2	104	48.8	213
Totals	2,876	281	29,607	74.4	9,391	23.6	790	2.0	29,731	74.7	10,057	25.3	39,788
6. Leather & rubber goods													
Belting & hose	20	302	361	73.1	97	19.6	36	7.3	409		85		494
Boots & shoes	119	279	11,703	89.0	1,424	10.8	15		8,287	63.0	4,855	37.0	13,142
Gloves, leather	2	292	52		1				20		33		53

197

Appendix F (continued)

Nature of industry	No. of establish-ments	Days in opera-tion	American No.	%	Foreign No.	%	Black No.	%	Male No.	%	Female No.	%	Total
Hides & skins	12	300	34		12		4		50				50
Leather, sole	41	298	3,270	58.6	2,305	41.3	4		5,525		54		5,579
Leather, tanned, curried, & finished	50	286	3,752	55.1	3,020	44.3	32		6,381		423		6,804
Leather goods	91	288	1,793	87.5	252	12.3	5		1,299	63.4	751	36.6	2,050
Rubber goods, not spec.	22	283	2,533	75.1	734	21.8	107	3.1	3,032	89.9	342	10.1	3,374
Trunks & suitcases	35	297	365	42.2	494	57.1	6		817		48		865
Leather & rubber goods, misc.	43	299	227	86.0	33	12.5	4		227	86.0	37	14.0	264
Totals	435	292	24,090	73.7	8,372	25.7	213	0.6	26,047	79.7	6,628	20.3	32,675
7. Liquors & beverages													
Carbonated beverages	214	282	664	88.8	72	9.6	12	1.6	725		23		748
Liquors, distilled	35	122	511	90.6	49	8.8	4		443	78.5	121	21.5	564
Liquors, malt	234	305	6,195	86.6	945	13.2	13		7,139		14		7,153
Table waters	19	302	116		8		4		122		6		128
Liquors & beverages, misc.	112	298	512		67		3		567		15		582
Totals	614	261	7,998	87.2	1,141	12.4	36	0.4	8,996	98.0	179	2.0	9,175
8. Lumber & its remanufacture													
Barrels, kegs & tanks	33	269	741	76.5	217	22.4	10		968				968
Billiard tables, supplies	4	300	32		11		4		46		1		47
Bobbins & spools	8	287	279	61.9	172	38.1			439		12		451
Boxes, cigar	54	259	1,436	99.0	15				696	48.0	755	52.0	1,451
Boxes, packing	46	291	1,290	80.5	288	18.0	25		1,593		10		1,603
Carriages, wagons, parts	242	291	2,518	92.3	208	7.6	3		2,719		10		2,729
Children's carriages, sleds	10	275	434	70.9	177	28.9	1		565		47		612
Cooperage, etc.	27	253	644	72.0	247	27.6	3		893		1		894

Furniture	212	284	7,881	79.0	2,065	20.7	35		9,868		113		9,981
Lasts	4	302	82						82				82
Lumber, timber products	116	215	2,624	76.7	764	22.3	31		3,408		11		3,419
Models, patterns, not paper	42	288	250	96.1	9		1		260				260
Planing mill products	306	286	7,376	86.1	1,004	11.7	182		8,447		115		8,562
Refrigerators, ice boxes	10	304	410	75.2	133	24.4	2		535		10		545
Washing machines, wringers	10	254	490	90.6	50	9.2	1		501		40		541
Wood, turned, carved	81	275	966	84.4	175	15.3	.3		1,037		107		1,144
Wood novelties	16	269	290	100.0					271		19		290
Lumber, manufacture, misc.	46	263	303	74.4	100	24.6	4		400		7		407
Totals	1,267	276	28,046	82.5	5,635	16.6	305	0.9	32,728	96.3	1,258	3.7	33,986

9. Paper & printing industries

Bags, paper	10	273	213	99.0	2				113	33.0	102	67.0	215
Boxes, fancy & paper	123	287	4,539	89.0	481	9.4	80		1,679	32.9	3,421	67.1	5,100
Card cutting, designing	15	303	200	84.4	35	14.8	2		178	75.1	59	24.9	237
Electroplating, engraving & dye sinking	59	292	1,039	98.5	15		1		716		339		1,055
Labels & tags	12	302	410	91.5	25	5.6	13	2.9	231	51.6	217	48.4	448
Paper goods, not specified	66	285	5,164	71.6	1,913	26.5	132		6,200	86.0	1,009	14.0	7,209
Photo engraving	21	313	517	93.8	27	4.9	7		532		19		551
Printing, publishing	1,556	299	22,794	96.3	500		383		19,271	81.4	4,406	18.6	23,677
Pulp goods	3		287	39.7	433	60.0	3		641		82		723
Roofing paper	13	257	597	61.5	354	36.5	19		970				970
Sand, emery paper, cloth	3		97	89.8	11				92		16		108
Stationery goods, not spec.	34	301	1,520	98.0	28		3		727	46.9	824	53.1	1,551
Stereotyping, electrotyping	12	279	291	96.0	2		10		296		7		303
Wall paper	17	287	1,207	90.2	113	8.4	18		1,143	85.4	195	14.6	1,338
Paper & printing industries, misc.	56	286	827	86.6	119	12.5	9		537	56.2	418	43.8	955
Totals	2,000	289	39,702	89.3	4,058	9.1	680	1.5	33,326	75.0	11,114	25.0	44,440

10. Textiles

Bags, other than paper	7	305	253	100.0					62	24.5	191	75.5	253

Appendix F (continued)

Nature of industry	No. of establishments	Days in operation	American No.	%	Foreign No.	%	Black No.	%	Male No.	%	Female No.	%	Total
Blankets, flannels, etc.	22	247	1,423	86.7	202	12.3	17		1,006	61.3	636	38.7	1,642
Braids, tapes, bindings	37	291	2,275	92.7	178	7.2	1		781	31.8	1,673	68.2	2,454
Carpets, rugs	57	278	4,755	86.7	726	13.2	4		3,617	65.9	1,868	34.1	5,485
Cordage, twine, jute and linen goods	19	243	904	51.4	843	47.9	12		960	54.6	799	45.4	1,759
Cotton goods	58	281	4,784	86.7	723	13.1	12		3,167	57.4	2,352	42.6	5,519
Curtains	16	287	2,084	86.1	334	13.8	1		1,012	41.8	1,407	58.2	2,419
Dyeing, finishing textiles	104	280	5,621	78.6	1,508	21.1	22		5,911	82.7	1,240	17.3	7,151
Haircloth	13	277	294	93.6	20	6.4			164	52.2	150	47.8	314
Hammocks	2	190	125	100.0					71	56.8	54	43.2	125
Handkerchiefs, embroideries	42	299	2,626	88.7	330	11.2	3		1,749	59.1	1,210	40.9	2,959
Horse blankets, robes	4	292	262	81.1	61	18.9			198	61.3	125	38.7	323
Shoddy	7	300	115	63.2	61	33.5	6		135	74.2	47	25.8	182
Silk, silk goods, throwsters	258	281	34,847	80.9	8,225	19.0	22		14,925	34.6	28,169	65.4	43,094
Thread	9	279	1,016	94.3	61	5.7			354	32.9	723	67.1	1,077
Towels	15	277	1,095	97.6	27	2.4			462	41.2	660	58.8	1,122
Waste	26	259	435	80.7	103	19.1	1		439	81.4	100	18.6	539
Wool pulling	7	268	62	26.3	173	73.3	1		230	97.5	6	2.5	236
Woolen, worsted, felt goods	65	285	6,962	79.8	1,754	20.1	6		4,723	54.2	3,999	45.8	8,722
Yarns	99	260	11,194	70.4	4,690	29.5	16		6,347	39.9	9,553	60.1	15,900
Textiles, misc.	60	290	1,728	85.8	265	13.2	22		1,371	68.0	644	32.0	2,015
Totals	927	275	82,860	80.2	20,284	19.6	146	0.1	47,684	46.2	55,606	53.8	103,290
11. Laundries													
Laundry work	338	281	8,778	90.9	687	7.1	197	2.0	3,210	33.2	6,452	66.8	9,662

12. Metals, metal products

Agricultural implements, machinery	32	276	1,650	96.1	46	37.2	21		1,712		5		1,717
Aluminum, its products	6	284	1,738	62.5	1,035	17.2	6		2,709		70		2,779
Automobiles, parts	69	295	5,469	82.4	1,143	17.2	28		6,584		56		6,640
Axes, edge tools	14	256	555	57.2	414	42.6	2		926		45		971
Axles	8	281	1,538	66.2	785	33.8			2,323				2,323
Babbit metal & solder	11	306	163	90.1	17	9.4	1		179		2		181
Bars, lead, lead sheets	4	243	56	26.8	96	45.9	57	27.2	209				209
Bars, iron, steel	38	269	13,846	50.0	13,540	48.9	311		27,625		72		27,697
Beds, bedsprings	14	272	460	60.6	295	38.9	4		700		59		759
Bicycles, motorcycles, parts	3	298	177	96.7	6				183				183
Billets, blooms, slabs	7	305	3,653	42.0	4,570	52.5	477	5.4	8,700				8,700
Boilers, tanks, stacks	79	325	4,662	73.9	1,593	25.3	52		6,305		2		6,307
Bolts, nuts, rivets	27	273	5,612	63.8	3,087	35.1	93		8,392		400		8,792
Brass, bronze products	106	287	8,248	75.7	2,607	24.0	38		10,854		39		10,893
Cars, car wheels	25	281	12,322	65.5	6,398	34.0	87		18,766		41		18,807
Castings, iron, steel	191	279	11,224	54.9	8,705	42.6	523	2.5	20,262		190		20,452
Chains	16	273	1,086	79.5	276	20.2	4		1,358		8		1,366
Cornices, ceilings, ventilators, etc.	30	286	284	85.8	43	13.0	4		331				331
Cutlery	11	273	347	87.6	48	12.1	1		369				396
Elevators, hoists	26	296	1,028	86.2	159	13.3	6		1,192		1		1,193
Engines, gas, gasoline	26	288	2,041	89.4	238	10.4	3		2,280		2		2,282
Engines, railroad	9	256	8,869	78.8	2,383	21.2	4		11,215		41		11,256
Engines, stationary	14	283	806	93.9	51	5.9	1		857		1		858
Engines, traction	4	296	330	98.5	5	1.5			335				335
Ferro alloys	10	292	667	33.0	1,208	59.8	146	7.2	2,019		2		2,021
Files	7	287	823	66.4	416	33.5	1		1,001	80.7	239	19.3	1,240
Fire escapes	3	305	46		19				65				65
Fire arms and ammunition	4	304	8,415	54.1	7,102	45.6	45		15,263		299		15,562
Fixtures, gas & electric	48	306	1,000	78.2	269	21.0	10		1,015		264		1,279

Appendix F (continued)

Nature of industry	No. of establish-ments	Days in opera-tion	American No.	%	Foreign No.	%	Black No.	%	Male No.	%	Female No.	%	Total
Forgings, iron and steel	35	290	4,262	58.7	2,282	31.4	713	9.8	7,251		6		7,257
Frogs and switches	5	298	752	68.4	346	31.5	1		1,095		4		1,099
Hardware & specialties	122	279	5,325	76.9	1,583	22.9	13		6,158		763		6,921
Hoops, bands & cotton ties	8	311	1,407	31.2	2,945	65.3	161		4,513				4,513
Horse shoes	3	309	740	69.5	323	30.4	1		1,064				1,064
Ingots, iron and steel	11	333	18,500	49.9	18,113	48.8	477	1.3	37,058		32		37,090
Iron, pig	38	276	4,639	45.0	5,350	52.0	304	3.0	10,259		34		10,293
Iron & steel work, orn.	7	251	74	60.7	46	37.7	2		122				122
Instruments, prof., sci.	45	289	1,110	86.5	165	12.9	8		1,204		79		1,283
Machinery and parts	266	287	15,626	85.4	2,576	14.1	91		18,210		83		18,293
Machine repair shops	199	287	2,542	94.0	159	5.9	2		2,695		8		2,703
Machine tools	44	289	2,515	87.0	354	12.2	22		2,883		8		2,891
Meters	12	304	945	87.5	131	12.1	4		1,050		30		1,080
Motors, dynamos, generators	14	244	6,115	55.6	4,830	43.9	61		9,936		1,070		11,006
Nails and spikes	11	280	749		362	32.1	18		1,096		33		1,129
Needles, pins, hooks, eyes	5	293	256	69.4	111	30.0	2		102	27.6	267	72.5	369
Piling, rolled sheet	1	305	3						3				3
Pipes and tubing	39	285	9,286	48.3	9,633	50.1	317	1.6	19,126		110		19,236
Plates, iron & steel	8	298	1,020	68.9	364	24.6	96	6.5	1,480				1,480
Plumbers' supplies	48	291	2,228	63.8	1,251	35.8	14		3,377		116		3,493
Pulleys, hangers, bearings	23	292	2,663	87.9	358	11.8	10		2,943		88		3,031
Pumps and valves	23	292	1,116	94.9	56	4.8	4		1,171		5		1,176
Rails, iron and steel	1	303	175	70.0	75	30.0			250				250
Radiators	9	272	534	61.4	329	37.9	6		869				869
Railroad supplies	18	264	3,932	70.4	1,651	29.5	5		5,510		78		5,588
Rods, steel, in coils	3	304	170	53.5	144	45.3	4		318				318

Safes, vaults & locks	11	293	927	95.8	38		3		952		16		968
Saws	14	296	1,881	97.6	47				1,843		85		1,928
Scales	5	250	213	69.4	94	30.6			307				307
Scrap iron & steel	59	295	424	43.5	478	49.1	72	7.4	929		45		974
Shafting, cold rolled, drawn & turned	8	302	1,349	54.7	1,116	45.2	2		2,467				2,467
Shapes, structural	42	295	4,498	55.8	3,458	42.9	111	1.4	8,067		1		8,067
Shapes, other iron & steel	54	293	1,550	59.6	1,043	40.1	9		2,601				2,602
Sheets	15	295	6,376	87.7	880	12.1	18		7,274				7,274
Shovels, scoops, spades	10	262	499	70.4	210	29.6			709				709
Silverware, plated ware	14	292	152	95.0	6	3.8	2		154		6		160
Smelting and refining	7	300	51	41.1	70	56.5	3		124				124
Springs	14	272	508	51.2	484	48.7	1		987		6		993
Stoves, heaters, ranges	75	269	4,455	91.0	421	8.6	19		4,874		21		4,895
Supplies, electrical	50	292	3,382	80.0	832	19.7	16		3,354	79.3	876	20.7	4,230
Tin & terne plate	8	274	7,456	83.3	1,438	16.1	59		8,668		285		8,953
Tinners' & roofers' supplies	8	300	125	77.6	36	22.4	0		161				161
Typefounding	9	304	245	95.0	5		8		229		29		258
Typewriters	2	300	489	99.2	4				473		20		493
Ware, tin & stamped	66	285	1,585	69.4	685	30.0	13		1,763	77.2	520	22.8	2,283
Ware, enamel, galvanized	16	237	1,693	47.5	1,843	51.8	25		3,428		133		3,561
Watches, clocks, jewelry etc.	66	292	1,400	94.4	82	5.5	1		1,359		124		1,483
Wire products	71	272	4,482	39.4	6,531	57.3	374		10,992		395		11,387
Garages, making repairs	515	323	2,802	93.5	105	3.5	90		2,976		21		2,997
Metals & metal products, misc.	83	291	707	77.9	195	21.5	5		856		51		907
Totals	3,092	287	231,048	62.9	131,192	35.7	5,092	1.4	360,019	98.0	7,313	2.0	367,332
13. Mines & Quarries													
Clay	16	235	274	83.0	24	7.2	32	9.7	330				330
Ore, iron	3	255	144	52.4	126	45.8	5		275				275

203

Appendix F (continued)

Nature of industry	No. of establish-ments	Days in opera-tion	American No.	%	Foreign No.	%	Black No.	%	Male No.	%	Female No.	%	Total
Sand & gravel	62	225	1,155	68.8	466	27.8	58		1,651		28		1,679
Slate, roofing	51	232	2,180	81.0	506	18.8	6		2,692				2,692
Slate, other than roofing	29	252	905	78.9	230	20.0	12		1,118		29		1,147
Stone	41	230	831	24.0	2,604	75.3	22		3,457				3,457
Stone, cut	30	262	469	56.8	225	27.2	132	16.0	826				826
Stone, crushed	70	205	1,092	44.3	1,292	52.4	82		2,466				2,466
Coal, anthracite	125	224	56,612	35.6	102,498	64.4	60		159,170				159,170
Coal, bituminous	672	218	49,429	32.1	102,819	66.9	1,505	1.0	153,753				153,753
Coke	125	213	6,508	48.8	6,540	49.0	297	2.2	13,345				13,345
Mines & quarries, misc.	8	229	59		37				96				96
Total	1,232	232	119,658	35.3	217,367	64.1	2,211	0.6	339,179	99.9	57	0.1	339,236
14. Public service													
Repair shops	136	342	36,198	62.9	21,122	36.7	227		57,412		135		57,547
Auto transit companies	4	333	150		14		12		176				176
Canal, navigation companies	4	252	135						135				135
Electric light, heat & power companies	181	356	5,361	90.0	545	9.2	49		5,947		8		5,955
Ferry companies	25	308	111	84.7			20	15.3	128		3		131
Gas companies	70	352	3,152	90.3	311	8.9	26		3,485		4		3,489
Gas companies, natural	125	342	4,750	85.7	791	14.2	3		5,493		51		5,544
Gas & electric companies	14	360	964	90.0	101	9.4	6		1,042		29		1,071
Inclined plane companies	6	297	72		2				74				74
Pipe line companies	14	316	940	98.9	7		3		944		6		950
Municipal sewage treatment works	12	354	32		2		3		37				37

Steam heating companies	12	285	98	83.0	20	17.0			118		105		118
Steam railroads	181	340	96,854	89.7	9,872	9.1	1,213	1.1	107,834		84		107,939
Electric railway companies	110	352	20,550	87.3	2,870	12.2	131		23,467				23,551
Telephone companies	278	351	13,345	98.8	151		8		5,165	38.2	8,339	61.8	13,504
Toll bridge companies	28	340	51						49		2		51
Turnpike companies	82	355	402		17		2		394		27		421
Water companies	355	346	1,388	60.5	897	39.1	10		2,288		7		2,295
Public service, misc.	2	187	234	56.5	65	15.7	115	27.8	346		68		414
Totals	1,639	324	184,787	82.7	36,787	16.5	1,828	0.8	214,534	96.0	8,868	4.0	223,402
15. Tobacco & its products													
Cheroots & stogies	53	275	1,229	73.8	395	23.7	41		375	22.5	1,290	77.5	1,565
Chewing tobacco	8	297	166	100.0					59	35.5	107	64.5	166
Cigars	851	262	22,903	71.3	8,902	27.7	329		11,409	35.5	20,725	64.5	32,134
Cigarettes	1	309	20	28.6	50	71.4			43	61.4	27	38.6	70
Smoking tobacco	13	256	156	88.6	20	11.4			58	33.0	118	67.0	176
Tobacco & its products, misc.	22	256	381		66		49		177		319		496
Totals	948	276	24,855	71.6	9,433	27.2	419	1.2	12,121	35.0	22,586	65.0	34,707
16. Miscellaneous													
Artificial flowers, feathers & plumes	16	299	657	83.5	129	16.4	1		96	12.2	691	87.8	787
Awnings, tents, sails	25	249	130	99.2			1		85	64.9	46	35.1	131
Asbestos products	14	298	985	47.9	1,007	49.0	65	3.2	1,928	93.7	129	6.3	2,057
Baskets, rattan & willow ware	16	286	110	75.3	35	24.0	1		132	89.0	14	11.0	146
Brooms	42	265	448	95.3	21	4.5	1		451	96.0	19	4.0	470
Brushes	36	276	411	85.4	64	13.3	6		428	89.0	53	11.0	481
Buttons	19	293	447	65.7	230	33.8	3		355	52.2	325	47.8	680
Caskets, undertakers' supplies	29	295	1,236	96.9	37		2		1,027	80.5	248	19.5	1,275

Appendix F (continued)

Nature of industry	No. of establish-ments	Days in opera-tion	American No.	%	Foreign No.	%	Black No.	%	Male No.	%	Female No.	%	Total
Cork cutting	8	279	1,266	84.7	210	14.0	18		931	62.3	563	37.7	1,494
Curled hair	5	291	116	32.3	242	67.4	1		293	81.6	66	18.4	359
Engineering service	16	289	171	73.7	55	23.7	6		231		1		232
Fancy articles, specialties	12	277	189	83.3	38	16.7			167	73.6	60	26.4	227
Flags, banners, regalia, emblems, etc.	21	284	190	99.0	2				74	38.5	118	61.5	192
Fuel, manufactured	7	267	163	62.5	98	37.5			189	72.4	72	27.6	261
Gold & silver leaf, foil	6	272	279	100.0					134	48.0	145	52.0	279
Hair work	18	308	113	83.1	21	15.4	2		65	47.8	71	52.2	136
Hand stamps, stencils, brands	32	308	276	96.8	6		3		244	85.6	41	14.4	285
Housefurnishing goods, not specified	1	268	141	100.0					135		6		141
Junk, paper, rags, etc.	25	294	95	58.6	60	37.0	7		104	64.2	58	35.8	162
Laboratory service	17	302	123	90.4	12	8.8	1		98	72.1	38	27.9	136
Mats & matting	5	222	210	94.6	6	2.7	6	2.7	140	63.1	82	36.9	222
Mattresses & bedding	47	278	815	78.1	213	20.4	15		704	67.5	339	32.5	1,043
Musical instruments, not specified	8	301	60		5				64		1		65
Nursery products	22	293	415	66.0	194	30.8	20	3.2	616		13		629
Oil cloth & linoleum	5	304	1,576	80.4	376	19.2	8		1,931		29		1,960
Optical goods	50	304	1,081	94.3	55	4.8	10		730	63.7	416	26.3	1,146
Packing, steam, etc.	13	271	98	88.3	12	10.8	1		104		7		111
Pens & pencils	7	276	191	91.4	18	8.6			107	51.2	102	48.8	209
Photographic apparatus, supplies	11	299	499	96.3	18		1		385	74.3	133	25.7	518
Pianos and organs	23	298	658	87.3	86	11.4	10		719		35		754
Pipes, tobacco	2	293	110	71.9	43	28.1			146		7		153
Plants & flowers	342	329	1,806	86.4	243	11.6	42	2.0	1,914	91.5	177	8.5	2,091
Signs	41	287	448	62.7	265	37.1	2		605	71.5	110	28.5	715
Ship & boat building	9	271	249	89.2	28	10.3	2		279				279

Soda water apparatus	5	276	200	87.0	27	11.7	3		225		5		230
Sporting & athletic goods	9	295	757	96.6	26	3.3	1		477	60.8	307	39.2	784
Statuary & art goods	2	300	4		2				5		1		6
Surgical appliances, artificial limbs	26	301	469	91.6	42	8.2	1		321	62.7	191	37.3	512
Teeth	9	300	1,308	98.3	18		4		461	34.7	869	65.3	1,330
Toys & games	13	281	538	74.0	187	25.7	2		539	74.1	188	25.9	727
Umbrellas & parasols	16	272	532	98.9	4		2		253	47.0	285	53.0	538
Upholstering	51	295	260	72.6	90	25.1	8		293	81.8	65	19.2	358
Wheelbarrows	2	279	25						25				25
Window shades, fixtures	12	278	119	88.1	15	11.1	1		106	78.5	29	21.5	135
Oil well supplies	22	291	968	79.8	242	20.0	3		1,211		2		1,213
Miscellaneous	22	274	446	92.1	31	6.4	7		247	51.0	237	49.0	484
Totals	1,130	286	21,388	81.7	4,513	17.2	267	1.0	19,774	75.6	6,394	24.4	26,168

207

Appendix G

ARRIVALS OF IMMIGRANTS AT THE PRINCIPAL PORTS OF THE UNITED STATES FROM FOREIGN COUNTRIES, 1884–1919

Year ending June 30	Boston	New York	Philadelphia	Baltimore	San Francisco	All other ports	Total U.S.
1884	35,036	354,702	18,931	35,507	1,735	70,602	518,592
1885	25,660	287,228	22,482	15,928	1,118	40,546	395,346
1886	25,046	266,370	20,822	13,500	1,428	4,610	334,203
1887	36,209	376,005	31,048	36,098	7,726	4,427	490,109
1888	44,873	418,423	37,325	33,297	2,935	5,600	546,880
1889	35,198	338,784	28,100	29,704	3,127	4,969	444,427
1890	29,813	364,086	22,658	27,178	3,606	5,479	455,302
1891	30,951	448,403	26,152	40,694	5,332	5,486	560,319
1892	32,343	489,810	31,102	55,820	6,425	6,446	623,084
1893	29,583	404,337	28,906	26,183	5,383	5,932	502,917
1894	17,558	253,580	19,861	13,425	5,743	3,058	314,467
1895	20,472	219,006	25,362	7,081	1,840	3,037	279,948
1896	21,846	263,709	24,977	13,374	1,411	17,950	343,267
1897	13,333	180,556	10,930	6,215	1,629	18,169	230,832
1898	12,271	178,748	8,360	10,735	2,274	16,911	229,299
1899	19,227	242,573	9,971	14,652	4,766	20,526	311,715
1900	15,754	341,712	16,134	27,564	5,165	42,243	448,572
1901	25,616	388,931	13,236	17,216	3,655	39,254	487,918
1902	39,465	493,262	17,175	39,679	5,271	53,891	648,743
1903	62,838	631,885	27,760	55,806	7,256	71,505	857,046
1904	60,278	606,010	19,467	55,940	9,036	62,130	812,870
1905	65,107	788,219	23,824	62,314	6,377	80,658	1,026,499
1906	62,229	880,036	23,186	54,064	4,138	77,082	1,100,735
1907	70,164	1,004,756	30,501	66,910	3,539	109,479	1,285,349

Year							
1908	41,363	585,970	16,458	31,489	3,608	103,982	782,870
1909	36,318	580,617	14,294	18,966	3,103		751,786
1910	53,617	786,094	37,641	30,563	4,233		1,041,570
1911	45,865	637,003	45,023	22,866	3,419		878,587
1912	38,782	605,151	43,749	21,667	3,958		838,172
1913	54,740	892,653	50,466	32,833	5,554		1,197,892
1914	69,365	878,052	56,857	39,048	6,716		1,218,480
1915	15,983	178,416	7,114	3,017	8,055		326,700
1916	12,428	141,390	229	124	7,955		298,826
1917	11,828	129,446	274	231	7,269		295,403
1918	3,392	28,867	386	268	9,812		110,618
1919	374	26,731	333	260	9,121		141,132
Total							21,130,475

SOURCE: United States Department of Labor, *Reports of the Commissioner General of Immigration, 1884–1919.*

Appendix H

NATIONALITIES OF IMMIGRANTS ARRIVING IN THE UNITED STATES THROUGH THE PORT OF PHILADELPHIA, 1880–1894

	1880	1881	1882	1883	1884	1885	1886	1887	1888	1889	1890	1891	1892	1894
Bohemia			5								41	49		50
Hungary	220	75	27	175	270	108	107	105	99	92	269	573	853	1,418
Other Austria except Poland	72	272	638	407	346	108	360	112	169	136	338	599	1,360	988
Belgium	201	258	94	87	25	77	26	273	342	143	199	217	537	455
Bulgaria														1
Denmark	286	329	435	120	149	116	206	111	130	327	395	481	358	93
France	81	442	103	252	63	52	62	185	188	314	86	76	156	51
Germany	3,686	11,192	9,278	3,288	2,661	2,913	1,744	5,084	5,353	4,580	3,619	5,494	8,368	4,344
Gibralter	5													
England	6,013	7,096	9,482	7,721	6,069	7,767	7,034	10,322	12,048	7,304	4,692	3,860	4,106	2,962
Scotland	132	142	135	223	187	1,129	1,278	1,593	3,435	2,207	1,000	804	595	196
Ireland	5,046	5,106	4,878	5,394	4,457	5,209	4,771	7,056	8,712	6,863	5,374	5,231	4,393	3,796
Wales	73	128	122	143	23	94	97	167	355	336	92	52	68	228
Great Britain, n.s.					63							1		
Greece		3	2	4		10	1		2	59	337	102	10	11
Italy	784	776	185	159	36	80	223	90	88	81	92	44	104	44
Sicily														
Malta														
Netherlands	80	419	111	84	17	80	19	16	138	27	28	16	235	133
Norway	2,011	2,957	2,872	1,566	1,659	1,234	900	980	1,258	1,344	1,005	947	877	344
Poland	260	911	1,467	824	420	694	758	1,494	1,381	1,284	1,676	2,303	2,797	658
Portugal		4	1			1	7						3	
Roumania		541				11				18	12	26	13	60

Russia except Poland	103		2,052	720	284	372	410	748	665	597	915	1,779	3,845	3,270
Finland	8	5	9		5		2	29	80	57	113	119	50	49
Spain	7	20	8		10		4	2	8	25	15	2	8	15
Sweden	2,543	4,014	3,585	2,125	2,381	2,751	2,551	3,352	1,958	1,830		342	2,189	563
Switzerland	101	152	72	79	17	23		63	38	23	41	40	43	52
Turkey in Europe				1		10				31	30	9	5	30
Asia, Africa, S. Amer., Other Europe		1		42	19	29		67		294	459	2,986	929	50
Total	21,712	34,753	36,278	24,773	18,981	22,482	20,822	31,048	37,325	28,100	22,658	26,152	31,102	19,861

NOTE: Statistics are not available by nationality for each port after 1894.

SOURCE: United States Treasury Department, *Annual Report and Statements of the Chief of the Bureau of Statistics on the Foreign Commerce and Navigation, Immigration and Tonnage of the United States for the Year Ending June 30 . . . (1880–1892; 1894)* (Washington, D.C.: Government Printing Office, 1880–1892, 1894. Statement, by Customs Districts, of the nationalities of immigrants arrived in the United States for the port of Philadelphia: 1880: Table 44, pp. 701ff; 1881: Table 44, pp. 725–26; 1882: Table 43, pp. 691–92; 1883: Table 43, pp. 683–84; 1884: Table 43, pp. 827–29; 1885: Table 41, pp. 719–21; 1886: Table 37, pp. 714–15; 1887: Table 37, pp. 728–29; 1888: Table 37, pp. 768–69; 1889: Table 37, pp. 764–65; 1890: Table 37, pp. 772–74; 1891: Table 37, pp. 850ff; 1892: Table 37, pp. 906ff; 1894: Table 4, pp. 14ff.

Appendix I

Professional

actor	1	fruit	1
artist	2	furniture	4
chemist	3	grocer	59(3*)
clergyman	13	hardware	1
editor	3	harnesses	2
lawyer	1	home furnishings	6
librarian	1	horseshoes	1
music teacher	2	huckster	7
musician	8	jewelry	3
nurse	1*	marble	1
optometrist	1	meat	47
orderly	1	men's furnishings	4
photographer	10	milk	5(1*)
physician	3	music	1
publisher	1	musical instrum.	1
secretary	1	news	1
stockbroker	1	novelties	2(1*)
teacher	3(1*)	paints	1
conductor, Phila. orch.	1	poultry	1
Total	57	pretzels	1
		produce	5(1*)
Executive/Managerial/Clerical		shoes	16
Executive	3	stationer	1
Manager	10	trimmings	1*
Superintendent	1	varieties	40(6*)
Bookkeeper	1	wagons	5
Purchasing agent	1	*Community services*	
Total	16	insurance agent	6
		notary	1
Self-Employed		printer	4
Mercantile/manufacturing		real estate	5
baker	48	steamship agent	2
baskets	1	undertaker	6(1*)
birds	1	dining	3
bottles	2	liquors	28
brooms	1	livery	2
candy	10(4*)	pool	9
church goods	1	teams	1
cigars	28(3*)	Total	405
coal	1		
druggist	5	*Services*	
drygoods	20(5*)	*General*	
florist	1	barber	39
flour	1	bellman	1

*Female.

212

bartender	28
bootblack	4
clerks	35
cook	10
elevator operator	1
housekeeper	1*
janitor	2
meterreader	1
midwife	19*
salesman	16
porter	2
sexton	2
waiter	19
watchman	14

Transportation

chauffeur	4
conveyancer	1
driver	64
hostler	1
mariner	1
railroads, electric:	
motorman	19
conductor	8
railroads, steam:	
engineer	15
fireman	29
stoker	3

Public service

collector (garbage)	3
police	2
post office carrier	3
telephone operator	1
U.S. Army	1
U.S. Navy	4
post office clerk	1
Total	354

Industry

Building and contracting
brick, cement and stone work:

bricklayer	10
cementworker	2
marbleworker	1
mason	1
stonecutter	3

*Female.

electrician	4
painting and decorating:	
painter	13
decorator	2
paperhanger	7
plumbing and heating:	
gas fitter	1
heater	1
pipefitter	10
plumber	9
steamfitter	1
roofer	9
contractor	4

Chemicals and allied products

gluemaker	2
paintmaker	2
soapmaker	1
temperer	1

Clay, glass & stone products

brickmaker	4
glass:	
bottlemaker	1
gasmaker	1
glassblower	2
glass cutter	1
glass worker	4
glazier	29

Food & kindred products;
beverages and liquors

baker	11
brewer	1
bottler	12
butcher	16
meatcutter	10
confectioner	8*
icemaker	1
sausagemaker	1
sugarboiler	1

Leather and rubber goods

hosemaker	1
leatherworker	99
moroccoworker	6
rubbermaker	8
shoemaker	62

shoe operator	1
tanner	4

Lumber and its remanufacture

cabinetmaker	18
carpenter	76
chipper	7
cooper	4
handlemaker	1
joiner	1
millwright	1
wagonbuilder	3
wagonmaker	3
woodworker	9

Paper and printing industries

paper:

boxmaker	2
papermaker	16
tagmaker	2

printing:

binder	3
engraver	1
lithographer	1
pressman	3
printer	15
stereotyper	1

Textiles

buffer	1
cordmaker	1
dyer	25
finisher	1
ironer	1
knitter	4
loomfixer	5
millworker	20
patternmaker	3
piecer	1
polisher	13
presser	2
roller	1
ropemaker	17
spinner	13
stitcher	1
stripper	1
textileworker	1
weaver	121

Clothing manufacture

dressmaker	10*
hatter	7
hosieryworker	1
hosieryoperator	3
milliner	3*
tailor	50
stockingmaker	1

Metals and metal manufacture

blacksmith	46
hammerman	2
boilermaker	17
brassworker	3
carbuilder	2
coppersmith	6
coremaker	1
cornicemaker	2
filemaker	3
filecutter	1
foundryman	1
grinder	1
harnessmaker	1
instrumentmaker	3
ironworker	110
locksmith	4
machinist	217
metalworker	3
riveter	8
rivetmaker	1
sawmaker	9
shovelmaker	1
smelter	1
springmaker	6
steelworker	28
tinsmith	5
watchmaker	1
wireworker	3

Tobacco and its products

cigarmaker	3

Miscellaneous

bambooworker	1
basketmaker	3
boxman	1
buttonmaker	20
calker	3

*Female.

craneman	1	reedworker	3
crane operator	6	repairman	1
designer	1	rigger	7
driller	4	umbrellamaker	1
estimator	1	upholsterer	6
foreman	26		
gas worker	1	*Laborer*	1,935
helper	1	Total	2,363
inspector	6		
longshoreman	1	*Other*	
machine operator	4	farmer	4
molder	15	gardener	3
oilclothmaker	4	miner	2
oiler	1	student	2
organmaker	1	Total	11
packer	2		

Appendix J

POLE-SEARCHING: PROBLEMS AND METHOD

Boyd's *City Directory* was used to locate Philadelphia's Poles in 1915. In the absence of meaningful political records and census materials, Boyd's *Directory* remains the most efficient way of discovering *where* the Polish people lived in Philadelphia and *what* their occupations were before the First World War. Nineteen-fifteen was chosen as the base year because it followed the period of peak Polish immigration to the United States (1907–1914), and it was a time when most of the Poles arriving in this country emigrated from the Russian sectors of Poland. By choosing 1915, Philadelphia's Polish community could be captured near the height of its development and after its period of largest growth. The community under surveillance would be mature, consolidated and amply represented by second-generation Polish-Americans (the native-born chidren of the foreign-born Pole) who would have reached adulthood by 1915.

Boyd's *City Directory* was published annually 186? to 1920 by the Catharine E. Howe Company of Philadelphia, which was founded in 1853 as an addressing and mailing service. Boyd, a relative of Catharine Howe, managed the *Directory* end of the business and thus the *Directory* bears his name. Boyd's aim in compiling the *Directory* was to list the names, addresses and occupations or places of business of all of the residents of the city who were gainfully employed and/or the heads of households. The *Directory* was intended to contain the names of all male breadwinners of the city. Women were listed only if they were widowed and the head of a household, or self-employed—a grocery store owner, a seamstress, a midwife, or the like.

The *Directory* itself was compiled like a census. Canvassers visited every home in the city. If there was no response, they returned again, and again. More information was gathered than was ever put into the published *Directory*—the number of children in each household and income level, for example. Unfortunately for future historians and social scientists all records and survey sheets were destroyed after use. It took approximately one year to complete the survey of the city. The 1915 listings were gathered throughout 1914 and were considered valid as of January 1, 1915. Advertising paid for part of the cost of producing the *Directory*. Other revenue came from the sale of the volume to banks, libraries, schools, municipal offices, police and fire departments, etc. No fee had to be paid in order to be listed in the *Directory*.*

Boyd's 1915 *City Directory* lists 4,464 persons (4,235 men and 229 women) who can be positively identified as either foreign-born Poles or the native-born children of Polish parents. This figure by no means represents all Poles or

*Interview with Mr. Frank Pitts, former employee of Catherine E. Howe Company, July 27, 1969.

persons of Polish origin residing within the city in 1915. All children and practically all Polish women were not included. For the most part, these 4,464 persons represent all Polish males who were gainfully employed at the time of the canvassing. This list was compiled from the *Directory* on the basis of surnames. Such a procedure presented two major problems which must be explained for the sake of accuracy.

First, hundreds of persons of Slovak, Ukrainian and Lithuanian origin, as well as hundreds of Polish and Lithuanian Jews, were included in the initial compilation—and deliberately so. The intention was to catch every Pole or every person who could possibly have been Polish. By using parish records and tracing descendents, most of these non-Polish persons were subsequently eliminated, leaving approximately 180 persons whose origins were doubtful or uncertain. These 180 individuals were either Poles, Lithuanians or Polish or Lithuanian Jews. Determining their nationality was further complicated by the fact that most of them lived in areas of high Polish and high Jewish or Lithuanian concentration, usually on those very streets that were the informal boundaries of the Polish and Jewish or Polish and Lithuanian communities. These 180 doubtful persons were finally eliminated for two reasons. First, their location in no way affected the distribution of the 4,464 persons who had been positively verified; and second, the occupational distribution of these 180 individuals did not influence the occupational distribution of the positive members. Had these 180 persons been included in the total listing, the results would have been exactly the same.

Second, many Polish persons could not be identified solely on the basis of surnames. Those from the German sectors of Poland often had German-sounding names: "Effenberg," "Kattein," "Petner." These persons were located through the parish records, crosschecked with the *City Directory* to find their place of residence and occupation, and added to the total list. As the existence of this problem was known before the study of the *Directory* was undertaken, it was possible to spotcheck for German names in the course of the survey in order to locate any addresses on streets or in areas known to be highly Polish in composition. These names, like the others, were subsequently checked to determine their correct nationality.

In the final outcome, therefore, 4,464 persons were listed in the 1915 *City Directory* who were definitely Polish or of Polish origin. The location and distribution of these people, plus crosschecking with parish records and descendent tracing, indicates that the list is both accurate and complete.

Appendix K

PARISH RECORDS

The records of Philadelphia's Polish parishes* contain a wealth of information for the historian, demographer or sociologist who wishes to study immigration to the United States before the First World War.

These records, however, are only as good as the priests who kept them. Some were very conscientious; others listed the bare essentials. Information is most consistent in parishes where one priest remained for a long time. Parishes experiencing frequent turnovers illustrate the problems involved: Father A used one schema or terminology; Father B used another. Many priests recorded information in Polish, others in Latin, while some used both languages. Finally, in several instances handwriting is absolutely illegible.

The parish sources consist of baptismal, death and marriage registers. Baptismal records usually list the name of the child, the names of its parents and godparents, and whether the child was legitimate or illegitimate. On occasion they also contain the birthplace of the child's parents. One conscientious pastor followed the life histories of the children baptized in his parish. If they died in childhood he indicated the date of their death. With this information it is possible to construct infant or child mortality schedules. These rates can then be compared to those of the city or the ward in which the Polish community was located.

Death records list the least information: date of death, place of burial and, possibly, age and place of birth, or age at time of death.

Marriage registers are by far the most informative. Some or all of the following information can be obtained from them:

1. Name of husband and wife.
2. Name of parents of husband and wife.
3. Date of marriage. Marriages took place on any day of the week and at any time of day.
4. Place of birth and/or place of baptism of husband and wife.

Details about precise origins in Poland depended solely on the priest recording the information. All parishes but one recorded the sector of Poland from which the people emigrated—Russian, German or Austrian Poland. German listings, for example, are registered as "Poznań," "West Prussia," or "Silesia." Austrian listings are always "Galicia." Russian listings are generally "Congress Kingdom," "Kingdom of Poland," or simply "Russian Poland." Many parishes supply more details—the province, town, village or parish of the immigrant. For these parishes it is possible to determine whether

---

*There are eight Polish parishes in Philadelphia. The records of seven were scrutinized in detail: St. Laurentius; St. Stanislaus, Bishop and Martyr; St. John Cantius; St. Josaphat; St. Adalbert; St. Ladislaus and St. Hedwig. The eighth, St. Mary of Częstachowa, was not founded until 1927, beyond the time limit of this study.

218

or not "chain migration" was at work; it is possible to determine if the Poles came from the same towns and villages of Poland or if their origins were random.

Knowledge of the Poles' birthplaces, coupled with knowledge of these various regions, reveals much about the immigrants who came to America. For example, a high percentage of Poles in one Philadelphia community were bakers. Marriage records revealed that these bakers came from a large city in Poland. Unlike the vast majority of Poles who immigrated to the United States, therefore, they were not peasant-farmers. They were urbanized individuals who had possessed skills and trades long before their journey to America.

The majority of Philadelphia's Russian Poles came from Płock, Łomża and Suwałki. These provinces were the least industrialized and least urbanized areas of Poland. They were the least able to absorb excess population and therefore were the most likely ones to export people.

Philadelphia had a larger representation of Galician (Austrian) Poles than the nation as a whole. Where approximately one-third of the Poles in the United States were Galicians, one-half of Philadelphia's Poles came from that province. For some reason, Philadelphia was especially attractive to Austrian Poles.

Information about place of birth also indicates the extent to which Poles married persons outside of their group (exogamous marriages). Marriages of persons from different provinces or sectors of Poland is even more revealing. In some parishes there was virtually no intermarriage of this type: Galicians married Galicians; Russian Poles married Russian Poles; very rarely did a Galician marry a Russian Pole. In other parishes, there was a high degree of marriage of persons from different sectors. Marriages of persons from the same village or province indicates that the group still maintained control over its members and that friends and family continued to exercise considerable influence. Lack of it indicates a breakdown of this control.

All parishes recorded very little exogamous marriage. Where this did occur, the Polish party usually married a person of some other Slavic group—Russian, Lithuanian, Slovak, or a German Pole married a German. Those marrying Italians, Irishmen, or other nationalities were almost exclusively American-born Poles; or they were women.

5. Date of birth or age at time of marriage. This information indicates the age at which the Poles immigrated to America. In one parish the majority of men did not marry until they were thirty or older; women on the other hand, were nineteen to twenty-three years old, quite a few years younger than their husbands. (This was the parish which also recorded a very low rate of intermarriage of persons from different Polish sectors.) In the rest of the parishes, the average of marriage for men was nineteen to twenty-three years; for women, seventeen to twenty-three years. In general, the younger the man at the time of marriage, the greater the likelihood that he married someone not of his province or sector; the influence of family and friends in Poland had already been weakened.

6. First marriage; widow or widower.

7. Religion of husband and wife if not Roman Catholic. The most common instances were Polish Catholics marrying Polish Lutherans from the German sectors of Poland, or German Poles (Catholic) marrying Germans (Lutheran). The Lutheran partner usually converted to Catholicism by the time of the wedding.

8. Place of present residence. This information reveals the distribution and location of the immigrants within the city. Were they scattered in space or did they settle close together? Did they predominate in certain areas, on certain blocks, and not in others? Three parishes supplied this information but only for disconnected periods of time.

9. Names of witnesses to the marriage.

10. Extenuating circumstances, dispensations, impediments, and the like. Most common was dispensation of the bans of marriage. Bans had to be read from the pulpit or posted in the church for three weeks before the wedding. The pastor had to petition the archbishop for permission to dispense with them. The reasons for this request varied: "Father, next Sunday I am off from work. That is the only day we can be married." "Father, marry us today, as I must be at work tomorrow in Wilkes-Barre." "Father, marry us tomorrow—we have been living together and cannot take the talk any more. . . ." "Father, marry us today because the child has already been born. . . ." Other routine dispensations were for permission to be married during Lent or Advent.

11. Annullments. If at some future time the marriage was annulled, the date and number of the decree granting the dissolution is recorded.

In general, the marriage records reveal one aspect of the Polish immigration which is very important: most Poles who came to America were single men between the ages of nineteen and thirty. They tended to come alone, unencumbered with wife or children. They married in America. Often marriage and the birth of children changed the migrant laborer into a permanent immigrant.

Notes

Introduction

The Wandering of Nations

1. "Immigrants and Their Children," *U. S. Bureau of the Census Monograph,* no. 7 (Washington, D.C., 1927), p. 40.
2. Arthur Meier Schlesinger, Sr., *The Rise of the City, 1878–1898* (New York: Macmillan Co., 1933; Chicago: Quandrangle paperback ed., 1971), p. 25; see chap. 2, "The Great West."
3. Schlesinger, *Rise of the City*, p. 61. For more information on rural depletion, see pp. 67–72; and W. F. Wilcox, "Decrease of Interstate Migration," *Political Science Quarterly* 10 (1895): 604–605; Adna Ferrin Weber, *The Growth of Cities in the Nineteenth Century: A Study in Statistics* (New York: Macmillan Co., 1899; Cornell University Press paperback ed.), pp. 251ff; and Charles N. Glaab and A. Theordore Brown, *A History of Urban America* (New York: Macmillan Co., 1967), p. 137: "As a result of internal migration during the decade [1880–1890], forty percent of the nation's 25,746 townships showed a decline in population. Portions of rural New England were particularly hard hit as nearly sixty percent of the townships (932 of 1,502) registered a drop. State studies recorded a widescale abandonment of farms—3,300 in Maine, 1,500 in Massachusetts, 1,300 in New Hampshire and 1,000 in Vermont. In the rapidly urbanizing Midwest, there were similar pockets of rural decay. Portions of central Missouri, eastern Iowa, northern and western Illinois, and central and southeastern Indiana were drastically depopulated, largely as a result of the movement of farmers to towns and cities. There were 7,500 fewer farmers in Michigan in 1890 than there had been ten years before, although the total population of the state grew by half a million. In Ohio, 755 of 1,316 townships and in Illinois, 800 of 1,424 decreased in population during the decade, though both states, like all midwestern states during the period, grew in total population." David Ward, *Cities and Immigrants: A Geography of Change in Nineteenth Century America* (New York: Oxford University Press, 1971), p. 58: "[B]efore about 1870 opportunities in the west for urban as well as agricultural employment competed with local urban centers within the areas of emigration. Thereafter, however, the proportion of long distance movements within the total internal migration declined, and even newly settled areas began to experience the effects of the cityward movement."
4. Adna Weber, pp. 27ff; Glaab and Brown, p. 136.
5. E. G. Ravenstein, "The Laws of Migration," *Journal of the Royal Statistical Society* 52 (1889); 241–301; Adna Weber, pp. 267, 257–58; Schlesinger, Sr., p. 61.
6. Glaab and Brown, p. 137; Schlesinger, Sr., p. 61: In the United States "the tendency was to move from the countryside to the nearest hamlet, from the hamlet to the town, and from the town to the city. The reasons that impelled a person to leave the farm to go to a crossroads village were likely to cause the ambitious or maladjusted villager to remove to a larger place, or might in time spur the transplanted farmer lad

221

himself to try his fortunes in a broader sphere. The results were seen in the records of city growth. The pyramid of urban population enlarged at every point from base to peak, and the countryside found itself encroached upon by hamlet, town and city."

7. Adna Weber, pp. 283, 259ff.
8. Ibid., p. 257.
9. Glaab and Brown, p. 135; 21.6% represented natural increase; 7.6% of the urban growth was due to annexation.
10. David Ward, p. 52; Adna Weber, p. 305: "In the entire country only 14.77 per cent of the population is foreign-born [1890]. The cities therefore contain more than their due proportion of foreigners. Expressed in another form, the 28 great cities, while constituting in 1890 15.5 per cent of the entire population of the United States, contained 12.4 per cent of all the American-born, and 33.4 per cent of the foreign-born in the United States. There is therefore a decided tendency on the part of the foreigners to settle in our largest cities."
11. This constitutes the primary thesis of Adna Weber's *The Growth of Cities in the Nineteenth Century* (1899), the first comprehensive analysis of urbanization in Europe and America, including its location, growth patterns and sources.
12. David Ward, p. 51.
13. The concept of *entrance status* was first developed by John A. Porter, *The Vertical Mosaic: An Analysis of Social Class and Power in Canada* (Toronto: Toronto University Press, 1965), and refers to the conditions for admission placed on the foreigner by the "charter group" (native or Anglo-Americans). In exchange for admittance, foreigners had to agree to perform certain economic roles, usually the lowest, which the charter group were not willing to perform themselves if they could avoid it.

Part I. The Context

Chapter 1. Philadelphia—Corrupt, Contented but Definitely American

1. "Philadelphia: Corrupt and Contented," *McClures* (July 1903).
2. New York, 1902, p. 5.
3. See Dennis Clark, *The Irish in Philadelphia: Ten Generations of Urban Experience* (Philadelphia: Temple University Press, 1973), pp. 71–72, 61–87, chap. 4, "Working to Live."
4. These estimates are based on the records of Philadelphia's Roman Catholic parishes and the listings of *Boyd's City Directory* for 1915 (see Appendixes J and K). Please note that these figures represent only the foreign-born segment of the Philadelphia Polish population, not the total community—foreign-born parent(s) plus American-born children.
5. W. Kruszka, *Historja Polska w Ameryce* (Milwaukee: Kuryer Publishing Co., 1937), 2:174; Emily Greene Balch, *Our Slavic Fellow Citizens* (New York: Charities Publication Committee, 1910), p. 264; anonymous estimate of the Chicago Polish *Press*, December 15, 1908 (see Appendix D); Paul Fox, *The Poles in America* (New York: George H. Doran Co., 1922), p. 63. In an article entitled "Poles in Philadelphia," the *Philadelphia Bulletin,* August 11, 1920, reported that there were

seven Polish colonies in Philadelphia totalling 75,000 people (foreign-born parents plus American-born children).

6. For discussion of Philadelphia's "southern character" see W. E. B. Dubois, *The Philadelphia Negro: A Social Study* (New York: Benjamin Blom, 1899). We may note that in 1910 New York City had the largest absolute black population of any city, north or south (91,709), but only 1.9% of the city's total population was black.

7. The unskilled or secondary labor market included those jobs that required little or no skill and were transient or temporary. Jobs in the primary labor market, in contrast, involved some skill and higher and/or more reliable wages. Blacks and Poles, for example, worked in identical jobs in Philadelphia—as coal shovelers in a steel plant. After ten years, however, when there would be an opening for foreman, a "primary" level job, it would be the Pole (or other white man) and not the black who would be promoted. Thus, the black, while utilized for the lowest jobs in the urban hierarchy, found stiff competition when it came to moving above the lower levels into the primary labor pool.

8. For additional discussion on this point, see Brinley Thomas, *Migration and Economic Growth* (Cambridge, Eng.: At the University Press, 1954), pp. 130–34; see also Niles Carpenter, *Immigrants and Their Children* (Washington, D.C., 1927), p. 34. Carpenter's was the first systematic study of immigrant and black migration patterns utilizing statistics of the U.S. Census.

9. For discussion of black migration, its scope and causes, 1860–1920, see C. S. Johnson, "The American Migrant: The Negro," *Proceedings, National Conference of Social Workers,* 1927, pp. 554–58; L. V. Kennedy, *The Negro Peasant Turns Cityward: Effects of Recent Migrations to Northern Centers* (New York, 1930), quote is from page 56; and George E. Haynes, "The Negro at Work in New York City: A Study in Economic Progress" (Ph.D. diss., Columbia University, 1912). For blacks in southern industry see Haynes, pp. 23ff. For industrialization, urbanization and black employment in the South see Schlesinger, Sr., chap. 1; Broadus Mitchell and George Sinclair Mitchell, *The Industrial Revolution in the South* (Baltimore: Johns Hopkins Press, 1930); Anthony Tang, *Economic Development in the Southern Piedmont, 1860–1950* (Chapel Hill: University of North Carolina Press, 1958); Kenneth Bailey, "A Judicious Mixture: Negroes and Immigrants in the West Virginia Mines 1880–1917," *West Virginia History* 34 (January 1973); Herman Bloch, "Labor and the Negro 1866–1910," *Journal of Negro History* 50 (1965): 163–84; Philip Foner, "The IWW and the Black Worker," *Journal of Negro History* 55 (1970): 45–64; Herbert Gutman, "Black Coal Miners and the Greenback Labor Party in Redeemer Alabama 1878–1879," *Labor History* 10 (1969): 506–36; Jerrell Shofner, "The Pensacola Workingmen's Association: A Militant Negro Labor Union During Reconstruction," *Labor History* 13, no. 4 (1972): 555–59; Paul Worthman, "Black Workers and Labor Unions in Birmingham, Alabama, 1897–1904", *Labor History* 10, no. 3 (1969): 375–407; Thomas Wagstaff, "Call Your Old Master—'Master'. Southern Political Leaders and Negro Labor during Presidential Reconstruction," *Labor History* 10, no. 3 (1969): 323–45; Joseph E. Walker, "A Comparison of Negro and White Labor in a Charcoal Iron Community," *Labor History* 10, no. 3 (1969): 487–97.

10. L. V. Kennedy, pp. 29–30.

11. Ironically, a similar situation prevailed in Italy: lack of convenient transportation made it easier for Italians to get to ships at Palermo, Naples or Messina and end up in New York harbor than to get to the industrializing, northern portions of their own

country. True to the rules of migration, it was the Italian population immediately surrounding Turin and Milan which were the first to feel the pull of that urban center's expanding economic opportunities.

12. *Third Annual Report of the Commissioner of Labor and Industry of the Commonwealth of Pennsylvania, 1915,* Part I: Statistics of Production, Wages, Employees for the Year 1915 (Harrisburg, 1918). See Appendix E for complete listing; Dubois, *The Philadelphia Negro,* chap. 9, pp. 97–146.

13. For impact of the First World War on black migration and movement into northern industry see L. V. Kennedy, pp. 23–29, 41–44, 74–76ff; Commonwealth of Pennsylvania, Department of Public Welfare, *Negro Survey of Pennsylvania* (Harrisburg, 1927); S. T. Mosell, "The Standard of Living among One Hundred Migrant Families in Philadelphia," *Annals* 98: 173–218, particularly pp. 173–75; and E. J. Scott, *Negro Migration during the War* (New York: Oxford University Press, 1920). Jane Lang and Harry N. Scheiber, "The Wilson Administration and the Wartime Mobilization of Black Americans," *Labor History* 10, no. 3 (1969): 433–58.

14. The labor shortage brought on by the war encouraged the recruitment of southern labor, both black and white, but it also accelerated the movement to Philadelphia of foreign-born persons who had been living and working in the smaller towns and cities of central and northeastern Pennsylvania, New Jersey and Delaware. Philadelphia's Polish community, as small as it remained, experienced its greatest period of growth during the war, but the expansion came from elsewhere in Pennsylvania or the nation and not directly from Europe.

15. A survey of Polish settlements throughout the country proves this to be true; see Glaab and Brown, p. 139; Charles Coulter, *Poles of Cleveland* (Cleveland: Americanization Committee, 1919); Sister Mary Adele Dabrowski, *A History and Survey of the Polish Community in Brooklyn* (Master's thesis, Fordham University, Department of History, 1946); Mieczysław Haiman, ed., *Poles of Chicago, 1837–1937* (Chicago: Polish Pageant, 1937); Sister Mary Theodosetta Lewandowska, "The Polish Immigrant in Philadelphia to 1914," *Records of the American Catholic Historical Society of Philadelphia* 65 (1954): 67–101, 131–41; Norman Thomas Lyon, *History of the Polish People in Rochester* (Buffalo: Polish Everybody's Daily Press, 1935); Mary Remigia Napolska, *The Polish Immigrant in Detroit to 1914* (Chicago: Polish Roman Catholic Union of America, 1946).

Chapter 2. Philadelphia in the Land of the Titan

1. *Philadelphia Yearbook* 1917, p. All.

2. Pennsylvania Department of Labor and Industry, *Monthly Bulletin* 1, no. 5 (October 1914): 33.

3. For discussion of decentralization: Leo F. Schnore, *The Urban Scene; Human Ecology and Demography* (New York: Free Press, 1965), pp. 79–113, "the population's movement away from the center of the city [Philadelphia] was proportionally greater in the fifty years between 1860 and 1910 than in the half century between 1900 and 1950." Schnore considered Philadelphia an example of an "extreme case" of decentralization; Adna Weber, pp. 202ff; Glaab and Brown, p. 277: "The building of industrial towns and cities in the early part of the twentieth century reflected a general pattern of decentralization clearly indicated in statistics of manufacturing. A Census Bureau study of twelve of the thirteen largest industrial districts showed that

from 1899 to 1904 the number of persons employed in industry in central cities increased by 14.9 percent while in the outlying zones the number increased by 32.8 percent. From 1904 to 1909 the increase in central cities was 22.5 percent while in the surrounding zones it was 48.8 percent. For the decade, the growth rate was over two times as great for the suburbs—97.9 percent to 40.8 percent." Hans Blumenfeld, "The Tidal Wave of Metropolitan Expansion," *Journal of the American Institute of Planners* 20 (1954): 3–14.

4. For discussion of "initial advantage" and relevance of technology to growth and location: Patrick Geddes, *Cities in Evolution,* rev. ed. (London 1949); Sir Patrick labels the stages of industrial technology as "paleotechnic," based on steam and iron, and "neotechnic," based on electricity, petroleum and steel. J. R. Borchert, "American Metropolitan Evolution," *Geographical Review* 57 (1967): 301–32, especially p. 327: "As the new epoch unfolded, a new pattern of 'initial advantage' also emerges: for certain advantages are created that could not have existed before." See also A. R. Pred, "Industrialization, Initial Advantage and American Metropolitan Growth," *Geographic Review* 55 (1965): 158–85; Pred, "Manufacturing in the American Mercantile City: 1800–1840," *Annals of the Association of American Geographers* 56 (1966): 307–38; Pred, "The Intrametropolitan Location of American Manufacturing," *Annals of the Association of American Geographers* 54 (1964): 165–80; Pred, *The Spatial Dynamics of U.S. Urban-Industrial Growth, 1800–1914: Interpretive and Theoretical Essays* (Cambridge, 1966); Eric Lampard, "Historical Aspects of Urbanization," in P. M. Hauser and L. F. Schnore, eds., *The Study of Urbanization* (New York, 1965), pp. 519–54; E. Lampard, "The History of Cities in the Economically Advanced Areas," *Economic Development and Cultural Change* 3 (1955): 81–136. For discussion of "diseconomies of congestion:" Pred, *Spatial Dynamics of U.S. Urban Industrial Growth,* p. 183; Edward E. Pratt, *Industrial Causes of Congestion of Population in New York City* (New York, 1911), pp. 109ff; Glaab and Brown, p. 275; Walter Isard, *Location and Space Economy* (New York, 1956), p. 83.

5. Sylvester K. Stevens, *Pennsylvania, Titan of Industry* (New York: Lewis Historical Publishing Co., 1948), vol. 1, pp. 297–98.

6. Ibid.

7. *Philadelphia Yearbook,* 1917, pp. Bl, A4.

8. *Philadelphia Yearbook,* 1917, pp. A13, 140–41.

9. Guy C. Whidden and W. H. Schoff, *Pennsylvania and Its Manifold Activities* (Philadelphia: Twelfth International Congress of Navigation, 1912), pp. 145, 147, 138–39, 133; see also H. L. Collins and W. Jordan, *Philadelphia: A Story of Progress* (New York: Lewis Historical Publishing Co., 1941), vol. 3, pp. 202–36.

10. U.S. Census, 1910, 1920; Balch, *Our Slavic Fellow Citizens,* p. 235; K. D. Miller, *Slovaks in the United States* (New York: George H. Doran Co., 1922), pp. 49–50; P. M. Rose, *The Italians in America* (New York: George H. Doran Co., 1922), pp. 53–54; F. J. Warne, *The Tide of Immigration* (New York: D. Appleton and Co., 1916), pp. 223–24.

11. F. J. Sheridan, *Italian, Slavic and Hungarian Unskilled Immigrant Laborers in the United States,* U.S. Bureau of Labor *Bulletin,* no. 72 (September 1907), pp. 412–15; U.S. Census, 1910, 1920.

12. Pennsylvania Department of Labor and Industry, "Report of Division of Immigration and Unemployment," *First Annual Report, 1913* (Harrisburg, 1914), pp. 232–35. Note that Pennsylvania's Bureau of Statistics and Information did not record the Jewish population by nationality group—i.e., Russian, Polish, Austrian, etc.—but

listed it in a separate category, "Hebrews." See also: Pennsylvania Department of
Labor and Industry, "Recent Immigration to Pennsylvania," *Monthly Bulletin* 1,
no. 5 (October 1914): p. 33.

13. For discussion of Pennsylvania's industrial activity and the labor that supported it,
see Stevens, *Pennsylvania, Titan of Industry*, vol. 1; Whidden and Schoff, *Pennsylvania and Its Manifold Activities;* Victor R. Greene, *The Slavic Community on
Strike: Immigrant Labor in Pennsylvania Anthracite* (University of Notre Dame
Press, 1968), chap. 1; Sheridan, *Italian, Slavic and Hungarian Unskilled Immigrant
Laborers in the United States;* Pennsylvania Department of Labor and Industry,
"Report of Division of Immigration and Unemployment," pp. 240–55; Pennsylvania
Department of Labor and Industry, "Racial Displacement in Pennsylvania Industries," *Monthly Bulletin* (November 1914), pp. 28–35.

14. Quoted in Pennsylvania Department of Labor and Industry, "Report of Division of
Immigration and Unemployment," p. 243; "Racial Displacement in Pennsylvania
Industries," pp. 28–29; F. J. Warne, *The Slav Invasion and the Mine Workers: A
Study in Immigration* (Philadelphia: Lippincott, 1904), chap. 3, pp. 39ff, chap. 5, pp.
52ff (good statistics, but takes the story only to 1901; greater displacement was yet
to come); Peter Roberts, *Anthracite Coal Communities: A Study of the Demography, the Social, Educational and Moral Life of the Anthracite Regions* (New
York, 1904), pp. 102ff; Peter Roberts, *The Anthracite Coal Industry* (New York:
Macmillan, 1901); Sheridan, p. 413; Greene, pp. 34–35; Pennsylvania Department of
Internal Affairs, *Annual Report, 1903* (Harrisburg 1904), 31: 431–32.

15. "Report of Division of Immigration and Unemployment," pp. 243–45; "Racial Displacement in Pennsylvania Industries," p. 30.

16. "Report of Division of Immigration and Unemployment," p. 246; "Displacement in
Pennsylvania Industries," p. 30; J. A. Fitch, *The Steel Workers* (New York:
Charities Publication Committee, 1910), pp. 30–31, 142–46; Charlotte Erickson,
American Industry and the European Immigrant, 1860–1885 (Cambridge, Mass.:
Harvard University Press, 1957); David Brody, *Steelworkers in America: The Non-Union Era* (Cambridge. Mass.: Harvard University Press, 1960); U.S. House Committee on the Investigation of the U.S. Steel Corporation, *Hearings,* 62 Cong., 2nd
Sess. (1911–1912), 4: 2889–93; U.S. Immigration Commission, *Report on Immigration,* 8, 9 and 11 (Washington, D.C., 1911).

17. Fitch, *Steel Workers,* pp. 142, 30–31.

18. "Report of Division of Immigration and Unemployment," p. 247.

19. Whidden and Schoff, pp. 45–54; 220–22.

20. Two statements by contemporary writers, one on coal mining, the other on steel
making, indicate Pennsylvania's industrial character: "The particular work the industry demands in the laborer's position needs very little more than physical
strength; the task requires quantity rather than quality of labor," F. J. Warne, *The
Slav Invasion,* pp. 77–78; and "Blast furnaces require little skilled labor. There is no
delicate machinery—it is simply a question of feeding the furnace with the raw material, and tapping out the molten product," J. A. Fitch, *The Steel Workers,* pp.
30–31.

Chapter 3. The Atlantic Economy and Its Migrant Workers

1. "Poland as an Independent Economic Unit," in *Poland's Case for Independence*
(New York: Dodd Mead and Co., 1916), p. 141.

2. Brinley Thomas, *Migration and Economic Growth: A Study of Great Britain and the Atlantic Economy* (Cambridge, Eng.: At the University Press, 1954). See also Frank Thistlethwaite, "Migration from Europe Overseas in the Nineteenth and Twentieth Centuries." Xle Congres International des Sciences Historiques, Stockholm, 1960; *Rapports 5: Histoire Contemporanie.*

3. For further discussion see, among others, Adna Weber, *The Growth of Cities in the Nineteenth Century;* Thistlethwaite, "Migration from Europe Overseas in the Nineteenth and Twentieth Centuries"; B. Thomas, *Migration and Economic Growth;* William D. Forsyth, *The Myth of the Open Spaces* (Melbourne: At the University Press, 1942).

4. Thistlethwaite, p. 75.

5. Thistlethwaite, pp. 73–74.

6. Marcus Lee Hansen, *The Immigrant in American History* (Cambridge, Mass: Harvard University Press, 1940), p. 192.

7. Victor Greene, *The Slavic Community on Strike*, p. 26.

8. Fitch, *The Steel Workers*, p. 149fn. For information on returning immigrants see Theodore Saloutos, "Exodus, U.S.A.," in O. F. Ander, ed., *In the Trek of the Immigrant* (Rock Island, Ill.: Augustana College Library, 1964), chap. 14; George Seibel, "Going Back and Why," *Nation* 109 (October 11, 1919): 493; *Reports of Immigration Conditions in Europe*, 61st Congress, 3rd Session, Sen. Doc. No. 748 (Washington, D.C., 1911), p. 40; W. F. Wilcox, "Restriction of Immigration: Discussion," *American Economic Review* 2 (March 1912): 68, supplement; Isaac A. Hourwhich, *Immigration and Labor* (New York, 1912), p. 50; U.S. Industrial Commission, *Reports* 15 (Washington, D.C., 1901): 161–64; W. B. Bailey, "The Birds of Passage," *American Journal of Sociology* 18 (November 1912): 392–93; Wilbur S. Shepperson, *Emigration and Disenchantment: Portraits of Englishmen Repatriated from the United States* (Norman, Oklahoma: University of Oklahoma Press, 1965); Shepperson, "British Backtrailers: Working-Class Immigrants Return," in Ander, ed., pp. 179–96; Francesco P. Cerase, "A Study of Italian Migrants Returning from the U.S.A.," *International Migration Review* n.s. 1 (summer 1967): 67–74; George R. Gilkey, "The United States and Italy: Migration and Repatriation," *Journal of Developing Areas* (1967), pp. 23–35; Victor Von Borosini, "Home-Going Italians," *Survey* 28 (September 28, 1912): 791, 793; Betty Boyd Caroli, *Italian Repatriation from the United States, 1900–1914* (New York: Center for Migration Studies, 1973).

9. Paul W. Gates has pointed out that newcomers wishing to farm around the turn of the century would need $500 to $1,500 in addition to money for land. Even free land was worthless to a person without capital. Virtually all immigrants and migrant-workers lacked the capital necessary to set up farming. ("Frontier Estate Builders and Farm Laborers," in Walker D. Wyman and Clifton B. Kroeber, *The Frontier in Perspective* [Madison: University of Wisconsin Press, 1957], pp. 144–63.)

10. Warne, *Slav Invasion*, p. 77.

11. Edward A. Ross, *The Old World in the New* (New York: Century Co., 1913), pp. 142–43.

12. Fitch, *Steel Workers,* p. 77.

13. According to the Immigration Commission (*Reports* vol. 1, 1911, p. 99), 26% of Jews were illiterate (unable to read or write), compared with 54% of southern Italians and 35% of Poles. Unlike the latter two groups, however, a high proportion of the Jews were women and children; hence, the literacy rate of the adult male population was probably much higher than 74%.

14. For general background on eastern European Jewish migration, see Louis Fin-kelstein, ed., *The Jews: Their History, Culture and Religion,* 2nd ed., (Philadelphia: Jewish Publication Society of America, 1960); Nathan Glazer, *American Judaism* (Chicago: University of Chicago Press, 1957); Nathan Glazer and Daniel Patrick Moyniham, *Beyond the Melting Pot* (Cambridge: MIT Press, 1963), pp. 143–85; Samuel Joseph, *Jewish Immigration to the United States from 1881–1910* (New York: Columbia University Press, 1914); Louis Wirth, *The Ghetto* (Chicago: University of Chicago Press, 1928; Phoenix ed., 1956); Ande Manners, *Poor Cousins* (Greenwich, Conn.: Fawcett Publications, 1972); Moses Rischin, *The Promised City: New York's Jews, 1870–1920* (Boston, 1962), chap. 1; Charles Bernheimer, ed., *The Russian Jew in America* (Philadelphia: John C. Winston Co., 1905); S. Dubnow, *History of the Jews in Russia and Poland,* 3 vols. (Philadelphia, 1916–1920); Maurice Fishberg, *The Jews,* (London, 1911); Harold Frederic, *The New Exodus* (London, 1892); Cecil Roth, *A History of the Jews,* 1961 ed., (New York: Schocken Books); Bernard J. Bamberger, *The Story of Judaism* (New York: Schocken Books, 1957); I. Abrahams, *Jewish Life in the Middle Ages,* 2nd ed. (London, 1932); S. W. Baron, *A Social and Religious History of the Jews,* 2nd rev. ed. (Philadelphia, 1952); Isaac M. Rubinow, *Economic Condition of the Jews in Russia, Bulletin* v. 15, U.S. Bureau of Labor (Washington, D.C., 1907), 487–583.

15. U.S. Foreign Commerce Bureau, *Labor in Europe, Reports of the Consular Officers of the United States* (Washington, D.C.: U.S. Government Printing Office, 1885), p. 326.

16. Immigration Information Bureau, *Morton Allen Directory of European Passenger Steamship Arrivals for the Years 1890 to 1930 at the Port of New York and for the Years 1904 to 1926 at the Ports of Philadelphia, Boston and Baltimore* (New York: Bernard Publishing Co., 1931).

17. Marcus Lee Hansen, in his classic study of the Old Immigration, was one of the first to document the importance of trade routes in determining where immigrants landed and settled in America; often disembarkation at a certain place was sufficient to ac-count for the formation of permanent colonies: *Atlantic Migration, 1507–1860,* 1961 ed. (New York: Harper Torchbooks), pp. 79–80, 172, 195–96, 249–50, 270, espe-cially pp. 178–98, 290–93; see also Oscar Handlin, *Boston's Immigrants: 1790–1880* (New York: Antheneum, 1969), pp. 48–50; Philip Taylor, *The Distant Magnet: Eu-ropean Emigration to the U.S.A.* (New York: Harper and Row, 1971), chaps 6, 7 and 8.

18. United States Treasury Department, Bureau of Statistics, *The Foreign Commerce and Navigation of the United States for the Year Ending June 30, 1896* (Washington, D.C., 1897), 1:lxx–lxxiii; 2: 851–52, 940–42, 947–48, 953, 955–57.

19. Rischin, *The Promised City,* p. 25.

20. Charles Bernheimer, ed., *The Russian Jew in America,* p. 124; for other cities and national comparisons, see Edward P. Hutchinson, *Immigrants and Their Children, 1850–1950* (New York: John C. Wiley and Sons, 1956), pp. 179–80, 189; Rischin, pp. 59, 69.

21. Bernheimer, pp. 122, 124; Joseph Willits, *Philadelphia Unemployment* (Department of Public Works, City of Philadelphia, 1915), published by the American Academy of Political and Social Science, 1916, p. 21. For needle trades in Philadelphia: Bernheimer, pp. 124, 126ff; Maxwell Whiteman, *The Jewish Exponent* (April 24, 1964); United States Industrial Commission, *Reports* (Washington, D.C., 1900–1902), 3: 192–97, 324–27; in New York City: Rischin, pp. 61ff.

22. Sheridan also observed that, unlike other Slavic groups, the "Hebrews" of Pennsylvania were not to be found in "heavier manual occupations": *Italian, Slavic and Hungarian Unskilled Immigrant Laborers in the United States*, p. 412.

23. See the *Morton Allen Directory of European Passenger Steamship Arrivals*.

24. Robert Foerester, *The Italian Emigration of Our Time* (Harvard University Press, 1919), pp. 40–41, 344, 362, 401 and passim for details on conditions in Italy and general character of the Italian migrations. See also Eliot Lord, John D. Trenor and Samuel J. Barrows, *The Italian In America* (New York: B.F. Buck and Co., 1905); Phyllis H. Williams, *South Italian Folkways in Europe and America* (New Haven: Yale University Press, 1936); Philip M. Rose, *The Italians in America* (New York: Doran Co., 1922); Humbert S. Nelli, *The Italians in Chicago 1880–1930: A Study of Ethnic Mobility* (New York: Oxford University Press, 1970); Francesco Cordasco and Eugene Bucchioni, *The Italians: Social Backgrounds of an American Group* (Clifton, New Jersey: Augustus M. Kelley, 1974); Grazia Dore, "Some Social and Historical Aspects of Italian Emigration to America," *Journal of Social History* (winter 1968); Francesco P. Cerase, "A Study of Italian Migrants Returning from the U.S.A.," *International Migration Review* n.s. 1 (summer 1967): 67–74; George R. Gilkey, "The United States and Italy: Migration and Repatriation," *Journal of Developing Areas* (1967), pp. 23–35; Frank G. Haughwont, "Italian Emigration," *U.S. Consular Reports* 11 (December 1883): 364–66; Henry G. Huntington "Italian Emigration to the United States," *U.S. Consular Reports* 44 (February 1894): 308–09; Lucrezio Monticelli, "Italian Emigration: Basic Characteristics and Trends with Special Reference to the Last Twenty Years," *International Migration Review* n.s. 1, (summer 1967): 10–24; Antonio A. Stella, *Some Aspects of Italian Immigration to the United States: Statistical Data Based Chiefly upon the U.S. Census and Other Official Publications* (New York: Putnam's Sons, 1924: reprinted., San Francisco: R & E Research Associates, 1970); Victor Von Borosini, "Home-going Italians," *Survey*, 28 (September 28, 1912): 791–93; Francis E. Clark, *Our Italian Fellow Citizens in Their Old Homes and Their New* (Boston: Small, Maynard & Co., 1919); Luciano J. Iorizzo and Salvatore Mondello, *The Italian Americans* (New York: Twayne Publishing Co., 1971); Joseph LoPreato, *The Italian Americans* (New York: Random House, 1970); Lawrence F. Pisani, *The Italian in America: A Social Study and History* (New York: Exposition Press, 1957); Giovanni E. Schiavo, *Italian-American History*, 2 vols. (New York: Vigo Press, 1947–1940); Silvano M. Tomasi and M. H. Engel, eds., *The Italian Experience in the United States* (Staten Island, N.Y.: Center for Migration Studies, 1970); Angelo M. Pelligrini, *Immigrant's Return* (New York: Macmillan Co., 1951); Alberto Pecorini, "The Italians in the United States," *The Forum* 45 (January 1911): pp. 15–29; Sister Mary Agnes Gertrude, "Italian Immigration to Philadelphia," *Records of the American Catholic Historical Society* 78 (1947): 133–43, 189–207, 256–57; Hugo V. Maiale, "The Italian Vote in Philadelphia Between 1928 and 1946" (Ph.D. diss. University of Pennsylvania,1950); Joan Younger Dickinson, "Aspects of Italian Immigration to Philadelphia," *The Pennsylvania Magazine of History and Biography* 90, no. 4 (October 1966): 445–65.

25. Foerester, pp. 21, 129–30, 215–16.

26. Walter F. Willcox ed., *International Migrations* (New York: National Bureau of Economic Research, 1929), vol. 2, p. 450.

27. Lord et al., p. 65.

28. Foerester, pp. 352–53, 355–60.

29. See Bianca Arcangeli, "The Italians in Philadelphia 1880–1920: Their Origins and Geographical and Occupational Distribution" (Master's thesis, University of Pennsylvania, Department of History, 1975), chap. 3.

30. Foerester, pp. 356–60; Sheridan, p. 421; Maiale, p. 12fn; U.S. Industrial Commission 15: 441.

31. Foerester, pp. 352–53, 355–60.

32. Foerester, pp. 143, 147.

33. Foerester, pp. 40, 343; U.S. Industrial Commission 15: 419.

34. Sheridan, pp. 416, 424.

35. John Koren, "The Padrone System and Padrone Banks," *Bulletin of the United States Department of Labor,* 9 (1897): 113–29, 123; Foerester, p. 355.

36. Koren, pp. 113–29; see also Maiale, p. 5; Edwin Fenton, "Italians in the Labor Movement," *Pennsylvania History* (1959), p. 135; Willits, *Steadying Employment,* pp. 32–33.

37. For information on Italian occupations see Emily W. Dinwiddie, "Some Aspects of Italian Housing and Social Conditions in Philadelphia," *Survey* 12 (May 1904): 490–93; Dinwiddie, *Housing Conditions in Philadelphia* (Philadelphia: Octavia Hill Association, 1904); Maiale, pp. 4–6, 9, 12fn; Lord et al., pp. 66–67, 97ff; Foerester, pp. 335–40; Rose, p. 57; Sheridan, passim: Hutchinson, pp. 137, 138, 178; Fenton, p. 136; U.S. Census 1900; Arcangeli, chap. 2.

38. Hutchinson, p. 138; Foerester, p. 349; Lord et al., p. 95; Foerester, p. 332, 347ff; Rose, p. 57; U.S. Industrial Commission 3: 324–27; Florence Lucas Sanville, "Sweated Homes in Philadelphia: An Unwelcome Corner of Industry upon Which the Law Has Turned Its Back," *Survey* 16 (September 1, 1905): 556.

Part II. The Polish Experience

Chapter 4. The European Background of Polish Migration

1. Władisław Reymont, *Chłopi (The Peasants)* (New York, 1925), 2:77.

2. This chapter is compiled from many sources. The more accessible references are: Stefan Kieniewicz, *The Emancipation of the Polish Peasant* (Chicago: University of Chicago Press, 1968)—by far the best book in English on the topic to date, relying heavily on primary data; William Thomas and Florian Znaniecki, *The Polish Peasant in Europe and America,* 4 vols. (Boston: Richard G. Badger, the Gorham Press, 1918–1920); Balch, *Our Slavic Fellow Citizens;* U.S. Immigration Commission, 1907–1910, *Abstracts of Reports with Conclusions and Recommendations of the Minority* (Washington, D.C., 1911); Greene, *The Slavic Community on Strike,* p. 26; Polish National Committee of America (Wydział Narodowy Polski w Ameryce), *Polish Encyclopedia,* 3 vols. (Geneva, Switzerland: Atar, Ltd., 1922–1924); William J. Rose, *Poland Old and New* (London: G. Bell and Sons, 1948), pp. 18–22; Roman Dyboski, *Outlines of Polish History* (London: Oxford University Press, 1924), pp. 213–29; Dyboski, *Poland* (London: Ernst Bevin, 1933), pp. 45–49; H. H. Fisher, *America and the New Poland* (New York: Macmillan Co., 1928), pp. 54ff; Henryk Frankel, *Poland: The Struggle for Power 1772–1939* (London: Linsay Drummond, 1946), pp. 56–63; F. E. Whitton, *A History of Poland from the Earliest Times to the Present Day* (New York: Charles Scribners Sons, 1918); Francis Bujak, *Poland's Economic Devlopment,* tr. from the Polish by K. Zuk-Skarszewska (Cracow: George Allen and Unwin, 1926): W. F. Reddaway, J. H.

Penson, O. Halecki and R. Dyboski, eds., *The Cambridge History of Poland,* (Cambridge: At the University Press, 1941); Roger Portal; "The Industrialization of Russia," *The Cambridge Economic History of Europe,* ed. by H. J. Habakkuk and M. Postan (Cambridge: At the University Press, 1965), vol. 6, chap. 9; M. Erasme Piltz, *Petite Encyclopedia Polonaise* (Paris: Librarie Payot & Cie., 1916); Alexandre Woycicki, *La Classe Ouviere dans la Grande Industrie Du Royaume De Pologne* (Louvain, 1909).

3. Ladislas Konopczynski, "Polish History," in *Polish Encyclopedia* 1: 489–90.

4. Stefan L. Zaleski, "General Demography," in *Polish Encyclopedia* 2: 77–79; Roth, *A History of the Jews,* pp. 265–70. Also see the references concerning Jewish history in Chapter 3, note 14, above.

5. Thomas and Znaniecki, 1: 118, 159: "The familial character of the farm should not be interpreted as if the family were an association holding a common property. The members of the family have essentially no economic share in the farm; they share only the social character of members of the group, and from this result their social right to be supported by the group and their social obligation to contribute to the existence of the group. The farm is the material basis of this social relation, the expression of the unity of the group in the economic world. The rights and obligations of the members with regard to it do not depend upon any individual claims on property, but upon the nearness of their social relation to the group."

6. Thomas and Znaniecki, 1: 108, 123ff, 113–14: ". . . every individual (except a future priest) is required to marry, if he is not hindered by a physical or an intellectual defect. The community demands from its members a steadiness of life which is necessary for its interior harmony; but a peasant individual can acquire this steadiness only after his marriage. The life of an unmarried man or woman bears essentially an unfixed character. A single person . . . cannot remain indefinitely with his family, for the latter is organized in view of the marriage of all of its members. He cannot carry on normal occupational activity alone—cannot farm or keep a small shop—he can be either only a hired laborer, living with strangers, or a servant. . . . A single person does not take an equal share with married couples in the life of the community. . . . He cannot even keep a house, receive, give entertainments, etc. He has nobody to provide for, no reason to economize. All these features of single life tend to develop either a spirit of revelry, vagabondage, and pauperism, or an egotistic isolation. . . . Accordingly, the community gives a positive sanction to the marriage of its members . . .in three ways . . . (1) Each wedding is a social event in itself, not limited to the families who intermarry, but participated in by the community. . . . (2) The community gives a higher social standing to its married members: after marriage they are addressed as 'you' instead of 'thou', they begin to play an active part in the commune, in the parish. . . . (3) The private life of married couples is much less controlled by the community than that of unmarried persons. . . . An individual who does not marry in due time is supposed not to be sufficiently controlled by the family, and the community allows him no privacy."

7. Kieniewicz, p. 53.

8. Kieniewicz, pp. 51–55.

9. "When a peasant emigrates, it is usually with the desire to earn ready money and return home and buy land. He goes where he can find a ready market for work involving no technical or intellectual preparation. . . . Astonishment and regret are often expressed that the peasant shows no decided inclination to become a farmer in America, but undertakes in mines, on railroads, and in steel works forms

of labor to which he is totally unaccustomed. But it will be found that the peasant has selected precisely the work which suits his purpose, namely, a quick and sure accumulation of cash"—Thomas and Znaniecki, I:192. See also H. J. Habakkuk. "Family Structure and Economic Change in Nineteenth Century Europe," *Journal of Economic History,* vol. 15, no. 1 (1955), pp. 1–12: "migration was not an escape from the peasant family, but a condition of its survival. The peasant went not to acquire a new occupation in a different society, but to improve his position in the old."

10. For detailed statistical information on German Poland, refer to *The Polish Encyclopedia* 1: 514–23, 2: 165–70, 3: 52–96, 106–28, 262–86.

11. *Reports of the Consular Officers of the United States: Labor in Europe,* communique dated Breslau, June 12, 1886, p. 157.

12. Kieniewicz, pp. 190–94.

13. *Polish Encyclopedia* 2: 138–39; Bujak, pp. 45–54. ·

14. *Polish Encyclopedia* 2: 140. See also Richard W. Tims, *Germanizing Prussian Poland: The H-K-T Society and the Struggle for the German Empire, 1894–1919* (New York: Columbia University Press, 1941), p. 115.

15. *Polish Encyclopedia* 2: 137–40; Lawrence Schofer, *The Formation of a Modern Labor Force; Upper Silesia, 1865–1914* (Berkley and Los Angeles: University of California Press, 1975).

16. For detailed statistical information on Galicia, see *Polish Encyclopedia* 1: 524–32, 2: 173–78, 3: 237–46, 246–49.

17. *Polish Encyclopedia* 2: 141–45.

18. See, among others, George W. Potter, *To the Golden Door: The Story of the Irish in Ireland and America* (Boston: Little, Brown and Co., 1960); Cecil Woodham-Smith, *The Great Hunger* (New York: Harper and Row, 1962); Carl Wittke, *The Irish in America* (Baton Rouge: Louisiana State University Press, 1956); and R. Dudley Edwards and T. Desmond Williams, eds., *The Great Famine: Studies in Irish History 1845–52* (Dublin: Browne and Nolan, 1956).

19. *Polish Encyclopedia* 2: 142.

20. *Polish Encyclopedia* 3: 248–50.

21. Kieniewicz, p. 139.

22. *Polish Encyclopedia* 3: 250.

23. Kieniewicz, pp. 214, 204, 203–16; *Polish Encyclopedia* 2: 143, 3: 239, 242; *Cambridge History of Poland,* pp. 438ff; Bujak, p. 52.

24. *Polish Encyclopedia* 3: 262–86, 343.

25. *Polish Encyclopedia* 3: 241, 341, 2: 142; Bujak, p. 53; Balch, p. 132.

26. Bujak, p. 53, Kieniewicz, p. 211, 213; *Polish Encyclopedia* 3: 241.

27. Balch, p. 139.

28. For a general history of Congress Poland, with statistical data, see *Polish Encyclopedia* 1: 533–51, 2: 184–92, 3: 385–99, 391–94, 400–18, 419–37; Kieniewicz, 77ff, 145ff, 221ff.

29. Kieniewicz, p. 145.

30. Kieniewicz, p. 222.

31. *Polish Encyclopedia* 2: 146–47.

32. Kieniewicz, p. 146.

33. *Polish Encyclopedia* 2: 147.

34. *Polish Encyclopedia* 2: 148; Kieniewicz, pp. 181, 182, 184.

35. *Polish Encyclopedia* 2: 148.

36. *Cambridge Economic History of Europe,* vol. 6, part 2, 818, 859; *Cambridge History of Poland,* p. 392; Bujak, p. 49.

37. *Polish Encyclopedia* 2: 185; Adna Weber, p. 105; *Russian Statistical Yearbook, 1913* (St. Petersburg: Central Statistical Committee, Ministry of the Interior, 1914), part I, pp. 46,50, 61.

38. *Polish Encyclopedia* 3: 419–30, esp. 423, 429; *Cambridge Economic History of Europe* 6, part 2, 859.

39. Kieniewicz, p. 223; *Polish Encyclopedia* 3: 395.

40. *Polish Encyclopedia* 3: 405.

41. Kieniewicz, p. 225.

42. U.S. Consular Reports, *Labor in Europe,* p. 1447.

43. *Polish Encyclopedia* 2: 151.

44. *Polish Encyclopedia* 2: 150.

45. *Polish Encyclopedia* 3: 397.

Chapter 5. The Polish Experience in Philadelphia

1. *Pennsylvania: Titan of Industry* (New York: Lewis Historical Publishing Co., 1948), vol. 3, pp. 970–71.

2. Warne, *Slav Invasion,* pp. 71–72; Fitch, *Steel Workers,* pp. 107ff.

3. Warne, *Slav Invasion,* p. 73.

4. Fitch, p. 142; other quotes, p. 146. See also Brody, *Steelworkers in America;* Crystal Eastman, *Work-Accidents and the Law,* vol. 2 of the *Pittsburgh Survey,* ed. by Paul U. Kellog (New York: 1909–1914); and U.S. Bureau of Labor, *Report on Conditions of Employment in the Iron and Steel Industry* 4 (Washington, D.C., 1911–1913).

5. "Report of Division of Immigration and Unemployment," pp. 231–32.

6. *Report of the Industrial Commission,* 1901, quoted in Lord et al., p. 96.

7. Lord et al., pp. 96–97.

Chapter 6. The Geography of Neighborhood

1. June 3, 1951.

2. Edward E. Pratt, *Industrial Causes of Congestion of Population in New York City,* p. 42.

3. See, for example, Herbert Gans, *The Urban Villagers: Group and Class in the Life of Italian Americans* (New York: Free Press, 1962), especially pp. 3–119; Michael Novak, *The Rise of the Unmeltable Ethnics* (New York: Macmillan Co., 1972); Thomas and Znaniecki, *The Polish Peasant in Europe and America,* vol. 1.

4. No definitive work has appeared on the history of Polish-Irish confrontation within the American Catholic Church nor has anything appeared that directly contrasts the two forms of Roman Catholicism. See, however, for starters, Daniel S. Buczek, "Polish Americans and the Roman Catholic Church," *The Polish Review* vol. 21, no. 3 (1976), pp. 39–61; Victor Greene, "For God and Country: The Origins of Slavic Catholic Self-Consciousness in America," *Church History* 35 (1966) and his more recent *For God and Country: The Rise of Polish and Lithuanian Ethnic Consciousness in America* (Madison: University of Wisconsin Press, 1975); Richard M. Linkh, *American Catholicism and European Immigrants* (New York: Center for Migration Studies, 1975); Colman J. Barry, *The Catholic Church and German Americans*

(Washington, D.C.: Catholic University of America Press, 1953); Hieronim Kubiak, *Polski Narodowy Kościo ł Katolicki w Stanach Zjednoczonych Ameryki w Latch 1897–1965; Jego Społeczne uwarunkowania i społeczne funkcje* (Warszawa; 1970); Daniel Buczek, *Immigrant Pastor* (Waterbury, Conn.: Hemingway Corp., 1974); Joseph J. Parot, "The American Faith and the Persistence of Chicago Polonia, 1870–1920" (Ph.D. diss., Northern Illinois University, 1971); Karol Gorski, *Od religijności do mistyki. Zarys dziejów życia wewnętrznego w Polsce. Część pierwsza, 966–1795* (Lublin: 1962), and his *Dzieje życia wewnętrznego w Polsce* (Lublin: 1969); *A History of Irish Catholicism,* ed. by Patrick Corish, vol. 6, no. 2: *The United States of America,* ed. by Thomas P. McAvoy, C.S.C., and Thomas N. Brown (Dublin: 1970); Novak, *Rise of the Unmeltable Ethnics;* Anthony J. Kuzniewski, "Faith and Fatherland: An Intellectual History of the Polish Immigrant Community in Wisconsin, 1838–1918" (Ph.D. diss. Harvard University, 1973); the quote is from *American Ecclesiastical Review* 19, 3rd series, vol. 9 (October 1903), p. 351.

5. Luciano J. Iorizzo and Salvatore Mondello, *The Italian Americans* (New York: Twayne Publishers, 1971); Henry J. Browne, "The 'Italian Problem' in the Catholic Church of the United States, 1880–1900," in *Historical Records and Studies of the United States Catholic Historical Society* 35 (1946): 52–60; Rudolph H. Vecoli, "Prelates and Peasants: The Italian Immigrant and the Catholic Church," *Journal of Social History* 1 (September 1969): 220–68; Sister M. Agnes Gertrude, "Italian Immigration into Philadelphia," and Richard A. Varbero, "Philadelphia's South Italians in the 1920's," in *The Peoples of Philadelphia,* ed. by Allen F. Davis and Mark H. Haller (Philadelphia: Temple University Press, 1973), 255–76.

6. Louis Wirth, *The Ghetto,* p. 229.

7. Wirth, p. 232.

8. "Report of Division of Immigration and Unemployment," *First Annual Report of the Commissioner of Labor and Industry, 1913,* pp. 277–78.

9. Joseph Willits, *Philadelphia Unemployment,* pp. 15, 16.

10. Willits, p. 2.

11. Willits, p. 5, 1–15.

12. See, for example, Daniel Buczek, *The Immigrant Pastor.*

13. Victor Greene, in his study of Polish communities in Pennsylvania's anthracite region, also noted the importance and diverse functions of saloons and nationality stores: "The proprietors, usually German Poles, had been the earliest arrivals, and, seeing the need for a neighboring center, they invested in a local establishment. They and their saloons provided necessary services such as holding the immigrants' earnings—the so-called 'immigrant banks'—notorizing papers, forwarding money orders home, acting as transportation agents, affording accommodations, interpreting and translating, giving generous credit to countrymen, and even writing letters for the illiterate. Their business hours were convenient, and the interested parties conducted negotiations over lager. Shopkeepers, then, wielded considerable local influence, and many acted as mediators and spokesmen for their countrymen. . . ." *Slavic Immigrants On Strike,* pp. 48–49.

14. See, for example, Stephan Thernstrom and Peter R. Knights, "Men in Motion: Some Data and Speculations about Urban Population Mobility in Nineteenth Century America" in *Anonymous Americans,* ed. by Tamara K. Hareven (Englewood Cliffs, N. J.: Prentice Hall, 1971), p. 32.

15. Random selections from interviews show, for example, that Anna L. had ten offers of marriage within three months of her arrival in America, Zofia S. had 8, Aniela R., 7, and so on. Anna L.s' brother told her that it was "not good" for a woman to be unmarried in America, so she chose one of her ten suitors, "The one from the best family"—the younger son of an impoverished noble family. They were married with great celebration; the inevitable photograph was taken and sent home to all the relatives. Had there been the opportunity to maintain the old traditions, the marriage of the two young people would have been arranged by the parents. This was no longer always possible in America. Rather, the "complicated process of courtship and selection" is reduced to "an offhand proposal to a girl who 'pleases' after a relatively short personal acquaintance. If the girl rejects the proposal, the boy tries to find another whom he 'likes' and repeats the performance" (Thomas and Znaniecki, 1: 127). Nevertheless, a man usually sought familial approval via letter before undertaking any marriage in America, even if the "approval" was sought in only a perfunctory statement that the wedding would soon take place and "your blessing upon us is requested."

16. "Report of Division of Immigration and Unemployment," *Annual Report of the Commissioner of Labor and Industry, 1916.*

17. Agnes Mary Hadden Byrnes, *Industrial Homework in Pennsylvania* (Commonwealth of Pennsylvania, Department of Labor and Industry, 1923).

18. Byrnes, pp. 18, 41, 42.

19. Byrnes, p. 18.

20. Byrnes, p. 7.

21. "We have every day 18 rooms to clean, and to cook and to wash linen. It is myself who wash every week about 300 pieces of linen, and iron it. But I have easy washing because I don't wash with my hands; the machines wash alone, I only cover the linen with soap and put five pieces into the machine at once. After 15 minutes I take them out and put in new ones, and so by noon I wash all the 300 pieces. I iron four days, from 6 a.m. to 8 p.m. I do nothing but iron for those four days"—Aleksandra Rembienska to parents in Poland, October 14, 1911 (Thomas and Znaniecki, 2: 251); "I walk very much, because from 6 o'clock in the morning till ten o'clock in the evening I have work and I receive $22 month, and I have seven persons and 16 rooms to clean and I cook; everything is on my head"—Aleksandra Rembienska, 1912 (Thomas and Znaniecki, 2: 254).

22. John and Leatrice MacDonald, "Urbanization, Ethnic Groups and Social Segmentation," *Social Research* 29 (1962): 446–48.

23. See Pennsylvania State Emergency Relief Administration, *Report of Philadelphia Real Estate Survey* (1934), 1: 233; 2:371; 3:233–34; 4:371–72; 5:114, 364 for Bridesburg/Frankford; 1:81, 253; 2:383; 3:81–82, 253–54; 4:383–84; 5:41, 124, 370 for Port Richmond; 2:137; 4:137–38; 4:252 for Nicetown; 1:133, 135; 3:133–36; 5:65–66 for Manayunk; 1:329; 3:329–30; 5:163 for Kensington; 1:45, 47, 49, 51, 71; 3:45, 47, 49, 51, 71; 5:23, 24, 25, 26, 36 for Northern Liberties; 1:17, 21; 5:9, 11 for Southwark; 1:43, 63; 3:43, 63, 44, 64; 5:22, 32 for Fairmount; and 2:123; 4:123; 5:245 for Southwest Philadelphia and the Bottom.

24. *See Report of Philadelphia Real Estate Survey,* 5 vols.; Helen L. Parrish, "The Housing Awakening: One Million People in Small Houses—Philadelphia," *Survey* 5 (May 6, 1911): 229–38; Northeast Philadelphia Chamber of Commerce, *The Great Northeast* (Philadelphia, 1928), pp. 36–37; A. F. Davies, "Land Values and

Ownership in Philadelphia," *Bulletin* of the Bureau of Labor, 9 (January 1904): 104–31; G. A. Weber, "The Improvement of Housing Conditions in Philadelphia," *The American City*, 1 (November 1909): 123–28; *Philadelphia Yearbook* 1917, pp. E6, 24; R. S. Glover, "A Survey of the Housing Situation in Philadelphia" (M. A. thesis, University of Pennsylvania, 1932); Henry M. Muller, *Urban Home Ownership: A Socio-Economic Analysis with Emphasis on Philadelphia* (Philadelphia, 1947); F. J. Shoyer, "Importance of Building and Loan Associations in Making Philadelphia the City of Homes," *Real Estate Magazine* (August 1925). "Bridesburg Leads in Homes Owned: Poles Form Biggest Part of Population of Historic Section," *Philadelphia Evening Ledger* (February 15, 1934): Bridesburg and the remainder of the 45th Ward "has the distinction of having the highest percentage of home ownership in Philadelphia, according to statistics compiled by the Philadelphia Housing Association." Muller, p. 130–149: Of 8,138 homes in Ward 45, 69.7% are owned by residents. "Bridesburg has done much to bring this average up. Ninety percent of the Polish families own their own homes."

25. For detailed list of origins of Philadelphia's Poles, see Caroline Golab, "The Immigrant and the City: The Polish Communities of Philadelphia, 1870–1920" (Ph.D. diss., University of Pennsylvania, 1971).

26. This is the thesis espoused by Theodore Hershberg, Harold Cox and Dale Light, Jr., for an earlier period of Philadelphia history, 1850–1880. ("The 'Journey-to-Work': An Empirical Investigation of Work, Residence and Transportation, Philadelphia, 1850–1880," typescript, the Philadelphia Social History Project, 1976.)

Conclusion

No History But Their Own

1. "The Ethnic Neighborhood: Leave Room for a Boccie Ball," in *Pieces of a Dream*, edited by Michael Wenk, S. M. Tomasi and Geno Baroni (New York: Center for Migration Studies, 1972), p. 55.

2. John Porter, *The Vertical Mosaic*, chaps. 1–2.

3. William Newman, *American Pluralism: A Study of Minority Groups and Social Theory* (New York: Harper and Row, 1973), pp. 135, 165.

4. Edward Hall, *The Hidden Dimension* (Garden City, New York: Doubleday, 1966).

Index

237